SSSP

Springer
Series in
Social
Psychology

SSSP

Mark R. Leary
Rowland S. Miller

Social Psychology and Dysfunctional Behavior

Origins, Diagnosis, and Treatment

Springer-Verlag New York Berlin Heidelberg
London Paris Tokyo

Mark R. Leary
Department of Psychology
Wake Forest University
Winston-Salem, North Carolina 27109
U.S.A.

Rowland S. Miller
Department of Psychology
Sam Houston State University
Huntsville, Texas 77341
U.S.A.

With 2 Figures

Library of Congress Cataloging in Publication Data
Leary, Mark R.
   Social psychology and dysfunctional behavior.
   (Springer series in social psychology)
   Bibliography: p.
   Includes index.
   1. Social psychiatry.   2. Interpersonal relations.
3. Mental illness—Social aspects.   4. Social psychology.
I. Miller, Rowland S.   II. Title.   III. Series.
[DNLM: 1. Behavior.   2. Counseling.   3. Interpersonal
Relations.   4. Psychology, Clinical.   5. Psychology,
Social.   WM 105 L438s]
RC465.L38   1986   616.89   86-6536

Typset by TC Systems, Shippensburg, Pennsylvania.
Printed and bound by R.R. Donnelley & Sons, Harrisonburg, Virginia.
Printed in the United States of America

9 8 7 6 5 4 3 2 1

ISBN 0-387-96325-1 Springer-Verlag New York Berlin Heidelberg
ISBN 3-540-96325-1 Springer-Verlag Berlin Heidelberg New York

To Wendy and Kevin, Gale and Christopher

Preface

A colleague recently recounted a conversation she had had with a group of graduate students. For reasons that she cannot recall, the discussion had turned to the topic of "old-fashioned" ideas in psychology—perspectives and beliefs that had once enjoyed widespread support but that are now regarded as quaint curiosities. The students racked their brains to outdo one another with their knowledge of the historical trivia of psychology: Le Bon's fascination with the "group mind," Mesmer's theory of animal magnetism, the short-lived popularity of "moral therapy," Descartes' belief that erections are maintained by air from the lungs, and so on.

When it came his turn to contribute to the discussion, one student brought up an enigmatic journal he had seen in the library stacks: the *Journal of Abnormal and Social Psychology*. He thought that the inclusion of abnormal and social psychology within the covers of a single journal seemed an odd combination, and he wondered aloud what sort of historical quirk had led psychologists of an earlier generation to regard these two fields as somehow related. Our colleague then asked her students if they had any ideas about how such an odd combination had found its way into a single journal.

One student suggested that the decision to stick abnormal and social psychology together must have been a financial one; perhaps the American Psychological Association did not have enough money to support a journal in both fields, and so they had thrown the two together. Another student thought that the enigma was more imagined than real—that "social psychology" must have had different connotations at one time than it does today.

Although neither our colleague nor her students knew the full story behind the *Journal of Abnormal and Social Psychology* (a topic we discuss in chapter 1), this anecdote makes an important point. Although many influential figures in psychology (such as Morton Prince and Gordon Allport) once viewed the study of interpersonal processes and the study of psychological difficulties as intimately related, social psychology and abnormal-clinical-counseling psychology historically have had little to do with one another.

Indeed, the schism has been so great that contemporary students may have difficulty imagining how the fields might be related at all.

However, a movement is under way that is restimulating interest in the role of social psychological processes in the development, diagnosis, and treatment of dysfunctional behavior. Researchers and practitioners alike are devoting increasing attention to the interpersonal determinants of emotional and behavioral problems. In doing so, they are finding not only that many psychological problems arise from people's relationships with others, but that the diagnosis and treatment of such problems necessarily involve an interpersonal relationship between a counselor and a client. As a result of this realization, social psychology, with its focus on interpersonal behavior, is being increasingly regarded as relevant to the concerns of clinical and counseling psychologists.

Excited by this recent development, we have set out in this volume to overview areas of inquiry in which theory and research in social psychology elucidate processes involved in behavioral and emotional problems. Our task was more formidable than it first appeared. Recent years have seen an explosion of interest in the interface between social and clinical-counseling-abnormal psychology, and we were forced to choose at every juncture among topics for inclusion. Thus, we thought it important to state up front the criteria (or, if you will, the biases) that guided our writing.

First, this book has a decidedly social psychological orientation. Although every page deals with phenomena of interest to clinical and counseling psychologists (and counseling and psychotherapy research appears throughout), our emphasis is on how basic interpersonal processes are involved in the genesis, diagnosis, and remediation of psychological difficulties. Thus, although we believe strongly that the literatures we review provide useful perspectives for the practicing psychologist, we have not tried to write a book on how to do counseling and psychotherapy. Nevertheless, trained therapists will find much of value in the book and will be able to incorporate the insights offered here into their own modes of dealing with troubled individuals.

Our goal throughout is to show how central topics and perspectives in social psychology can help us better understand and treat certain sorts of psychological difficulties. We have sampled broadly from areas of interest in social psychology, including attribution, social cognition, impression management, relationships, the self, attitude change, expectancy effects, and self-esteem, to name some of the more central. In many instances we discuss work that has explicitly integrated social psychological perspectives into studies of clinical phenomena, whereas in others we speculate about the interpersonal aspects of psychological problems and their treatment on the basis of basic research.

In several chapters, we provide a brief introduction to basic social psychological constructs before delving into the implications of those constructs for abnormal, clinical, and counseling psychology. We ask those readers who are well versed in social psychology to bear with us during these brief introductions; we thought it would be helpful to readers who are less familiar with work in social psychology if we provided a bit of background on such topics.

We feel strongly that social psychology has much to offer to our understanding and treatment of dysfunctional behavior, and that, in turn, counseling and clinical psychology can shine considerable light on the interpersonal processes that interest social psychologists. The potential for dialogue among these areas is extensive but has barely been tapped, and we hope that this volume will serve as a further impetus to cross-fertilization among these fields.

We would like to express our deepest thanks to Jane Reade, Teresa Hill, and Jodi Steiner for typing the reference list, to Robin Kowalski for her work on the author index, to Jim Maddux for extraordinarily helpful comments on an earlier draft of the manuscript, and to the staff at Springer-Verlag for their unflagging encouragement and support.

Winston-Salem, North Carolina   Mark R. Leary
Huntsville, Texas   Rowland S. Miller

Contents

Chapter 1
Introduction

Since the earliest days of psychology, researchers and therapists alike have recognized that interpersonal processes play a role in the development and treatment of emotional and behavioral problems. Although his theory of psychoanalysis is often described as *intra*psychic, even Freud traced many of his patients' difficulties to their social relationships with parents and lovers and wrote extensively about the interpersonal complexities of the relationship between therapist and patient.

In recent years, a wide range of theoretical and therapeutic approaches have increasingly emphasized the importance of social factors in understanding and treating dysfunctional or "abnormal" behavior. It is now widely accepted that many psychological problems are caused or exacerbated by interpersonal events. Not only is mental health customarily defined in terms of socially relevant criteria such as social competencies, effective relationships, and self-esteem (Orford & Feldman, 1980), but the issues, stresses, doubts, and problems for which people seek professional help are often social in nature. As we will see, phenomena as diverse as depression, anxiety, schizophrenia, alcoholism, and hypochondriasis may be developed, exacerbated, and prolonged by people's social interactions and relationships.

Further, the identification or diagnosis of psychological difficulties, whether by a highly trained professional or by anyone else, is necessarily a social process, involving one person's perception and categorization of another. Indeed, the mere identification of an individual's behavior as abnormal or deviant requires a comparison with the behavior of relevant others (Artiss, 1959; Langer, 1982). As Carson (1969, p. 225) observed, "personality disorder . . . is a matter of how one *behaves* (including what one *says*) in the presence of others; its definition is public and social in nature."

Finally, the treatment of dysfunctional reactions necessarily entails interpersonal processes, involving a therapist and a client or group of clients. Thus, a full understanding of what happens in the course of counseling and psychotherapy requires an appreciation of the interpersonal dynamics involved (Frank, 1973; Strong, 1968; Strong & Claiborn, 1982). In fact, C. Hendrick (1983) flatly stated that "psychotherapy is first and foremost a species of human interaction" (p. 67).

Given that the role of interpersonal processes in the development and treatment of psychological problems has been recognized for some time, one might expect an intimate connection to exist between psychologists interested in dysfunctional behavior (predominantly clinical and counseling psychologists) and those interested in interpersonal processes (social psychologists). Not only do theory and research in social psychology seem to be relevant to understanding, diagnosing, and treating behavioral and emotional problems, but knowledge of the nature and treatment of such problems would be likely to elucidate phenomena of interest to social psychologists. However, for reasons we will discuss momentarily, a schism has existed between the two fields for many years, slowing the development of what would appear to be a meaningful and productive interchange.

There exists today, however, a new current moving toward the study of dysfunctional phenomena by social psychologists (Leary, Jenkins, & Shepperd, 1984; Weary & Mirels, 1982), the integration of social psychological principles and findings into clinical practice (Brehm, 1976; Maddux & Stoltenberg, 1983a), and the collaboration of clinical and social psychologists in research (Haemmerlie & Montgomery, 1984), graduate training (Harvey & Weary, 1979), and even therapy (Harari, 1983; C. Hendrick, 1983). In this introduction we provide an overview of this emerging area, first by describing the history of the rocky relationship between social psychology on the one hand and clinical, counseling, and abnormal psychology on the other, and by enumerating factors that have hindered a meaningful exchange between them. We then examine the changes within psychology that have precipitated the recent interest in the interface among these areas. The chapter then concludes with a brief overview of topics in which social psychological perspectives have been applied to clinically relevant phenomena, and with a preview of the remainder of the book.[1]

---

[1] Throughout the book, we will generally not distinguish between the fields of clinical and counseling psychology, nor between clinical and counseling psychologists or psychotherapists and counselors. This is not meant to imply that there are no important differences among these fields (see Osipow, Cohen, Jenkins, & Dostal, 1979; Watkins, 1984), but the differences are generally not germane to the purpose and scope of this book. Further, we often use the terms *therapist* and *counselor* in a generic sense, thereby including not only clinical and counseling psychologists (narrowly defined), but all professionals who provide psychological services, such as school psychologists, social workers, psychiatrists, members of the clergy, and even lay helpers.

Why So Long?

Despite clear indications that the development, diagnosis, and treatment of dysfunctional behavior are influenced by social psychological processes, a meaningful dialogue between social and clinical-counseling psychologists has been slow to develop. Not only have practicing clinicians and counselors paid little attention to relevant work in social psychology, but researchers interested in psychopathology and psychotherapy have shown little inclination to borrow from social psychological theory and research. On the other side of the fence, social psychologists have been equally remiss in ignoring theory and research dealing with dysfunctional behavior and have seemed reluctant to foray into clinically relevant areas.

The extent of the schism between the two camps was starkly portrayed by the bifurcation of the *Journal of Abnormal and Social Psychology* into the *Journal of Abnormal Psychology* and the *Journal of Personality and Social Psychology* in 1965. Morton Prince established the *Journal of Abnormal and Social Psychology* in 1921 in an attempt to promote work at the interface of abnormal and social psychology (Hill & Weary, 1983). He maintained that researchers in social and abnormal psychology were interested in many of the same phenomena and believed that a journal that focused on abnormal *and* social behavior would provide both an outlet for such work and an impetus for its development. Gordon Allport, who was editor of the journal from 1938 to 1950, shared this sentiment, but observed that most of the journal's articles dealt with topics in either social *or* abnormal psychology and rarely attempted to capitalize upon the integration of the two fields. For this and other reasons, the decision was ultimately made to split the journal in two (Hill & Weary, 1983). Thus, even a journal devoted expressly to the interface between social and abnormal psychology was unable to stimulate research at the nexus of the two fields. As Goldstein (1966, p. 39) observed at about that time, "for the most part, researchers interested in psychotherapy and their colleagues studying social psychological phenomena have gone their separate ways, making scant reference to one another's work and, in general, ignoring what appear to be real opportunities for mutual feedback and stimulation."

Historical Considerations

There appear to us to be three broad reasons why it has proven difficult to integrate social psychological perspectives with abnormal, clinical, and counseling psychology. The first of these is historical. The World-War-II era had a profound effect on social, clinical, and counseling psychology, setting them upon the separate paths we know today (C. Hendrick, 1983; Reisman, 1976; Steiner, 1979).

Clinical psychology. Before the war, clinical psychologists were chiefly diagnosticians, blocked from doing psychotherapy by the powerful monopoly of psychiatry. The enormous need created by the war for psychological services forced the psychiatric establishment to admit psychologists as therapists, but the money and the institutional structure provided by the Veterans Administration and the National Institute of Mental Health still tied clinicians to psychiatric settings. Sarason (1981) feels that this was a grave mistake: "Clinical psychology became part of a medically dominated mental health movement that was narrow in terms of theory and settings, blind to the nature of the social order, and as imperialistic as it was vigorous" (p. 833). Immersed in medical settings, surrounded by psychodynamically oriented psychiatrists, and serving mainly patients with severe disturbances, clinical psychologists tended to deemphasize interpersonal processes and problems in their work.

In addition, as a function of both self-selection and training, clinical psychologists of the day were trained primarily as diagnosticians and therapists and only secondarily (if at all) as researchers. Although the Boulder Conference (Raimy, 1950) endorsed the importance of training clinical psychologists both as "scientists" and as "practitioners," the emphasis in clinical psychology has remained on assessment and treatment (Sheras & Worchel, 1979).

Social psychology. Social psychology, by contrast, increasingly emphasized basic research in the years following World War II, often ignoring potential applications of its findings and displaying little interest in applied topics, including those relevant to adjustment and psychopathology. This had not always been so. Under the guiding presence of Kurt Lewin, often regarded as the father of contemporary social psychology, the new specialty focused on broad social problems with an "action-orientation" toward *solving* those problems (Lewin, 1948). Although Lewin emphasized the importance of theory and rigorous experimentation, he also stressed the importance of addressing real-world problems. Indeed, among his other interests, Lewin himself explored processes involved in dysfunctional phenomena such as childhood emotional disturbances and mental retardation.

However, after Lewin's untimely death in 1947, social psychology became more experimental and laboratory based, focusing primarily on the behavior of single individuals (Steiner, 1979). Moving from applied field research to the readily controlled confines of the laboratory, experimental settings became more sterile and the focus of investigations more minute as social psychologists began testing specific details of emerging theories in earnest. In addition, social psychologists employed the ever-present college undergraduates as research subjects in increasing numbers. Moreover, to some observers, social psychologists seemed to be "deliberately insulating themselves from clinical, sociological, anthropological, and a variety of other sources of knowledge about human behavior" (Jones, 1983, p. 11). The pendulum has begun to swing back, and contemporary social psychology no longer relies so heavily on controlled experiments on university students; nevertheless, the field remains wedded to experimental approaches to research based on a somewhat positivistic notion of the philosophy of science (Gergen & Gergen, 1984).

Professional Identities and Stereotypes

These disparate histories have resulted in very different professional identities for social and clinical psychologists, accompanied by different objectives, priorities, theoretical bases, skills, and methodological perspectives. Clinical and counseling psychologists, particularly those who do not work in academic settings, tend to be interested primarily in service delivery, and have little interest in the research process that so fascinates many social psychologists. This difference in orientation arises both from self-selection into graduate programs and from differing emphases in graduate and postgraduate work. The result is that the two groups (practitioners and researchers) do not understand each other's professional world view and hold unflattering stereotypes of one another that foster misunderstanding and poor communication.

Practicing psychologists often perceive the empirically oriented social psychologist as out of touch with issues of real relevance to psychological adaptation and dysfunction. They point to the sterile, contrived, unrealistic settings in which much social psychological research is conducted, to the use of artificial and deceptive methodologies, to the nonrepresentativeness of research samples, and to the clinically meaningless (though statistically significant) findings. Further, practicing clinical and counseling psychologists often contend that, because of the methods and samples employed, the results of social psychological inquiry "can't be generalized to the real world."

Social psychologists' stereotypes of the practicing psychologist are probably no more flattering. Clinical and counseling psychologists often are perceived as nonscientific (if not antiscientific) professionals who prefer to base psychological treatment on intuition and untested armchair theories rather than on empirical fact. Further, clinical-counseling psychologists are often berated for their lack of methodological and statistical sophistication. Social psychologists respond in frustration that quality research often requires the controls possible only in laboratory settings, that external validity is a minor concern when testing hypotheses (Mook, 1983), and that single research studies should *never* be generalized to the real world regardless of how and upon whom they are conducted. The social psychologists maintain that the purpose of experiments is not to create real-world settings in the lab, but rather to test theories, which, when deemed reasonably useful, are then applied to real-world settings.

In fact, these stereotypes are partially accurate and are to some degree, proudly fostered by each of the two groups. Many clinicians and counselors do endorse nonempirical, intuitive approaches to understanding human behavior and derogate the importance of research. In turn, many social psychologists, by choice, have little experience or interest in clinical settings, study relatively microcosmic phenomena in controlled studies, and ignore, if not avoid, applications of their work. Thus, given these different professional identities, unflattering stereotypes, and negative attitudes, it is not hard to understand why each group finds it difficult to understand and trust the other's contributions to psychology.

Practical Problems

Aside from the barriers arising from historical and professional factors, there have been practical problems in stimulating an interface between psychologists interested in social behavior and those interested in people with psychological problems. For one, the structure of most academic departments (in which most clinically relevant research is conducted) does not encourage collaboration among faculty, either within or between subspecialties. As a result, there is little departmental incentive for social and clinical-counseling psychologists to collaborate.

Further, as Hill and Weary (1983) observed, the researcher who tries to cross disciplinary barriers often faces a loss of professional identity. This is particularly true for younger researchers who have not yet established their careers. Riding the fence between social and clinical psychology, for example, may leave them without full recognition by either area (Harari, 1983).

A further problem is that of becoming knowledgeable in two disparate areas (Leary, 1983a). Both time constraints and a myopic view of psychology have led clinical and counseling psychologists to fail to appreciate the real breadth and utility of social psychology, and social psychologists to fail to understand clinical problems and practice. This problem becomes apparent when social psychologists draw naïve connections between their work and areas of clinical or counseling psychology, and vice versa. Not only do the members of each group tend to read and publish in different publications and belong to different organizations, but they are highly specialized within their own fields. Rigid training of new students only widens the gap, as few students obtain training outside of their primary area (Harvey & Weary, 1979; C. Hendrick, 1983; Maddux & Stoltenberg, 1983a).

In sum, a conglomeration of historical, professional, and practical barriers exist between factions within psychology that appear on the surface to be "made for each other." These barriers have created a situation in which the parties involved lack full appreciation of each other's work, view one another with skepticism and distrust, and have little professional contact. Even so, the last ten years have seen an increasing interest in the interface between social psychology and clinical-counseling and abnormal psychology, as well as improved dialogue between experimental social psychologists on the one hand and researchers and practitioners in counseling and psycho-therapy on the other.

The Emerging Interface

This new interest in the social–clinical-counseling interface is manifested in several books that use social psychological perspectives in examining dys-functional behavior (Dorn, 1984; Leary, 1983b; Sheras & Worchel, 1979; Strong & Claiborn, 1982; Weary & Mirels, 1982; this volume), the creation of a new *Journal of Social and Clinical Psychology* (Harvey, 1983), articles discussing aspects of the emerging interface (C. Hendrick, 1983; S. Hendrick, 1983; Maddux & Stoltenberg, 1983a, 1983b, 1984a), convention sym-posia and presentations regarding applications of social psychology to clini-cal and counseling practice (Maddux & Stoltenberg, 1984b), and hundreds of research articles that examine interpersonal facets of dysfunctional behav-ior. The extent of recent interest within social psychology is demonstrated by a content analysis of the articles in five major social psychological jour-nals from 1965 to 1983 (Leary et al., 1984). Overall, the percentage of clini-cally relevant articles in major social psychological journals more than dou-bled from 1965 to 1983.

To what may this change be attributed? Although it is risky to attempt an answer to such a question, we see three central factors.

First, during the 1970s, social psychology experienced a self-described "crisis" of confidence, a period of critical evaluation of the direction and usefulness of the field (Elms, 1975; Gergen, 1973; McGuire, 1973; Schlenker, 1973). Serious questions were raised regarding the relevance of research findings for real-life problems, the appropriateness of prevailing research methods, and the general viability of the discipline as a social science. One consequence of this self-examination was that many social psychologists turned their attention to research topics that were directly relevant to social life outside of the laboratory, such as eyewitness identification, jury behav-ior, consumer behavior, personnel management, organizational issues, ur-ban crowding, and health-related behavior. The current interest in the social psychology of dysfunctional behavior reflects one manifestation of this heightened attention to applied topics.

In addition, as interest in applied social psychology has grown, more research has been conducted in field settings, with a wider variety of sub-jects than those found in universities and colleges (see Reich, 1982). This is not to suggest that social psychology has lost its taste for controlled labora-tory experimentation; it has not. However, nonexperimental research on applied topics has become increasingly accepted and commonplace. Not only has this furthered many social psychologists' interest in topics relevant to dysfunctional behavior, but it has stimulated the interest of their colleagues in applied settings who, for the first time, have begun to see something of value in social psychological research.

The second factor contributing to the budding interface has been the emergence of counseling psychology as a field specializing in "normal" adjustment difficulties. Although counseling psychology emerged as a distinct specialty out of vocational and educational guidance in the 1950s (Super, 1955), early counseling psychologists tended to use predominantly intrapsychic models borrowed from psychiatry and clinical psychology (Tyler, 1972). During the 1960s and 1970s, however, counseling psychologists became increasingly interested in the interpersonal dimensions of behavior, in organizational behavior, and in facilitating group interactions (Tyler, 1972). This shift made social psychology more clearly relevant to the interests of counseling psychologists. Further, the research interests of counselors in academic settings began to coincide closely with those of social psychologists as they began to examine the counselor-client relationship, social processes in counseling, and the genesis of common adjustment difficulties.

Finally, with the improved professional climate, all that was needed was a few catalytic publications to ignite widespread interest in the social psychology of dysfunctional processes and therapy. This impetus was provided by writers such as Goldstein (1966), Goldstein, Heller, and Sechrest (1966), Strong (1968, 1978), Brehm (1976), Sheras and Worchel (1979), and Weary and Mirels (1982). Although differing in focus, each of these writers—some of whom are clinicians or counselors, and others social psychologists—made a strong case for integrating aspects of social psychology with the study and treatment of psychological problems. We hope that the present volume will contribute further to the growth of this hybrid area.

Current Topics at the Interface

Social psychological perspectives have been applied to a wide range of topics dealing with the development, diagnosis, and treatment of dysfunctional behavior. Before examining these topics in detail in the following chapters, we offer a broad overview of the areas in which social psychology interfaces with abnormal, clinical, and counseling psychology.

These areas fall roughly into three categories (Leary, in press-a). The first, *social-dysgenic psychology,* is the study of interpersonal processes involved in the development and maintenance of dysfunctional behavior. Several such phenomena are listed in Table 1-1, along with representative, clinically relevant topics that have been studied. As noted earlier, much maladaptive behavior is caused, exacerbated, or maintained by interpersonal processes, and a considerable amount of research has been devoted to these processes in recent years.

The second area, *social-diagnostic psychology,* focuses on the role of interpersonal processes in the identification and classification of psychologi-

Table 1-1. Social Psychological Processes in the Development of
Dysfunctional Behavior

Social psychological phenomenon	Relevance to dysfunctional phenomena
Attribution	Interpretation of bodily and psychological states
	Reactions to negative events
	Self-blame
	Perceived helplessness; depression
	Health-maintenance behavior
Aggression	Child and spouse abuse
	Rape
	General hostility
Self-presentation	Evaluation apprehension
	Malingering
	Impression management of psychopathology
Relationships	Marital difficulties
	Interpersonal conflict
	Communication deficits
	Loneliness
	Jealousy
	Social support
Social comparison	Self-concept formation and change
	Inferences about one's own mental health
Conformity	Drug and alcohol use; smoking
The self	Self-esteem
	Identity problems
	Self-defeating behavior
	Deindividuation and antisocial behavior
Modeling	Social-skills deficits
	Styles of coping
Roles	Maladaptive role behavior
	Role conflict

cal problems. At its heart, the diagnosis of emotional and behavioral difficulties involves problems of social inference. Thus, the extensive literatures in person perception, attribution, judgmental heuristics, inferential biases, and labeling are all quite germane. Table 1-2 lists several topics relevant to the social psychology of clinical inference.

The third category of topics, which we call *social-therapeutic* psychology, deals with the study of interpersonal processes in counseling and psychotherapy. At its base, counseling and psychotherapy involve an interpersonal relationship between two individuals: a client and his or her therapist. Thus, much of what occurs, for good and for bad, during the course of treatment can best be understood in terms of this relationship. Topics relevant to social-therapeutic psychology are listed in Table 1-3.

From the variety of topics listed, we have selected for this book those that are most firmly rooted in social psychological theory and research and have attracted the most research attention. Chapters 2 through 7 examine social

Table 1-2. Social Psychological Processes in the Diagnosis of
          Dysfunctional Behavior

Social psychological phenomenon	Relevance to diagnosis
Person perception	Forming impressions of clients
	Stereotypes of specific disorders
Judgmental heuristics	Diagnosis under uncertainty
Attribution	Attributions of causes of client's problems
Labeling	Effects of diagnostic labels on subsequent diagnoses
	Self-fulfilling labels
Inferential biases	Biases in clinical judgment
Conformity	Violation of residual rules

psychological processes relevant to understanding the development of dysfunctional behavior, including work in attribution, control, impression management, the self, and interpersonal relationships. Chapter 8 explores the
processes involved in the identification and diagnosis of behavioral and emotional problems, drawing on social psychological research on person perception, attribution, social inference, and labeling. Chapters 9 through 11 examine the interpersonal aspects of counseling and psychotherapy. In these

Table 1-3. Social Psychological Processes in the Treatment of
          Dysfunctional Behavior

Social psychological phenomenon	Relevance to treatment
Attitudes	Attitude change in therapy
Social influence, power	Therapy and counseling process
	Power strategies among hospitalized patients
Resistance to influence	Client resistance
	Compliance with treatment regimen
	Paradoxical therapy
Interpersonal attraction	Therapist-client relationship
Group dynamics	Group therapy
Self-fulfilling prophecies	Expectancy effects in treatment
	Hope
Cognitive dissonance	Effort justification in therapy
The self	Self-serving resistance in therapy
	Denial, repression
Modeling	Role playing
	Social-skills training
Relationships	Social support
	Coping with stressful events
	Transference

chapters, we focus on processes involving social influence, attitude change, cognitive dissonance, self-perception, self-efficacy, impression manage-ment, and expectancy effects. Finally, in Chapter 12, we briefly mention topics in social-dysgenic, social-diagnostic, and social-therapeutic psychol-ogy that we do not cover elsewhere in the book, and we address current issues within the field.

Part I

Interpersonal Origins of Dysfunctional Behavior

Chapter 2

Attributional Processes

Imagine that you are a counselor meeting a client who is newly divorced. When you ask about the circumstances, he has a ready explanation: Although he partly blames his ex-wife, he shoulders most of the responsibility himself. With somber affect, he declares that his wife's faithlessness was surely a result of his own inadequacy, that his failure with her shows he is not cut out for marriage, and that, indeed, he cannot imagine anyone ever being attracted to him again. For him, the evidence is clear: He simply does not measure up in the interpersonal marketplace.

Your depressive client would make clear two important points. First, people seek explanations for important (and for trivial) events in their lives; they spontaneously engage in causal analyses of their own and others' behavior, seeking to understand why it occurred (Weiner, 1985; Winter, Uleman, & Cunniff, 1985). Thus, any newly divorced person would be likely to have a set of working hypotheses explaining why he or she had become divorced (Hill, Rubin, & Peplau, 1976). Second, these explanations, or attributions, have important psychological consequences. One's emotional reactions, self-esteem, expectations for the future, and judgments of oneself and others are all influenced by one's causal beliefs. How well a person copes with diabetes (Tennen, Affleck, Allen, McGrade, & Ratzen, 1984), an industrial accident (Brewin, 1984), an abortion (Major, Mueller, & Hildebrandt, 1985), or a relationship's end (Hill et al., 1976), for example, will depend on how the person explains the traumatic event. Attribution theories in social psychology have attempted to describe the manner in which people decide what factors underlie and explain some event. In addition, attribution theorists have studied the effects these attributions have on subsequent feelings and behavior (cf. Antaki, 1982).

There are a variety of possible explanations for most of the events in our lives, and the causes we identify can be described by several different dimensions. Causes may be relatively internal, reflecting our own personalities, abilities, and efforts, or they may be more external, reflecting the influence of the situations (and other people) surrounding us. For instance, students who do well on exams usually attribute their performance to internal causes (e.g., their preparation and talent), whereas students who do poorly blame their performances on external factors (e.g., "ambiguous" tests). Causes may also be rather stable and lasting, as our abilities are, or unstable and impermanent, such as moods that come and go. In addition, causes may be relatively global, affecting many situations in our lives, or specific, affecting only a few. These three dimensions—internality, stability, and globality—have been used most frequently in the research we will discuss (e.g., Abramson, Seligman, & Teasdale, 1978; Weiner, Russell, & Lerman, 1978), but more recently a fourth dimension has been identified: We perceive some events as caused by factors we can control, others by factors that are uncontrollable. As we will see later, attributions to uncontrollable factors may be especially related to dysfunctions such as shyness and depression (Anderson & Arnoult, 1985).

In general, events are attributed to the apparent cause with which they seem to covary (Kelley, 1973). However, it is possible for two perceivers to formulate quite different attributional explanations for the same event from the same objective information, and this possibility makes attributional processes particularly relevant to the clinician and counselor. A person who attributes a moment of embarrassment to lasting, unchangeable, and broad personal deficiencies is likely to be much more humiliated than one who shrugs it off by seeing temporary, specific, manageable, environmental causes at work. Indeed, maladaptive attributions may create psychological problems, and more adaptive attributions can minimize them. We will later find that some practitioners suggest that most therapies involve some sort of attributional analysis and reinterpretation of a client's problems (Brewin & Antaki, 1982; Frank, 1973; Sloane, Staples, Cristol, Yorkston, & Whipple, 1975). This and the next chapter will address these issues, seeking to explicate the role of attributional processes in dysfunctional behavior.

Maladaptive Attributions

Molehills can appear to be mountains if we look at them the wrong way. Our explanations for an event can exaggerate its importance, and our attributions for small problems can make them seem much worse than they are. In the first half of this chapter we consider three examples of self-defeating attributional processes. First, we examine the manner in which attributional judgments may exacerbate dysfunctional behavior, creating sizeable problems out of trivial concerns. Second, we will find that some people employ damning judgmental patterns that are chronic enough to be termed "styles" of attribution. Finally, we investigate the mistakes, or misattributions, that complicate and confuse our perceptions of our own internal states.

The Emotional Exacerbation of Dysfunctional Behavior

Skilbeck (1974) described the case of Nancy N., a 21-year-old student who reported to a university counseling center in a state of agitation. She had been having trouble concentrating and felt she was doing badly in her abnormal psychology course. She attributed her woes to emerging psychopathology; her father and sister had undergone psychiatric hospitalization (and had recently visited her), and Nancy felt that her recent distraction was an indication that she, too, must be emotionally disturbed. Skilbeck reported, however, that Nancy's "symptoms" began with the announcement of an exam in her dreaded psychology course. In fact, she seemed to be experiencing apprehension and anxiety just like that of her classmates—but explaining it very differently. Skilbeck's intervention encouraged Nancy to explain her feelings not as free-floating pathology, but as a reasonably normal response to the anxiety-arousing test. With this less threatening explanation in hand, Nancy's feelings seemed much less troublesome, and her anxiety greatly diminished. It appears that Nancy's original attribution for her anxiety—thinking it indicative of incipient psychopathology—had actually added to her distress, making her even more anxious and distraught.

Indeed, Storms and McCaul (1976), elaborating an idea introduced by Storms and Nisbett (1970), argued that certain attributions can sometimes inflame unwanted behavior, making it worse. For many psychological conditions, an internal or personal attribution implies personal inadequacy and/or a lack of control that is frustrating, threatening, or embarrassing. Such attributions increase the sufferer's emotionality or "anxiety," and thereby fuel the original problem. This may occur because of increased physiological arousal (which would exacerbate insomnia, for example) or enhanced drive states (which would potentiate habitual responses, and increase stuttering), or because of self-deprecating cognitions that interfere with successful coping (as with shyness and test anxiety). Whatever the reason, the unwanted behavior is exacerbated by damning self-blame that sets the cycle in motion (see Figure 2-1).

Consider a male who, after drinking too much, finds himself impotent. If, instead of rightly blaming the alcohol, he formulates an internal attribution and begins to worry that there is something wrong with him, he may enter the exacerbation cycle that Storms and McCaul (1976) described. He may

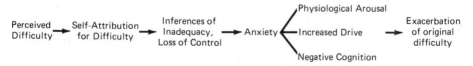

Figure 2-1. The emotional exacerbation of psychological dysfunction. Based on material in "Attribution Processes and Emotional Exacerbation of Dysfunctional Behavior" by M. D. Storms and K. D. McCaul. In J. H. Harvey, W. J. Ickes, & R. F. Kidd (Eds.), *New Directions in Attribution Research*, Vol. 1, 1976, Lawrence Erlbaum Associates, Inc.

ruminate about his inadequacy to the extent that, when he next finds himself in a sexual encounter, he is so tense and preoccupied with the possibility of another sexual failure that he is again unable to maintain an erection. One can imagine his dismay and his certainty that his is a serious problem; yet had he dismissed the first occurrence as an isolated, drug-related event, the "problem" would have never developed.

Storms and McCaul suggested that this exacerbation model is applicable to any behavioral syndrome in which the primary symptoms are increased by anxiety or emotionality. Thus, the model helps explain some instances of insomnia, shyness, phobia, depression, and even schizophrenia. As Storms and McCaul (1976) demonstrated, the model is certainly applicable to stuttering. They taped interviews with 44 males and then informed each of them that he had displayed a high number of speech dysfluencies (stammers, pauses, and repetitions). Half of the men were told that this was a normal result of experimental participation, but the remaining subjects were informed that the errors were attributable to their personal (and, apparently, deficient) speech patterns and abilities. When they were later asked to make a public speech, the self-attribution subjects evidenced a significantly greater increase in stammering than did those blaming their awkwardness on the unusual situation. The concern generated by their internal attributions made their dysfluencies worse, a finding that closely fits the experiences of real stutterers (e.g., Van Riper, 1971).

The exacerbation model is also relevant to the plight of insomniacs who, frustrated at their sleeplessness, become so restless that their insomnia lasts even longer. Van Egeren, Haynes, Franzen, and Hamilton (1983) randomly sampled the thoughts of subjects awaiting sleep and found that, unlike the rest of us, insomniacs focus on their insomnia, fretfully ruminating about their sleep problems. Moreover, as Storms and McCaul (1976) suggested, the more strongly insomniacs attribute their problems to internal causes, the more concerned they are about their sleeplessness, and the more elusive sleep becomes.

These findings suggest that insomniacs would profit by avoiding attributions that exacerbate their insomnia. Lowery, Denney, and Storms (1979) suggested two ways this might be done. In their study, some insomniacs received a placebo, which, they were told, would arouse them; participants in this "pill-attribution" treatment could logically attribute their restlessness to the pill, escaping any troublesome self-blame (cf. Storms & Nisbett, 1970). Other subjects in a second treatment were told that they were personally responsible for their insomnia, but that they should not worry; they were shown bogus physiological data indicating that their arousal levels were higher than average but were still completely normal. Lowery et al. found that, compared to no-treatment controls, subjects in both treatments found it easier to get to sleep; in addition, they found that subjects in the second, "nonpejorative" self-attribution group reported falling asleep more quickly.

Thus, an exacerbation cycle may be blocked either at its inception, by changing the individual's self-attribution, or by ameliorating the emotionality and anxiety a self-attribution would cause. However, as our later discussion will indicate, some self-attributions are easier to change than others. Moreover, internal or personal attributions for undesirable behavior are not necessarily disadvantageous. A self-attribution that precipitates exacerbation probably involves characteristics that are not only internal, but stable and uncontrollable as well (cf. Brewin & Antaki, 1982; Van Egeren et al., 1983). In contrast, a self-attribution that emphasizes the person's ability to control and change unwanted behavior is likely to be beneficial. For these reasons, the precise nature of the judgments that both trigger and prevent exacerbation warrants close consideration.

Interestingly, the second strategy of reducing a client's emotionality is, in one sense, already a component of established therapies. For example, Ascher and Efran (1978) reported that paradoxical intention is successful in treating insomnia. Urging an insomniac to *try* to remain awake, they believe, reduces the performance anxiety and frustration that make the insomnia worse. In addition, the nonpejorative analysis Lowery et al. (1979) employed bears a fundamental similarity to Ellis' (1977a) rational-emotive therapy; in both, the exaggerated importance clients attach to certain troublesome events is disputed.

The exacerbation model, then, emphasizes the role of a client's interpretation of his or her condition in exacerbating or minimizing some disorder. It clearly does not apply to all psychological dysfunction, but it may substantially affect some problems that have an emotional basis. Importantly, since exacerbation cycles are triggered by internal attributions, they may affect some people more often than others; people differ in their tendencies to make dispositional "self"-attributions. It is to these individual differences in attribution, or attributional styles, that we now turn.

Attributional Styles

It is well known that depressed people make "logical errors" in their thinking, magnifying the importance of negative events and minimizing whatever successes they do achieve (Beck, Rush, Shaw, & Emery, 1979). In fact, people who believe that they are chronic failures may be using a maladaptive attributional style that keeps them thinking so. A style of attribution is a "habitual way of anwering questions about causality" (Layden, 1982, p. 64). Such a habit could lead people to blame themselves routinely for failure even when they are not at fault; it could even become an attributional rut that contributes to dysfunctions like depression (see Peterson, Schwartz, & Seligman, 1981, and chapter 3).

In fact, chronic patterns of attribution appear to be rather commonplace. Weiner and Kukla (1970) have noted that persons high in achievement motivation take more personal responsibility for their successes than do those with lesser motivation. Ickes and Layden (1978) discussed the tendency of people with low self-esteem to externalize success and internalize failure to a greater extent than those high in self-esteem. Shy (Teglasi & Hoffman, 1982) and lonely (Anderson, Horowitz, & French, 1983) people, like depressives, attribute failures in their interactions with others to internal, stable defects in themselves. Even children show evidence of using specific attributional styles (Seligman et al., 1984).

Attributional styles and dysfunctional behavior. Such attributional styles may put some individuals at risk for emotional and behavioral problems. When a shy woman attributes another's antagonism or disinterest to her own personal inadequacy, she reinforces her shyness, perpetuating her inhibition and social anxiety. By seeing herself as the cause of another person's grumpy mood, she paints herself as inept and unskilled and makes future interactions all the more threatening. She may in fact be socially maladroit, and the unfavorable responses she receives from others may partially be of her own making. Still, her inability to distinguish her own awkwardness from other, external causes of uneasy interaction is likely to make her shyness more intractable.

In fact, Anderson (1983a) showed that certain attributional styles can lead to motivational and performance deficits in social situations. Using a pretest that assessed subjects' attributional styles, Anderson selected subjects who tended to blame interpersonal failures either on their own imperfect characters (with attributions to stable, uncontrollable abilities and traits) or on their inappropriate, but changeable, behavior. When he then asked his subjects to persuade others to donate blood (a task in which several failures were likely), the character-attribution group expected less success, displayed less motivation, improved less quickly, and—as one would guess—actually enjoyed fewer successes than those who blamed their failures on inappropriate behavior. Their habit of blaming failure on deficient traits appeared to rob the character-attribution group of the motivation and interest that would help them to improve.

In addition, Anderson (1983a) tried to convince some of his subjects that success at this novel task was due to the "basic persuasiveness of the caller"—that some people were simply good at recruiting blood donors, and others simply were not. By contrast, other subjects were led to believe that success was a matter of strategy and that good recruiters had merely found the most persuasive tactics. The subjects were thus led to anticipate success as a result of either their abilities and traits or their strategies and effort, respectively. The two groups behaved very differently. Whatever their natural attributional style, subjects who were led to make ability/trait attributions expected and enjoyed fewer successes than those who considered strategy and effort more important determinants of success.

Thus, Anderson found that naturally occurring attributional style differences are associated with actual behavioral differences, as studies of shy, lonely, and depressed persons would suggest. Importantly, he also demonstrated that experimentally changing an individual's attributional outlook can change one's motivation and performance as well.

Anderson's work clarifies the question of whether maladaptive styles precede and help create dysfunctional behavior, or whether they emerge as a result of the dysfunction (and then help perpetuate it). Metalsky and Abramson (1981) suggested, for instance, that attributional styles may exist either because people are constantly confronted with the same attributional data or because they rely on strong, generalized beliefs about causality that are sometimes inappropriate. In the first case, an internalizing, character-blaming style could result because a person really is inept and is accurately assessing his or her failures. In the second case, however, a person's mistaken beliefs could lead to chronic patterns of attribution that unfairly underestimate his or her skills. Anderson's (1983a) study provided evidence that belief-based styles *can* exist independently of any behavioral deficit: When equipped with a more desirable attributional set (in the strategy/effort condition), characterological self-blamers behaved just as effectively as other subjects. Their characteristically lower motivation and performance appear to have resulted more from their chronic style of cognition than from any lack of social skill. Thus, maladaptive attributional styles may often reflect existing behavioral deficits, but they can also help create dysfunctional behavior that would otherwise not exist.

The measurement of attributional style. Several different instruments have been used to measure attributional styles, but as we review them two related points should be kept in mind. A first consideration is that maladaptive attributional styles are often quite specific. Cutrona, Russell, and Jones (1984) found scant evidence for broad cross-situational styles of attribution, and, indeed, the self-defeating styles examined in other studies are usually limited to particular problem areas. Shy and lonely people, for instance, display unique patterns of attribution only for interpersonal failure situations; their judgments of personal performances that do not involve interaction with others and their perceptions of interpersonal successes do not differ from those of nonshy and nonlonely people (Anderson & Arnoult, 1985; Teglasi & Hoffman, 1982; cf. Watson & Dyck, 1984). Nevertheless, the apparent specificity of maladaptive attributional styles may be partly due to the use of measurement scales that assess respondents' attributions for hypothetical outcomes. When people are asked to explain actual events in their lives over a period of time, broad, cross-situational patterns of attribution may emerge (Zautra, Guenther, & Chartier, 1985).

A second point is that habitual use of particular attributions may be more damaging than others. In an examination of this issue, Anderson and Arnoult (1985) assessed subjects' depression, shyness, and loneliness and then measured their attributional styles with the Attributional Style Assessment Test developed by Anderson et al. (1983). Regression analyses indicated that subjects who routinely attributed events in their lives to causes they could not control were particularly likely to be shy, lonely, or depressed. People who blamed themselves for failure were also likely to suffer these dysfunctions, but whether people made stable or unstable, global or specific attributions did not matter much. Thus, certain types of attributions may be more debilitating than others. In particular, our (perceived) ability to control the events in our lives seems to be of fundamental impact, a matter we will consider in more detail in chapter 3. For now, let us note that efforts to measure (and, perhaps, to change) maladaptive patterns of attribution need to address the particular importance of uncontrollable, internal attributions as correlates of dysfunction.

Three different scales have been used to measure attributional style, and though they are conceptually similar each has a unique format. The first was developed by Ickes and Layden (1978); it consists of 24 hypothetical events and their positive or negative outcomes (e.g., "You got an 'A' on a class project"), which the respondent is asked to explain. Each item is followed by four possible causes, which are internal or external and stable or unstable (e.g., "You worked hard to prepare this project," or "The project was relatively easy"), and the perceived influence of each is rated on 5-point scales. The scale thus assesses only the internality and stability of respondents' explanations, but it has been successful in identifying chronic patterns of attributions (e.g., Sober-Ain & Kidd, 1984).

The Attributional Style Questionnaire (ASQ) developed by Peterson et al. (1982) expands on Ickes and Layden's (1978) effort by distinguishing interpersonal situations (e.g., "You go out on a date and it goes badly") from achievement situations (e.g., "You become very rich"). Again, half of the items describe positive events, half negative. Subjects are asked to envision the situation and write down the one major cause that comes to mind; that freely chosen cause is then rated on separate 7-point scales assessing its internality, stability, and globality. The ASQ has the advantage of not constraining the subject's judgments of causality, and several studies (e.g., Seligman et al., 1978) point to its usefulness, but its psychometric properties have been recently criticized (Cutrona et al., 1984; Johnson, Petzel, & Sperduto, 1983).

Anderson and his colleagues (1983a; Anderson et al., 1983) have since developed their own Attributional Style Assessment Test (ASAT). It is the most elaborate of the three, consisting of 36 interpersonal or noninterpersonal successes or failures, which, in the latest version of the scale (Anderson & Arnoult, 1985), are judged using the same response format as that of the ASQ. Unlike the ASQ, however, the ASAT asks for ratings of each cause's *controllability* in addition to ratings of its internality, stability, and globality. Given the importance of the controllability dimension (Anderson & Arnoult, 1985), the ASAT thus seems to be the most useful of the three scales. Nevertheless, it is likely that they have all enjoyed some success because they all use items that contain minimal situational information and so are causally ambiguous (Metalsky & Abramson, 1981). For instance, one ASAT item describes this interpersonal failure: "You have just attended a party for new students and failed to make any new friends.'' The lack of detail forces respondents to rely on their own generalized beliefs or past histories, allowing their personal patterns of attribution to emerge.

Modifying attributional styles. To the extent that a shy, lonely, or depressed person actually lacks the social skills necessary for rewarding interactions with others, some self-blame is appropriate, and a behavioral therapy that teaches the needed skills is desirable. Still, as we have seen, a maladaptive style can create dysfunction in the absence of any behavioral deficit, keeping sufferers from recognizing and appreciating the successes that they already enjoy. In this case, as Layden (1982) notes, it may be useful to attempt to change their attributional habits, asking them ''to scan success situations for internal causes, to focus on abilities and personality traits they normally ignore, and to make realistic estimates of the amount of effort they expend'' (p. 72).

This may be easier said than done, however. Convincing a client that his or her perceptions of events are inaccurate may be quite difficult. Layden (1982) suggests that clients frequently deny that they have an attributional habit, or, if they do recognize the patterns in their judgments, insist that their perceptions are accurate. They may have to be shown why it would be to their advantage to change, and even then they may consider it immodest not to blame themselves for their troubles. Indeed, Ickes and Layden (1978) found that merely getting low self-esteem subjects to practice making attributions that were inconsistent with their styles (i.e., encouraging them to internalize success and externalize failure) did not consistently change their styles. Ickes and Layden asked their subjects to list as many possible causes—of the appropriate type—they could think of for 15 positive and 15 negative specific events occurrring during the 5-week study. The subjects were not given a rationale for this procedure and were not shown how some attributions were better than others. Perhaps as a result, this minimal intervention did not produce consistent effects; still, when subjects' styles did change, there was a concomitant increase in their self-esteem.

Thus, interventions designed to change a client's attributional style probably should strive to demonstrate *why* such changes are both feasible and desirable, thereby providing the client with needed incentive and purpose. In support of this, Sober-Ain and Kidd (1984) compared Ickes and Layden's (1978) alternative-attribution treatment with a condition in which an active, supportive experimenter consistently rewarded ''appropriate'' attributions, stressed the advantages of such attributions, and boosted the egos of self-blaming subjects. This ''supportive suggestion'' treatment appeared to be more effective than Ickes and Layden's strategy in changing the subjects' styles, but the changes, although beneficial (cf. Layden, 1982), came grudgingly. It appears that attributional styles can be so habitual that clients may need considerable help in altering them. Indeed, Sober-Ain and Kidd warned that, ''since attributional style is a pervasive, and possibly a dispositional, characteristic of the person, global change is apt to take place slowly, if at all'' (p. 134).

Misattributions: Mistaken Causality

As the preceding discussion of attributional styles implies, our judgments regarding the causes of our—and others'—feelings and behaviors are not always accurate. We do not always know why we do what we do, and we may occasionally believe that we are influenced by particular factors that in fact have little effect. In short, *mis*attributions, or mistaken perceptions of causality, are possible. Moreover, they can help develop or maintain dysfunctional behavior.

Johnson, Ross, and Mastria (1977) presented a case study that exemplifies this point. A 37-year-old male was institutionalized with the belief that he was being sexually aroused by an unseen "warm form." He never masturbated but had been brought to orgasm several times by this mysterious entity. Understandably, he was quite concerned. When Johnson et al. encouraged him to attribute his sensations to normal sexual desire (he had no steady partner) and inadvertent masturbation through leg movements, his delusions disappeared and he had no further problems. In this case, the misattribution to a fictional cause was the problem.

Misattribution can inflame existing dysfunctions as well. For instance, Borkovec, Wall, and Stone (1974) provided speech-anxious subjects with bogus heart rate feedback, which indicated that a brief speech had caused their pulse rates to increase. When later they gave another speech, they become more discombobulated than they had been earlier, becoming more anxious and displaying more speech dysfluencies. In addition, they were more uneasy than other subjects who had heard feedback suggesting either that their heart rates had decreased or that they had not changed. The mistaken belief that they had been physiologically aroused by the prior talk apparently led them to suppose that their speech anxiety was even more serious than they had thought. Indeed, one of the present authors has forsworn caffeinated coffee because he realized, in retrospect, that he sometimes misattributed his caffeine-induced arousal to performance anxiety in stressful situations.

In a related vein, alcoholics who believe they are drinking vodka-and-tonics, but who are actually drinking straight tonic water, develop the same craving for additional liquor that they do when drinking real vodka. Similarly, tonic water gets male subjects just as aggressive as vodka does (alcohol increases aggression), if the men think there is vodka in the drink (Marlatt & Rohsenow, 1980). Examples like these illustrate that what we think does influence what we feel, and our wrongful perceptions can create problems where none would otherwise exist.

Mistaking the level of arousal. Two broad types of misattribution are possible. In the first, one misperceives one's *level* of arousal in response to some stimulus. In studies of this phenomenon, subjects are led to believe that they are or are not being influenced by surrounding events (manipulating, in Kelley and Michela's [1980] terms, selective "arousal" or "quiescence"). The first studies to manipulate either arousal or quiescence were both performed 20 years ago by Valins (1966; Valins & Ray, 1967). In his first study, Valins showed men photographs of female models while they listened to an amplified rhythmic sound that they believed was their own heartbeat. For half of the photographs, subjects heard the "pulse rate" change, either increasing or decreasing; in truth, the subjects heard a tape recording that could be controlled by the experimenter. The subjects' heart rates had not actually changed, and different photos were associated with the pulse change for different men. Nevertheless, when they were later asked to judge the photos, the men generally liked best whichever pictures they could reasonably assume had "turned them on." The bogus information regarding their internal arousal had affected their choices of which photos were the most compelling.

Valins and Ray (1967) soon followed with a provocative study that had more obvious clinical implications. They attempted to convince participants that they were not being greatly affected by a stimulus that actually did arouse them. They recruited subjects with mild phobias toward snakes and showed them slides of reptiles while they listened to bogus heart rate feedback. The snake photos were intermixed with photos of the word "shock," and when "shock" appeared, the viewers were actually given a mild electric shock. The subjects found that their "heart rates" increased when they were confronted by "shock" but remained steady when snakes appeared. They were thus led to believe that the snakes did not affect them particularly much, and compared to a control group who believed the "heartbeat" rhythm to be extraneous noise, the misattribution subjects seemed less wary of snakes, becoming more likely to approach and even touch live snakes.

Influencing a person's perceived level of arousal, then, may minimize, as well as exacerbate, dysfunctions. Koenig (1973), for instance, provided test-anxious subjects with manipulated information about their emotionality, confronting them with a galvanic skin response meter that indicated high, average, or low arousal. As the preceding discussion suggests, subjects' belief that they were strongly aroused debilitated their subsequent performance on math problems; attributing their apparent anxiety to the testing situation made it an even more threatening stimulus. By contrast, subjects given low-arousal feedback, indicating relative calm and relaxation, did better than average, answering more problems correctly and working more quickly. The belief that they were not experiencing their usual anxiety apparently facilitated their performance, largely obviating, for the moment at least, their very real problem.

Mistaking the cause of arousal. Thus, changing a person's perceptions of how much he or she is reacting to some event can have desirable as well as undesirable outcomes. There is, however, a second broad type of misattribution that was once believed to have even greater therapeutic potential. People may misunderstand not only the level but the *source* of their arousal as well. Studies of this kind of misattribution induce subjects to attribute troublesome emotional reactions not to their actual cause but to less threatening, emotionally neutral sources. In this way, fear or anxiety can be reinterpreted as innocuous "stimulation" or "activation," thereby making one's feelings less worrisome. Unlike Valins' paradigm, which might try to convince subjects that they are not much aroused, this approach attempts to get subjects thinking that their obvious arousal is not aversive.

Dienstbier and Munter (1971) provided a good example of this technique. All of their subjects took a placebo pill, and half of them were told to expect noticeable arousal as a result. The subjects then encountered failure on a contrived vocabulary test and were given an opportunity to change their answers covertly to improve their scores. Dienstbier and Munter suggested that the tension and guilt that usually accompany cheating normally inhibit wrongdoing. However, half of their subjects could reasonably assume that any nervousness was being caused by the pill rather than by personal guiltiness, and with that misattribution cheating would be less aversive. In fact 49% of the pill/arousal group cheated by changing their answers, versus 27% of a control group. The results suggested that "even naturally occurring emotion is subject to this apparent ease of reinterpretation" (p. 213).

Studies like these imply that we are not always certain of our feelings and that misattributions of the cause and extent of our emotions are possible. Moreover, whereas certain misattributions may create or exacerbate dysfunctions, other attributional mistakes may have a beneficial effect. To complete our discussion of misattributions, therefore, we need to address their potential therapeutic uses and begin consideration of the adaptive applications of attributional processes.

Adaptive Attributions

Misattributions

Under the impetus of provocative studies like that of Valins and Ray (1967), misattribution research flourished in the 1970s, and the term *attribution therapy* was introduced (Ross, Rodin, & Zimbardo, 1969). It was thought that misattribution procedures might be readily applied to clinical settings as treatments; in particular, interventions that led people to misattribute internal arousal to external sources often seemed to have therapeutic effects. A well-known study by Storms and Nisbett (1970) exemplified this approach. Insomniacs, it was argued, exacerbated their sleeplessness by attributing it to internal causes and making it a threatening, anxiety-arousing event. If they could be supplied a plausible cause for their restlessness that did not create further anxiety, their worry and arousal would be reduced, and they would be more likely to fall asleep. Accordingly, Storms and Nisbett assigned insomniacs to one of three conditions. One group was given a placebo pill that, they were told, would arouse them. A second group believed that the pill would calm them down, and a third, control group was given no pill at all. Of course, the placebo did not actually affect the subjects' insomnia, but the "aroused" group could reasonably attribute their sleeplessness to the pill; by contrast, the relaxation group found themselves just as restless as ever despite the supposed sedative. As a result, the aroused subjects reported getting to sleep 12 minutes faster, and the relaxation group 15 minutes slower, than they had before the experiment.

Further studies extended these effects. For instance, Barefoot and Girodo (1972) led smokers to believe that the effects of nicotine withdrawal were due to a pill they had taken, thereby substantially reducing their craving for cigarettes. Brodt and Zimbardo (1981) bombarded shy women with aversive noise just prior to an interaction with an attractive male, enabling them to explain their apprehension and social anxiety not as shyness but as a result of the noise. This simple manipulation temporarily "cured" shyness; the behavior of shy subjects who misattributed their anxiety to the external noise was no different from that of normal controls.

Here, then, was a set of techniques that were reasonably simple, quick, inexpensive, and often provocatively effective. Unfortunately, they did not always work. Storms and Nisbett's (1970) "insomnia" study was shortly followed by two failures to replicate that called the generality of their work into question (Bootzin, Herman, & Nicassio, 1976; Kellogg & Baron, 1975). Singerman, Borkovec, and Baron (1976), using a procedure much like that of Brodt and Zimbardo (1981), were unable to convince speech-anxious subjects that their nervousness was due to noise bombardment; the subjects (correctly) continued to believe that it was their speechmaking that was upsetting them. These studies suggested that the implementation of a therapeutic misattribution was no sure thing. The effect depended on the creation of a plausible, convincing, neutral source that could explain untoward arousal, and if a person's arousal (or fear or anxiety) was high (Nisbett & Schachter, 1966) or was very familiar (Ross et al., 1969; Singerman et al., 1976; Slivken & Buss, 1984), this was hard to do.

Similar problems beset the Valins and Ray (1967) paradigm, which attempted to change subjects' perceptions of the level of their arousal. Borkovec and Glasgow (1973) found that false heart rate feedback helped reduce subjects' snake phobias only when they had not recently encountered a real snake; contact with a snake just before the misattribution procedure apparently made their fear so salient that they could not be readily convinced of their newfound calm. In addition, Conger, Conger, and Brehm (1976) showed that it was easier to modify the snake-avoidance behavior of low-fear than of high-fear subjects; again, the greater one's arousal, the harder it was to change one's perception of it.

Thus, despite the excitement and interest generated by misattribution techniques, the adaptive uses of misattributions now appear to be limited, for two interrelated reasons: First, it is difficult to convince subjects that strong emotions that have troubled them for some time either are not particularly potent or are largely caused by innocuous factors they had not considered. This can be done, of course, given enough experimental control, but such misattributions are unlikely to last (and this is our second reason) because they are inherently deceptive. The beneficial belief that one's insomnia is being caused by a stimulant pill depends on both the presence of the pill and the fragile fiction that, without it, one's insomnia would be reduced. Such misattributions are difficult to maintain in a person's normal environment simply because they are falsehoods. Indeed, therapists may be reluctant to employ them at all for this reason. Misattribution may be quite useful for treatment of infrequent events and novel symptoms (Fincham, 1983), but at bottom, the alternative use of adaptive *reattributions* probably has wider applicability.

Reattributions

Instead of trying to mislead people, however kindly, about the level or the source of their symptoms, why not try to equip them with an *accurate* but nevertheless more desirable attribution for their feelings? In providing *reattributions*, one suggests explanations for a person's experience that point to (at least potentially) veridical causes that are less threatening than those the person has already identified. To promote coping, the person's dysfunction is interpreted as less severe and more manageable than it now seems. Reattributions follow the same lines as, but are usually much more specific than, efforts to retrain a person's broad attributional style; whereas style interventions must break an enduring habit of pejorative self-attribution, reattributions are most often designed to facilitate coping with a particular delimited problem. For instance, Valins and Nisbett (1972) described the distress encountered by sufferers of the "FNG [for "fucking new guy"] syndrome" in Vietnam. New arrivals in the war zone were often met with suspicion and hostility by field veterans, a situation that greatly disturbed many of the new men. To deal with the syndrome, the newcomers were urged to replace the attribution "They hate me" with the more tolerable explanation "They hate the FNG." Reattributing the others' hostility to situational role requirements instead of some personal deficiency made the adjustment period easier to endure.

The concept of reattribution is quite similar to processes already at the heart of many psychotherapies. Whether one uses psychoanalysis or behavior modification, for instance, one relies on new causal interpretations of a client's dysfunction in order to motivate and direct his or her coping responses (Sloane et al., 1975). Strong (1978) has argued that, "changing . . . causal attributions is the therapist's first order of business" (p. 27), and

Hoffman and Teglasi (1982) suggested that all counseling therapies provide new interpretations and frames of reference for the client. In fact, Hoffman and Teglasi found that providing shy clients with *any* causal attribution for their shyness increased their motivation, involvement, and expectations of success beyond those of clients who were not provided some explanation of their problem (cf. Strong, Wambach, Lopez, & Cooper, 1979). Thus, social psychological reattribution is not a new idea. However, as we are about to find, most reattribution training explicitly addresses the preferred use of particular attributional dimensions, and is thus more specific than most "interpretations" (cf. Försterling, 1985).

A well-known study by Dweck (1975) is a good example. She identified 12 children with extreme, helpless reactions to failure and placed each child into one of two 25-day treatments. Half of the children encountered constant success on arithmetic problems (and were given personal credit for their achievements), whereas the other subjects met with both success and failure. When the latter children failed, however, they were implicitly urged to attribute their failure to a lack of effort: "You should have tried harder." When all the children were later given difficult (i.e., failure-producing) problems, the failure-reattribution children persisted in their attempts to solve the problems, but the success-only children quickly gave up. Learning to attribute failure to controllable, unstable factors such as effort promoted perseverance and achievement better than did getting a taste of success.

Similar results have been obtained with children's reading behavior (Chapin & Dyck, 1976) and perceptual reasoning (Andrews & Debus, 1978), and two provocative studies by Wilson and Linville (1982, 1985) have even extended these effects to college freshmen. In their studies, students who were instructed that low first-term grades were due to unstable causes (and thus were likely to improve) actually achieved higher grades in subsequent semesters and were somewhat less likely to drop out of school than were "untreated" control subjects.

Importantly, such reattributions may have more profound and lasting effects than mere persuasive advice, especially when they influence a person's self-perceptions. Miller, Brickman, and Bolen (1975) compared the effectiveness of an attribution treatment stressing ability or effort (e.g., "You really work hard in arithmetic") to persuasive exhortations (e.g., "You should work harder") and positive reinforcements (e.g., a "math award") in improving student achievement in mathematics. The attribution treatments clearly had more effective and lasting impact, leading to significantly more long-term improvement. Leading the students to internalize desirable behavior by identifying the personal, controllable causes at work was thus a much more valuable approach than either instructing them how to act or rewarding them for their successes.

Indeed, a series of studies by Haemmerlie and Montgomery (1982, 1984; Haemmerlie, 1983; Montgomery & Haemmerlie, in press) has successfully ameliorated heterosocial anxiety in college students not by teaching them new skills, but by leading them to think differently about the ones they already have. In this procedure, anxious subjects engage in "purposefully biased" 10-minute interactions with each of six different opposite-sex peers. These "interaction assistants" need not know the purpose behind these meetings, and are merely instructed to carry on pleasant conversation (without being negative, discussing sex, or making any dates). Whether or not the subjects think they are getting "therapy" and whether their expectations are positive or negative, the procedure seems to be quite beneficial, substantially reducing the subjects' anxiety. It is much more effective, in fact, than an imaginal therapy in which subjects envision successful interactions without actually engaging in them (Haemmerlie & Montgomery, 1984). Admittedly, this treatment is unlikely to work with persons who have real social-skills deficits. Nevertheless, for reasonably skillful people, the procedure may lead to a reattribution of the occasional successes they do enjoy; subjects are implicitly taught not only that they can have enjoyable interactions with others, but that they are more adept than they might have believed. In this and other reattribution research, learning how to explain successes (and failures) more profitably appears to be as important as experiencing the successes themselves.

Recent research does suggest that personal and contextual variables can influence the effectiveness of adaptive reattribution, however. Forsyth and Forsyth (1982), for example, found that a counseling session that invited subjects to attribute their social anxiety to internal and controllable (and thus manageable, changeable) causes was more helpful for subjects with an internal, rather than an external, locus of control (cf. Brewin & Shapiro, 1985). Moreover, the timing of the reattribution intervention may be important (Altmaier, Leary, Forsyth, & Ansel, 1979). Forsyth and Forsyth were led to conclude that, "an even-handed analysis suggests that a guided exploration of the causes of behavioral and psychological problems may be helpful for only (unfortunately) some of the people some of the time" (1983, p. 457).

Still, when they are wisely chosen and are applied to selected individuals (they are obviously unlikely to palliate paranoia, for example), reattributions may have considerable beneficial impact. Storms and his colleagues have now forsworn misattribution therapies for insomnia in favor of veridical reattributions that explain the problem as normal, albeit high, levels of autonomic arousal (Storms, Denney, McCaul, & Lowery, 1979). The procedure is ethical and effective and often leads to improvement over time. Indeed, as Storms et al. noted, adaptive attributions can also facilitate the *maintenance* of desirable change in behavior over long periods of time, well beyond the end of any organized therapy.

The Maintenance of Behavior Change

The long-term success of a therapeutic intervention may depend on the perceptions with which a client leaves therapy. The client who judges external factors (such as an ingenious therapist or a calming drug) to be the primary cause of his or her improvement may find it hard to maintain his or her gains when the external agents are withdrawn. If a person suffering from sleeplessness thinks 1) "I'm an insomniac, but, " 2) "this medication helps me sleep," imagine his or her dismay on finding the medicine bottle empty. By contrast, if the client sees himself or herself as personally capable of managing the dysfunction, the treatment gains may be more likely to last. When faced with sleeplessness, the client might think, "I *can* deal with this." This approach to maintenance touches on issues we will also address in chapters 3 (perceptions of control) and 11 (self-efficacy). Nevertheless, the specific manner in which a person attributes desirable change seems to be a central concern.

Again consider insomnia. In one of the first tests of the attributional maintenance hypothesis, Davison, Tsujimoto, and Glaros (1973) provided insomniac subjects a treatment package in which they scheduled a specific time for settling down to sleep, received relaxation training, and took 1,000 mg of a hypnotic (chloral hydrate) each night before bedtime. For a week thereafter the subjects reported the latency and quality of their sleep, and for most the treatment was effective; most of them fell asleep in less than half their usual time. At the end of that week, however, the subjects were divided into two groups: Some were told that they had been taking an optimal dosage of the drug, making it "a very effective sleep aid"; the others were informed they had been taking a minimal, "very ineffective" dosage. The subjects were thus led to perceive the drug either as an important active agent in their improvement or as a largely inconsequential adjunct. They then went home without the drug and were told to rely on their scheduling and relaxation for the next several days. The optimal-drug group slipped badly, requiring an average 45 minutes longer to get to sleep than they had needed the preceding nights. By contrast, the minimal-drug group regressed less precipitously, taking only 13 minutes longer and, unlike their drug-oriented counterparts, retaining some of their treatment gains. A check of the subjects' attributions showed that the two groups had indeed made different attributions for their prior improvement: The optimal-drug group believed that the drug had been mostly responsible, whereas the minimal-drug subjects credited themselves. As a result, Davison et al. asserted that the favorable self-attributions of the minimal-drug subjects had facilitated the maintenance of their behavioral change (cf. Davison & Valins, 1969).

Their argument received further support from subsequent studies that extended this framework to methods of weight reduction and smoking cessation. Behavioral weight control techniques are often successful, but they are plagued by clients' failures to maintain their new lower weights (Stunkard & Penick, 1979). Jeffrey (1974) provided suggestive evidence indicating that these failures could be reduced if clients were taught a greater sense of self-control. In his study, obese subjects were placed in one of two treatment groups. For the first group, the therapist controlled the rewards they received (which consisted of cash refunds from money they had deposited with the program) for meeting weight-loss goals. The other participants doled out their own rewards, and their personal responsibility for managing their weight was stressed. Everybody lost weight during the 7-week treatment, but only the self-control subjects maintained their progress over a 6-week follow-up period; on average, the external-control subjects regained 55% of the weight they had lost. In a partial replication, Sonne and Janoff (1979) specifically assessed subjects' attributions for their weight loss and even more obviously supported the attributional maintenance hypothesis: The more personal control over their weight subjects perceived, the more likely they were to continue to lose weight over a 3-month follow-up period. Colletti and Kopel (1979) obtained similar results in a smoking cessation study over an even longer posttreatment period of 1 year. Indeed, they flatly argued that, "superior maintenance is associated with a greater degree of self-attribution (p. 616; cf. Chambliss & Murray, 1979).

The size of the behavioral differences that are obtained between external-attribution and self-attribution subjects in studies like these, although statistically significant, is sometimes small (e.g., Sonne & Janoff, 1979). This fact has not been lost on some critical observers (Grimm, 1980). Nevertheless, the wide applicability of the attributional maintenance model—to alcoholism (Davies, 1982) and drug therapies with hyperactive children (Whalen & Henker, 1976) among other examples—and the weight of the empirical evidence clearly point to its usefulness and importance. This is also true in that a person's sense of self-responsibility and self-control in a specific therapeutic treatment is usually *modifiable,* and can be enhanced by a judicious therapist.

There are several ways to do this. Kopel and Arkowitz (1975) suggested using the "least powerful reward or punishment" that will work in any behavior modification procedure. Bowers (1975) echoed this idea with his concept of "subtle control." The external response contingencies facing a person should not be so overwhelming that self-attributions for desirable change are undermined. Similarly, Kopel and Arkowitz advocate allowing a client to play an active role in the planning and execution of his or her therapy whenever possible. Both of these tactics are likely to enhance the client's sense of behavioral freedom (Sonne & Janoff, 1982), maximizing his or her feelings of self-direction and self-control. Sonne and Janoff also suggested showing clients how capable they are through videotape replays of their own behavioral successes. At the very least, these clinicians agree, therapists should be alert to the potential value of appropriate self-attribution in helping maintain therapeutic change.

Conclusions

Our perceptions of why we behave the way we do appear to be centrally involved in the development and, perhaps, the amelioration of dysfunctional behavior. It seems to be advantageous to consider one's problems changeable and controllable, and one's causal attributions either facilitate or preclude that view. Indeed Brewin and Antaki (1982) raised the provocative argument that the usefulness of the various etiological models used in psychotherapy (that is, whether one's problems are described in psychoanalytic, behavioral, or other terms) depends largely on how well they help clients reattribute their problems in desirable directions. This is not to imply, of course, that modification of a person's causal attributions is always readily accomplished. We have seen that general attributional styles are difficult to change, and Peterson (1982) has wisely reminded us that we should not approach attributional beliefs "as if they were removable like psychological tumors" (p. 107). Nevertheless, attributional processes remain a key focus of the social/clinical interface because of their primary importance: "attributions affect our feelings about past events and our expectations about future ones, our attitudes toward other persons and our reactions to their behavior, and our conceptions of ourselves and our efforts to improve our fortunes" (Kelley & Michela, 1980, p. 489).

Chapter 3
Attributions, Perceived Control, and Depression

Many theories in psychology are based on the assumption that an individual's sense of psychological well-being is augmented by a belief that he or she has some degree of control over personally relevant events. As early as 1930, the neo-Freudian Alfred Adler observed that the need for control is "an intrinsic necessity of life" (Adler, 1930, p. 398)—a point that has been reiterated by many other theorists (e.g., Bandura, 1977; deCharms, 1968; Langer, 1983; Lefcourt, 1973; White, 1959; Woodworth, 1958). As usually defined, control is said to exist when an individual's outcomes are dependent upon his or her responses (Seligman, 1975). *Perceived* control is more important than control per se, however. As we shall see, people's *beliefs* about how much control they have are more closely associated with functional and dysfunctional reactions than is their objective level of control.

Perceived control fosters a sense of personal well-being for many reasons. Control over one's environment allows the individual to achieve desired goals while avoiding outcomes that are aversive. As a result, it is rewarding to feel that one is in control of personality relevant events, and frustrating or threatening to feel that one is not.

Further, studies show that the mere belief that one can control one's outcomes has positive psychological effects, even when one's perception of control is mistaken and, in reality, no control exists. For example, people are less anxious about experiencing painful stimuli (such as electric shocks) when they *think* they can control their onset, and aversive stimuli are perceived as less painful when people think they can control them, *even when no control exists or they choose not to exert control* (Bowers, 1968; Glass & Singer, 1972; Kanfer & Seidner, 1973). Similarly, information that leads surgery patients to believe they can control their pain through cognitive means reduces the need for pain killers and sedatives (Langer, Janis, & Wolfer, 1975). In another intriguing line of research, Pennebaker and his colleagues have found that perceived failure to control one's environment leads people to report an increased number of physical symptoms (Pennebaker, Burnam, Schaeffer, & Harper, 1977). As these studies demonstrate, perceived control over one's outcomes generally has positive effects, whereas perceived lack of control has dysfunctional consequences.

The effects of perceived control have been of particular interest in real-world settings that lead people to conclude that they have little control over their lives. Langer and Rodin (1976) explored the impact of perceived control upon elderly residents in a nursing home, an environment conducive to feelings of helplessness (see also Schulz, 1976). An administrator gave two different talks to samples of the residents; one talk emphasized the residents' responsibility for themselves, admonishing them to make their own decisions about their lives in the facility, whereas the other talk emphasized the staff's responsibility for the residents. In both cases, the responsibility and options stressed by the administrator were already available to the residents, so the groups differed chiefly in the degree to which their freedom, responsibility, and choice were explicitly stressed.

Compared to the other residents, those who heard the talk that emphasized their personal control and responsibility became more active and alert, rated themselves as happier, and became more involved in activities within the facility. The nursing staff rated them as more interested, sociable, self-initiating, and vigorous than other residents, and follow-up data collected 18 months after the intervention showed long-term psychological and physical effects (Rodin & Langer, 1977). Overall, the residents who experienced greater personal control showed a greater improvement in health and a lower mortality rate.

As this brief review demonstrates, people's beliefs regarding their personal effectiveness and control have important implications for their psychological and physical well-being. Not surprisingly, a great deal of attention has been devoted to identifying the factors that foster a sense of personal control, and to understanding the emotional and behavioral consequences of losing perceived control. In this chapter, we examine dysfunctional reactions that can occur when people feel they have lost control, focusing on how these problems are affected by the kinds of attributions they make.

Learned Helplessness

As hard as they might try, people cannot always control what happens to them. Despite their best efforts, people become ill; lose their jobs; have accidents; fail in business, school, and love; and experience a host of other negative events that they try hard to avoid. Because their responses to such events affect the quality of people's lives, a great deal of research has explored how people react to instances in which they lose control over aspects of their lives.

Interestingly, the earliest work on this topic was conducted not on human beings, but on dogs. In 1967, Overmeier and Seligman showed that dogs that had been exposed to electric shocks that they were unable to escape later had great difficulty learning to escape shock in a new situation. Unlike animals that had earlier experienced escapable shock or no shock at all, dogs that had previously suffered uncontrollable shock failed to exert control even when avoidance of the shock became possible. This debilitating effect of uncontrollable events, termed *learned helplessness,* has since been demonstrated in a variety of species, including cats, rats, fish, pigeons, and humans. This extensive research is far beyond our capacity to review here, and so we will focus our attention on only one portion of the literature, that dealing with helplessness and depression in humans, and suggest that the interested reader see Garber and Seligman (1980) for a more extensive review of the helplessness literature.

Learned Helplessness and Depression

In an early statement of his theory of learned helplessness, Seligman (1975) noted the similarities between the behavioral consequences of learned helplessness in animals and the concomitant features of reactive depression in humans. Specifically, he observed that depression and learned helplessness share several common features, including passivity in the face of aversive outcomes, difficulty in learning that outcomes are controllable, and affective correlates involving depression and/or anxiety. On the basis of these similarities, Seligman (1974, 1975) suggested that reactive depression in humans, like learned helplessness in animals, may result from the perception that one has no control over important outcomes.

In his original statement of the theory, Seligman maintained that helplessness occurs when an organism learns to expect that its behavior will not influence the likelihood of certain outcomes. The expectancy that one's outcomes are independent of one's responses (or "noncontingent") was assumed to produce the motivational, cognitive, and affective consequences associated with both learned helplessness and depression.

However, Seligman's (1975) original theory had difficulty accounting for some aspects of learned helplessness in depressed humans (Abramson et al., 1978). For example, the theory did not specify the conditions under which the perception of noncontingent outcomes leads to helplessness. As Abramson et al. (1978) noted, many events in life that people regard as uncontrollable do not depress them. Second, the original theory did not explain why depression is often accompanied by low self-esteem. Third, the theory did not easily account for the paradoxical finding that depressed individuals tend to blame themselves for events over which they think they have no control (Abramson & Sackheim, 1977). Perhaps most importantly, the original model did not address either the chronicity or the generality of depression; the time course of depression can vary from minutes to years, and encompass all of a person's life or only part.

The Attributional Model of Helpless Depression

In a reformulation of learned helplessness theory, Abramson et al. (1978) proposed that helplessness effects in humans are mediated by the causal attributions people make when they find themselves unable to control important outcomes. Specifically, the reformulated model posits that learned helplessness occurs when individuals make attributions that lead them to expect that they will be unable to control their outcomes in the future. Further, using three of the attributional dimensions introduced in chapter 2 (internal-external, stable-unstable, global-specific), Abramson et al. showed how a person's attributions might affect the cognitive, motivational, and affective aspects of depression.

Internal-external. According to Abramson et al. (1978), attributing one's helplessness to internal factors—characteristics of oneself—results in "personal helplessness," in which the person believes that his or her lack of control is due to a personal deficiency. As a result, personal helplessness is often accompanied by lowered self-esteem. However, when a person makes an external attribution, explaining helplessness in terms of the situation or other people, "universal helplessness" results. Because an external attribution implies that *no one* would be able to control the outcome, self-esteem is not affected, although helplessness and depression may still occur.

Stable-unstable. Some causes of helplessness are perceived as stable and unchangeable (such as a physical deformity or an incurable disease), whereas others are regarded as unstable and potentially changeable (e.g., temporary fatigue). The attributional reformulation of learned helplessness posits that attributions to stable factors result in deeper depression and in greater motivational decrements than do attributions to unstable factors, because the individual expects that the helplessness will persist over time. When the cause of one's difficulty is thought to be temporary or modifiable, the individual may continue to work toward control and show few helplessness deficits. Thus, the chronicity or time course of a depressive episode may be related to the stability of the perceived causes.

Global-specific. The perceived causes of one's helplessness may be ones that affect many areas of one's life (i.e., global) or just a few (i.e., specific). The more global the apparent causes of one's helplessness are, the deeper the depression and the more it generalizes to many areas of life.

Thus, from the standpoint of the individual confronting an uncontrollable situation, the most dysfunctional attributions are those that emphasize internal, stable, and global causes, and the least dysfunctional involve factors that are external, unstable, and specific.

Research on the Attributional Model

Attributional style and depression. Abramson et al. (1978) speculated that certain people may be more likely to become depressed than others because they have a "depressive attributional style" characterized by a tendency to attribute negative events to internal, stable, and global factors. Persons who tend to make these sorts of attributions should be particularly prone to general and chronic helpless depression that is accompanied by lowered self-esteem.

In fact, research prior to the appearance of the attributional model of learned helplessness did show that depressed subjects are more likely to make internal attributions for their failures than are nondepressed individuals (e.g., Klein, Fencil-Morse, & Seligman, 1976; Kuiper, 1978; Rizley, 1978). The first study explicitly designed to test the relationship between attributional style and depression, however, was conducted by Seligman, Abramson, Semmel, and von Baeyer (1979). In this study, depressed and nondepressed college students completed the Attributional Style Questionnaire (ASQ), which assessed the internality, stability, and globality of their attributions (see chapter 2). As predicted by the model, depressed students' attributions for negative outcomes were more internal, stable, and global than the attributions made by nondepressed students. Further, depressed students made more external and unstable attributions for positive outcomes than did less depressed students. Consistent with the theory, then, certain patterns of attributions were associated with higher levels of depression.

Subsequent research has generally supported the hypothesized link between attributional style and depression using a variety of populations, including children (Seligman & Peterson, in press), depressed patients in a Veterans Administration hospital (Raps, Peterson, Reinhard, Abramson, & Seligman, 1982), lower-class women (Navarra, 1981, cited in Peterson & Seligman, 1984), and, of course, college students (Metalsky, Abramson, Seligman, Semmel, & Peterson, 1982; Peterson, Schwartz, & Seligman, 1981). Further, support has been obtained using both cross-sectional and longitudinal designs, and employing both the ASQ and open-ended measures of attributional style (see Peterson & Seligman, 1984, for a review).

Importantly, however, although each of these studies has obtained support for one or more predictions derived from the attributional model, few of them have confirmed the importance of all three attributional dimensions within a single study. For example, Metalsky et al. (1982) found that depression correlated with the tendency to make internal and global (but not stable) attributions, whereas Hammen and Cochran (1981) obtained effects only on the globality dimension. Although this is not an indictment of the theory per se, it highlights the need to explore other variables that may mediate between perceived lack of control and depression (see Ickes & Layden, 1978; Peterson & Seligman, 1984). It may be that the perceived *controllability* of the cause, rather than its internality, stability, or globality, may best predict depression (Anderson & Arnoult, 1985; Wortman & Dintzer, 1978). Further, a few studies have failed to find support for any relationship between attributions and depression (see Coyne & Gotlib, 1983; Hammen & Mayo, 1982), although these are in the minority.

In considering the implications of the attributional style research for the attributional model, three points should be kept in mind. First, the theory does not imply that a depressogenic attributional style is either a sufficient or a necessary cause of depression. For example, the theory hypothesizes that attributional style should predict depression only in the face of negative events. Put another way, the tendency to make internal, stable, and global attributions for negative events is best regarded as a risk factor for depression. Because few of the subjects in these studies had recently faced traumatic events (and therefore most were not particularly depressed), only a moderate relationship between attributional style and depression would be expected.

Further, even individuals who do not usually make internal, stable, or global attributions for negative life events may do so in particular instances. As a result, many depressed individuals are not characterized by a general tendency to make such attributions, thereby lowering the correlation between attributional style and depression. In addition, even proponents of the attributional model recognize that depression may be caused by noncognitive factors, such as biochemical disturbances. In these cases, no relationship between attributional style and depression would be expected at all.

Finally, Cutrona et al. (1984) have recently presented evidence that casts doubt upon the adequacy of the ASQ (Seligman et al., 1979) as a psychometric instrument. Their data demonstrate that this scale, which has been used in much of the research described above, is neither a sufficiently reliable nor a valid measure of attributional style. Still, although the psychometric weaknesses of the ASQ have been addressed even by its proponents, there is considerable evidence that the measure *is* useful as a measure of individual differences in attributional style and that such differences are related to reactions to aversive events (see Anderson, 1983a; Anderson et al., 1983; Peterson & Seligman, 1984; chapter 2, this volume).

In brief, although the attributional style literature provides only moderate support for the attributional model of helpless depression, several factors have militated against stronger findings. Thus, it is difficult at this juncture to adequately evaluate the strength of the theory on the basis of existing studies of attributional style, although the evidence is by and large supportive.

Characterological versus behavioral self-blame. Janoff-Bulman (1979) refined the attributional categories emphasized by other researchers by distinguishing between two qualitatively different kinds of internal attributions: characterological and behavioral. She asked depressed and nondepressed subjects to imagine themselves experiencing several negative events (such as a car accident or rejection by a lover) and to rate how much of the blame was due to "the kind of person you are" (a characterological attribution) and how much to "what you did" (a behavioral attribution). Her data showed that, although depressed and nondepressed subjects did not differ in the degree to which they made generally internal attributions, depressed subjects were more likely than less depressed subjects to make characterological attributions for bad events. In addition, she found that depressed subjects made stronger attributions to luck and chance, and scored higher in external locus of control (the belief that one's outcomes in life are largely beyond one's control). In short, depressed subjects were more likely to attribute negative events to aspects of their own character and other uncontrollable factors than were nondepressed subjects, a finding that is consistent with the attributional model.

Other studies have replicated the positive correlation between characterological self-blame and depression, as well as demonstrating that behavioral self-blame is negatively correlated with depression (Anderson et al., 1983; Peterson et al., 1981). Together, these studies suggest that whether individuals make internal attributions per se is less important than whether their internal attributions emphasize stable, characterological deficiencies or unstable, behavioral factors, such as the momentary use of an inappropriate strategy. Even so, the research on characterological and behavioral self-blame provides further evidence that attributions are related to the experience of depression.

Depression and Perceptions of Control

Another implication of the learned helplessness approach to depression is that some people may be particularly prone to depression either because they have difficulty detecting contingencies between their actions and outcomes or because they tend to underestimate the degree of contingency that does exist. Such perceptual tendencies may lead people to conclude, erroneously, that they have little control over their outcomes, the results being helplessness and depression. However, as plausible as this notion sounds, research evidence clearly refutes it. Not only is there no reason to suspect that depression-prone individuals are deficient in their ability to assess behavior-outcome contingencies, but there is strong evidence that depressed people are *better* at doing so than nondepressed, "normal" individuals.

Support for this point comes from research on the "illusion of control," or the tendency for people to perceive uncontrollable events as controllable (Langer, 1975). Several studies have demonstrated that people sometimes act as if they can influence the occurrence of chance events, such as the roll of dice and the random selection of lottery winners (Langer, 1983). Research has shown that nondepressed subjects are more susceptible to the illusion of control than are depressed subjects; that is, normals are more likely to overestimate the degree of control they have over uncontrollable events (Alloy & Abramson, 1979, 1982; Golin, Terrell, & Johnson, 1977; Golin,

Terrell, Weitz, & Drost, 1979). Put another way, depressed people are more accurate in assessing contingencies between their behavior and outcomes than are nondepressed subjects, leading Alloy and Abramson (1979) to characterize them as "sadder but wiser."

At first glance, it would appear that learned helplessness theory has difficulty accounting for these results, because depressed people do not appear to underestimate their control over events. It is possible, however, that depressed individuals maintain the perception that they have little control over their outcomes even though they accurately assess behavior-outcome contingencies (see Alloy & Abramson, 1979). For example, depressed persons may recognize that certain behaviors lead to certain outcomes, but doubt that they can execute the requisite behaviors. Phrased in terms of Bandura's (1977) self-efficacy theory (see chapter 11, this volume), depressives may accurately assess outcome expectancies but underestimate efficacy expectancies, or the probability that they can successfully execute the behavior needed to produce the outcome. Further research is needed to assess this possibility (see Kanfer & Zeiss, 1983).

Alternatively, the research on illusion of control suggests that depression results not so much from perceived lack of control as nondepression results from perceived control. In other words, the tendency to overestimate one's degree of control provides a buffer against depression, and people who do not overestimate their control are more prone to depression. This raises the provocative possibility that the incidence of depression would be higher if everyone accurately perceived the minimal control they have over many objectively uncontrollable events.

Critique of the Attributional Model of Depression

Despite a fair amount of empirical support for the attributional model of helpless depression, questions remain regarding the usefulness of the attributional model as an explanation of both helplessness effects and naturally occurring depression.

First, virtually all of the research that has studied attribution and depression has been correlational in nature. Thus, at best, the data demonstrate that certain kinds of attributions and depressive symptoms covary, but we are unable to conclude that certain attributions actually *cause* depression as the attributional model suggests (Abramson et al., 1978). An alternative explanation of the attribution-depression relationship is that depression leads people to make "helpless" attributions. This possibility is strengthened by research showing that depressed subjects whose moods are temporarily raised by an experimental induction succumb to the illusion of control (i.e., their perception of control increases), whereas depressed subjects whose moods are not raised do not (Alloy, Abramson, & Viscusi, 1981). Similarly, there is evidence that, although depressed people engage in more characterological self-blame for negative events, characterological self-blame does not appear to *cause* depression directly (Peterson et al., 1981; see also Danker-Brown & Baucom, 1982). In all likelihood, the relationship between attribution and depression is reciprocal: Certain attributions lead to depression, and a dysphoric mood increases the likelihood that the person will make pessimistic, "helpless" attributions. This possibility may explain why it is difficult to "think" oneself out of depression (see Kuiper, Derry, & MacDonald, 1982). In any case, more research is needed that explores the nature of the relationship among attribution, expectancy, and depression.

Second, both Seligman's (1975) original theory and the reformulation offered by Abramson et al. (1978) assume that, for helplessness effects to occur, the individual must first become consciously aware that outcomes are not contingent upon behavior. Recent research by Oakes and Curtis (1982) challenges this assumption. In their study, subjects shot a "light gun" at a target that had a photoreceptor cell in the bull's-eye. Because of the lighting in the room, subjects were unable to determine their accuracy visually whenever they hit the bull's eye (thereby allowing the researchers to experimentally manipulate subjects' perceptions of their accuracy). Results showed that actual noncontingency (when accuracy feedback was truly independent of subjects' performance) produced helplessness effects, whereas subjects' *perceptions* of noncontingency did not. In other words, learned helplessness seemed to occur even when subjects did not consciously realize that their behavior and outcomes were independent. Further, cognitive measures, such as attributions and moods, were unrelated to helplessness effects. Other failures to demonstrate a mediating role of perceptions and attributions in learned helplessness have been reported by Tennen, Gillen, and Drum (1982) and Tennen, Drum, Gillen, and Stanton (1982). The latter study showed that neither perceived uncontrollability of outcomes nor the internality, stability, and globality of attributions mediated learned helplessness effects.

What are we to make of such findings? For psychologists who assume that cognitions mediate between stimuli and behavior, findings such as these are difficult to interpret. In a response to these studies, Alloy (1982) pointed out that they do not adequately address two important aspects of learned helplessness theory. First, as noted earlier, *expectations* of future response-outcome noncontingency, rather than attributions per se, are assumed to mediate helplessness effects. Although certain patterns of attributions should lead to such expectations, "helpless" expectations may occur for other reasons. Thus, it is possible for a person to hold a low response-outcome expectancy without having made relevant attributions about previous performance. Because none of these studies assessed expectations directly, they do not adequately test the theory.

Second, Abramson et al. (1978) explicitly stated that the expectation of future uncontrollability is a sufficient, but not necessary condition for helplessness effects. Thus, behavioral deficits that characterize learned helplessness may occur for other reasons, and it is possible that the effects observed in these studies fall into this category. In short, it is not clear that studies such as these do much damage to the attributional model of learned helplessness, although they do raise several important questions that the theory does not explicitly address (see Alloy, 1982).

However, even if these particular studies do not provide evidence against the learned helplessness model, they raise an important question that psychologists interested in attributional processes have not adequately addressed: Do people spontaneously make attributions that resemble those elicited in research settings? It is quite possible that, although people provide researchers with attributions when asked to so, they do not spontaneously make such attributions as a matter of course (Hanusa & Schulz, 1977; Wortman & Dintzer, 1978).

To investigate this question, Peterson, Bettes, and Seligman (1982) asked subjects to describe the worst two events that happened to them during the past year. Even though the subjects were not prompted to explain or account for the events, each description included at least one explanation. Further, many of these explanations could be classified along the internality, stability, and globality dimensions. Thus, it appears that people do make spontaneous attributions, at least in regard to particularly traumatic events.

A remaining question regards the attributional dimensions that are most important in producing helplessness and depression. The Abramson et al. (1978) model posits three—internality, stability, and globality—and research attests that these dimensions are related to helplessness and depression. However, are they the most important? Wortman and Dintzer (1978) suggested that whether the individual believes the factors responsible for his or her state of helplessness are controllable may be far more important than whether they are seen as internal, stable, or global.

Recent work by Anderson and Arnoult (1985) supports this notion, showing that controllability is the single most important attributional predictor of depression. Further, they found that, once the controllability dimension is considered, the three attributional dimensions posited by Abramson et al. (1978) add little to predicting one's level of depression. The importance of attributions of controllability is also suggested by Janoff-Bulman's (1979) work on characterological and behavioral self-blame. As we saw earlier, internal attributions to characterological factors (which are uncontrollable) are more strongly associated with depression than are attributions to behavioral and strategy factors (which are more controllable).

One way to reconcile the Abramson-Seligman-Teasdale model with more recent research is to postulate an attributional hierarchy. According to this view, certain "lower order" attributional dimensions, such as stability and globality, may be subsumed by "higher order" dimensions such as controllability. Put another way, whether people's attributions involve controllable or uncontrollable factors may depend upon the kinds of "lower order" attributions they make. In any case, taken together, research attests to the importance of attributions—particularly those relevant to controllability—in the development of reactive depression.

Therapeutic Implications of Learned Helplessness Theory

As noted earlier, the attributional theory posits that helpless depression occurs when the attributions people make lower their expectancies of control in the future. Thus, broadly speaking, helpless depression should be reduced by changing depressed individuals' perceptions of powerlessness (Beach, Abramson, & Levine, 1981). Such an approach may be used either to attenuate an ongoing depressive episode or to reduce the individual's vulnerability to future bouts of depression.

It should be noted, however, that directly modifying clients' attributions (as discussed in chapter 2) is only one possible way to do this. Other steps may be taken to give clients a greater sense of control over their lives. For example, it may be necessary to lower their unrealistically high goals (e.g., Bandura, 1969; Ellis, 1962; Rehm, 1977), to provide training in skills in the domain in which they feel helpless (Bellack & Hersen, 1979), or to improve clients' ability to detect behavior-outcome contingencies. Beach et al. (1981) argued that practitioners should carefully assess the specific locus of a depressed client's difficulties, remembering that feelings of helplessness may arise from a number of sources. The interested reader should refer to Beach et al. (1981) for a detailed discussion of the implications of the reformulated attributional model for the treatment of depression.

Egotism as an Alternative Explanation of Helplessness

Any psychological phenomenon is open to multiple interpretations and explanations. Although the attributional model of helpless depression enjoys a great deal of popularity and empirical support, Frankel and Snyder (1978) have offered an alternative explanation of helplessness effects based on a self-esteem maintenance or "egotism" model. According to this approach, the perception that one is unable to control important outcomes threatens the individual's self-esteem, resulting in a sense of failure and, often, depression. Further, when faced with an opportunity to reexert control, the individual may fear a second failure and another loss of self-esteem. To avoid such damning feedback, the individual may exert minimal effort in subsequent attempts to exert control. By doing so, one can attribute a continuing failure to control one's outcomes to inadequate effort rather than personal incompetence, thereby preserving self-esteem. (Many readers will recognize this esteem-maintaining strategy as a type of "self-handicapping" [Berglas & Jones, 1978; Jones & Berglas, 1978], a topic covered in the next chapter.) Thus, the decreased motivation observed after depressing failures may result from people's attempts to avoid future failures, rather than from perceived helplessness.

Two studies have supported this explanation of helplessness effects (Frankel & Snyder, 1978; Snyder, Smoller, Strenta, & Frankel, 1981). In the experiment by Snyder et al. (1981), subjects first worked on unsolvable problems, and then worked on solvable problems in the presence of music that they thought would either hinder or facilitate their performance. Learned helplessness theory predicts that subjects should experience greater helplessness when an allegedly debilitating factor is present, thereby lowering their expectations regarding performance. An egotism model, on the other hand, posits that distracting music provides subjects with an external attribution for failure, thereby allowing them to exert full effort on the task without risking their self-esteem should they fail. Consistent with the egotism hypothesis, but contrary to learned helplessness theory, subjects solved more problems when the noise during the second task was ostensibly distracting.

The egotism explanation for helplessness and depression is similar to one suggested by Rothbaum, Weisz, and Snyder (1982), who distinguish between two ways of exerting control. Rothbaum et al. suggested that, when attempting to control events, people may try either to change the environment to fit their desires ("primary" control) or to change themselves to fit the environment ("secondary" control). When people believe they are unable to exert primary control over events, they may become passive and withdrawn in order to avoid the disappointment and possible loss of self-esteem that would result from repeated attempts to control seemingly uncontrollable events. Thus, rather than representing helplessness, decreased motivation in uncontrollable situations may be an attempt to exert "secondary" control by managing one's cognitive and affective reactions to such events.

Although promising, the egotism and secondary control models are underdeveloped as explanations of helplessness and depression and have been tested only in relation to performance on laboratory tasks. Whether they can be extended fruitfully to an analysis of naturally occuring helpless depression has yet to be seen.

Reactance as a Reaction to Loss of Control

Although there is little question that helplessness is a common reaction to perceived loss of control, another, opposite tendency is often observed. Reactance theory (Brehm, 1966, 1972) proposes that when a person's freedom of behavioral choice is threatened, he or she will experience "reactance" and become motivated to restore the freedom. This effect is easily observed in the "lure of the forbidden fruit"; when people find they cannot have something they may become more strongly motivated to attain it.

A moment's thought should show that reactance is precisely the opposite of learned helplessness. In helplessness, loss of control decreases one's motivation to pursue the goal; in the case of reactance, loss of control heightens this motivation. Importantly, the same conditions that produce helplessness, such as noncontingent outcomes and internal attributions for failure, have been found to produce an *increase* in performance in some studies (Hanusa & Schulz, 1977; Roth & Kubal, 1975).

In a paper addressing the apparent discrepancy between the learned helplessness and reactance formulations, Wortman and Brehm (1975) suggested that when a person expects to be able to influence a certain outcome but finds his or her control and freedom threatened, reactance is the *initial* response as the individual first tries harder to exert control. However, if after continued effort the individual becomes convinced that further attempts will not produce the outcome, helplessness results. The results of a study by Roth and Kubal (1975) directly support this integration of the theories. In their study, one instance of noncontingent feedback produced an improvement in subsequent performance (i.e., reactance), whereas three instances of noncontingent feedback produced a performance decrement (i.e., helplessness).

The Wortman-Brehm (1975) model highlights the need for an overriding theoretical framework that encompasses both reactance and helplessness effects. One possibility is that, when people first encounter events they have difficulty controlling, they find it hard to assess the stability, globality, and controllability of the problem. Because it is more facilitative to assume initially that the cause of the difficulty is unstable and specific, they may exert increased effort in an attempt to reexert control. However, if after repeated attempts to exert control they are still unable to do so, they may begin to assume the outcome is truly uncontrollable and experience helplessness.

Individual Differences in Response to Loss of Control

Whether people experience helplessness or reactance in response to uncontrollable outcomes may also be related to certain personality characteristics. Although individual differences in reactions to loss of control have not received a great deal of attention, two lines of research seem particularly promising.

Gender Differences

A great deal of research has shown that women become depressed more frequently than men (Weissman & Klerman, 1977). This fact suggests that there may be differences in the ways in which men and women tend to respond to uncontrollable outcomes. Specifically, sex differences in response to helplessness-producing situations may be mediated by so-called "sex roles," or the degree to which an individual possesses instrumental (i.e., masculine) and expressive (i.e., feminine) personality attributes (see chapter 7).

Baucom (1983) predicted that an instrumental sex-role orientation would be associated with attempts to regain control under conditions that normally produce helplessness. To test this, female subjects took what they believed was an intelligence test and received feedback that either was or was not contingent upon their performance. They were then told that the study involved a problem-solving task in which two people would work together, and they were given a choice regarding their participation on this task. They were told that they could take part in the task but not have control over the team's decision, take part in the task and have control over the team's decision, or not take part in the task at all.

As expected, results showed that, whereas women low in instrumentality avoided control of the group task, a great majority of the highly instrumental women chose to be in control. To the degree that helplessness results in depression, these results suggest that women who are low in instrumentality may be particularly predisposed to depression because they do not attempt to regain control in situations in which they feel they have lost it. The mediating effects of traditional socialization on depression in women deserve additional research attention.

Desire for Control

People's reactions to a loss of control may also be mediated by the degree to which they are motivated to exercise control over their lives. Burger (1985; Burger & Cooper, 1979) has introduced the concept of "desire for control," which he views as a stable personality characteristic reflecting the extent to which individuals are motivated to control the events in their lives.

Individuals who score high on the Desirability of Control Scale (Burger & Cooper, 1979) persist longer and exhibit greater effort when confronted by impediments (Burger, 1985). Thus, people who have a high desire for control may be more likely to experience reactance when their sense of control is first threatened. However, such people may also be more susceptible to depression, possibly because they want to have more control over events than is often possible (Burger & Arkin, 1980). Thus, such individuals try harder to exercise control but are more often frustrated or depressed at their inability to do so.

In short, the available data suggest a link between an individual's desire for control and reactions to loss of perceived control. Further work is needed, however, to fully explore the relationship between this characteristic and dysfunctional reactions such as helplessness and depression.

Negative Reactions to Control

Throughout this chapter, perceived lack of control has been consistently associated with dysfunctional reactions, including lowered motivation and increased depression. Evidence that perceived lack of control has deleterious effects is quite extensive, but there are also circumstances in which people react negatively to having control. For example, Rodin, Rennert, and Solomon (1980) found that subjects who were given control over a simple laboratory task subsequently showed decrements in self-esteem compared to subjects who did not have control. Likewise, Miller (1980) showed that subjects who had control in a reaction-time experiment were more hostile and anxious than those who relinquished their control to a partner.

Two different explanations of this effect have been suggested. Miller (1980) and Rodin et al. (1980) suggested that personal control carries a burden of personal responsibility that people sometimes find aversive. However, Burger, Brown, and Allen (1983) proposed that having control is aversive only when it raises concerns that the individual will be unable to demonstrate his or her competence. Faced with the possibility of appearing incompetent to themselves and others, people often prefer not to be in control and are willing to relinquish control to others. When control is voluntarily relinquished to others in order to avoid negative consequences, helplessness and depression should not occur.

Conclusions

People generally prefer to believe that they are able to control events that affect them, and they experience negative psychological and physical effects such as stress, depression, and feelings of helplessness when they perceive that they are unable to do so. The mediating role of attributions and expectancies in these phenomena has been explored extensively, and although the data are not unequivocal, most would agree that people's reactions to uncontrollable events are affected by the attributions they make. However, despite widespread interest in attributional processes among social psychologists, we think that the utility of attributional models of dysfunctional behavior has not yet been fully explored. Existing attributional models need to be elaborated, the critical attributional dimensions identified, measures of attributional style refined and validated, and more research conducted using clinical and subclinical populations. Only then will we be able to assess the full value of attributional models for understanding and treating dysfunctional reactions.

Chapter 4

Self-Processes and Behavioral Problems

The capacity for self-reflection is one of the most fundamental human attributes. Although there is evidence that other primates can recognize themselves in a mirror (Gallup, 1977), the ability to think consciously about oneself in abstract terms is a uniquely human characteristic. Much of our behavior may be performed "mindlessly," without conscious consideration of its implications for oneself (Langer, 1978), but many behaviors that we consider uniquely human require the ability to hold ourselves as the object of our thoughts. Without the ability to think consciously about ourselves, we could not contemplate alternative courses of action, consider the impact of our behaviors upon other people, ponder the "meaning" of our actions and lives, systematically plan for the future, or purposefully attempt to better ourselves. Each of these actions requires the capacity to consciously self-reflect.

However, the ability to think about oneself comes at a price. Psychological difficulties can arise from this capacity for self-reflection. It allows us to agonize over past misfortunes, contemplate our shortcomings, worry about the future, and dread our inevitable deaths, thereby setting the stage for a variety of psychological problems such as depression, loneliness, guilt, and anxiety.

Although the role of self-processes in dysfunctional behavior has long been discussed within certain circles of psychology (notably the humanistic, existential, and phenomenological schools of thought; see Rogers, 1959), the study of the self has gained momentum within experimental social psychology somewhat more recently (Schlenker, 1985; Wegner & Vallacher, 1980). In this chapter, we discuss two topics that have been of special recent interest to social psychologists and that provide useful frameworks for understanding maladaptive behavior: self-esteem maintenance (with a focus on self-handicapping and self-reported handicapping) and self-awareness.

Self-Esteem Maintenance

Just as people evaluate the objects and events that they encounter in their lives—their jobs, the people they know, the music they hear, the quality of the food they eat, and so on—they also evaluate themselves. It is to this self-evaluation that we refer when we speak of "self-esteem" (Rosenberg, 1965). Within personality and social psychology, it is axiomatic that people are motivated to maintain and enhance their self-esteem. That is, it is nearly universally accepted that people desire to evaluate themselves as positively as possible (Wells & Marwell, 1976). This is not a new idea; years ago, Adler (1930) proposed that inherent feelings of inferiority motivate people to strive for self-improvement and feelings of superiority. Similarly, Horney (1950) assumed that people desire to value themselves positively, and Allport (1955) asserted that self-enhancement was a central property of the self (or what he called the "proprium"). Further, social psychologists have connected a wide variety of specific interpersonal behaviors to people's attempts to maintain self-esteem, including prejudice (Katz, 1960), reactions to others' evaluations (Jones, 1973), social comparison choices (Bramel, 1963), dissonance-produced attitude change (Aronson, 1969), reactions to receiving aid (Nadler, Altman, & Fisher, 1979), and self-serving attributions (Weary Bradley, 1978). Although theorists disagree regarding the origin of this motive, it is clear that people generally prefer to regard themselves positively rather than negatively, become anxious at the prospect of receiving self-deflating information (Leary, Barnes & Griebel, in press), and behave in ways that protect and/or enhance their view of themselves (see Tesser, in press).

Given the pervasiveness of the self-esteem motive, it is likely that it serves important functions for the individual. The most obvious, of course, is the maintenance of positive affect; people experience positive affect when their self-esteem is bolstered and negative affect when it is deflated. Thus, they prefer esteem-enhancing rather than esteem-diminishing feedback and behave in a manner designed to attain it.

Beyond that, however, high self-esteem and self-confidence provide instrumental benefits. Regarding oneself and one's abilities positively prompts people to undertake and persist on difficult tasks, thereby increasing the likelihood that they will be effective and successful (Bandura, 1977; Greenwald, 1980). In other words, high self-esteem provides people with the motivation to attempt to achieve their goals and to persevere in the face of adversity.

Unfortunately, the desire to preserve one's self-esteem can also result in negative consequences if people adopt maladaptive ways of protecting their self-esteem. The first half of this chapter focuses on potentially dysfunctional effects of our efforts to maintain self-esteem.

Self-Defeating Behavior: Self-Handicapping

It is a source of puzzlement to psychologists and laypersons alike that people often behave in ways that work against their own best interests. After all, it is difficult enough to get by in life under the best of circumstances without adding to one's struggles through self-defeating behavior. Nonetheless, examples of such behavior are legion: the bright student who receives bad grades because she won't study, the problem drinker whose drinking interferes with his effectiveness on the job, the lonely single who doesn't take advantage of available social opportunities, the athlete who doesn't practice sufficiently before an important game, the premed student who fails to get enough sleep the night before the MCAT exams. Although self-defeating behavior has been discussed since the earliest days of psychology, social psychologists have recently offered new perspectives on such behavior, and in this section we examine instances in which people behave in ways that work against their academic, occupational, social, or athletic success.

Several social psychological theories assume that people are motivated to maintain an accurate view of the world and of themselves because veridical knowledge increases their ability to behave effectively. For example, the central proposition of social comparison theory is that people have a drive to evaluate their opinions and abilities accurately (Festinger, 1954). This view suggests that people generally behave in ways that allow them to receive diagnostic information about themselves.

However, it is becoming increasingly clear that people do not always want to know the truth about themselves. In many if not most cases, people would just as soon avoid information that casts undesirable aspersions upon their positive views of themselves (Jones, 1973). Understandably, people are unenthusiastic about receiving information that highlights their failures, weaknesses, and personal deficiencies, and they may engage in behaviors that allow them to avoid such information. Unfortunately, in doing so, people often use behavioral strategies that are self-defeating.

Specifically, when faced by the prospect of unflattering evaluative feedback, people may procure an impediment or *self-handicap* that will provide them with a plausible excuse for failure. As defined by Berglas and Jones (1978, p. 406), self-handicapping involves "any action or choice of performance setting that enhances the opportunity to externalize (or excuse) failure and to internalize (reasonably accept responsibility for) success." Thus, as in the examples listed above, people may stack the cards against themselves in order to ensure that failure, should it occur, will be attributed to factors other than their lack of competence. For example, the student may not study so that failure can be blamed on inadequate effort rather than lack of ability, and the lonely single may decline social opportunities in order to preclude the chance of unequivocal rejection. These tactics allow the self-handicapping individual to maintain that he or she *could* be successful in school or social life, for example, if only he or she devoted sufficient effort to studying or socializing.

Of course, setting up such a handicap makes success on the ego-threatening task difficult, if not impossible. One is unlikely to do well in class without studying or to make friends without socializing. Thus, we would expect people to self-handicap chiefly in situations in which the self-relevant implications of failure are more threatening to the individual than is failure itself. People should be willing to risk failure by self-handicapping only when the possible threats to self-esteem outweigh the other potential consequences of failure.

Experimental studies. In the first experimental study of self-handicapping, Berglas and Jones (1978) reasoned that self-handicapping may be a common response to noncontingent success (i.e., situations in which an individual succeeds on an important task, but remains unsure of how success was obtained). Under such circumstances, people would like to make an internal attribution and accept personal responsibility for their performance, thereby enhancing their self-esteem. However, for all they know, their subsequent performances will be less successful, thereby demonstrating that their initial success was a fluke and that they are not as bright, skilled, or competent as they first seemed. To prevent such negative feedback, they may decide not to risk another fair test of their abilities; they may instead self-handicap on subsequent tasks so that, should they fail, their failure can be attributed to the handicap rather than to lack of ability, preserving their initial success.

To test this notion, Berglas and Jones (1978) presented subjects with success feedback that was either contingent or noncontingent on their actual performance on a test of intellectual ability. Prior to taking a second version of the test, subjects were given the option of taking a drug that ostensibly would either facilitate or hinder their performance on the second exam. Results showed that male subjects who had experienced noncontingent success on the first test were far more likely to handicap themselves by choosing to take the performance-debilitating drug before the second test than were subjects who had received contingent success feedback. They had all done well on the first test, but 70% of the noncontingent group chose to interfere with their future performances, whereas only 13% of the contingent group did so.

Berglas and Jones' explanation of this effect is straightforward: Subjects who had received noncontingent success were uncertain that they could repeat their success on the second test. Thus, they arranged conditions so that, if they did poorly on the second test, the failure would be attributed to the debilitating drug rather than to their lack of ability.

Sachs (1982) conceptually replicated the Berglas and Jones (1978) study, giving subjects the option of working on items that were either highly diagnostic of or irrelevant to their ability. As self-handicapping theory predicts, subjects who had previously experienced noncontingent success subsequently preferred to work on items that were *low* in diagnosticity, indicating that they were attempting to avoid a close examination of their ability on the second test.

Other studies have also replicated and extended Berglas and Jones' findings, demonstrating that subjects threatened by the prospect of failure often choose to take performance-debilitating drugs, including alcohol, prior to performing (Gibbons & Gaeddert, 1984; Kolditz & Arkin, 1982; Tucker, Vuchinich, & Sobell, 1981). In addition, Rhodewalt and Davison (1984) showed that people may also self-handicap by arranging the testing conditions in a way that interferes with their performance. In their study, subjects who had performed well but who were uncertain of future success elected to take a second test while listening to distracting music instead of music that could enhance their performance.

Another self-handicapping strategy involves expending less than full effort on a threatening task. By not exerting full effort on a task on which success is uncertain, people are able to attribute a poor showing to lack of effort rather than low ability. This strategy may be the modus operandi of the underachiever (Jones & Berglas, 1978). People who are highly threatened by the possibility of being incompetent and who harbor doubts about their ability may chronically exert less than total effort, resulting in underachievement. Such a strategy *is* likely to lead to failure, but it protects the person's self-image from the damaging implications of failure. For many, it is better to be an underachiever who doesn't perform up to full potential than to risk the possibility of definitively learning than one is not as capable as one would like to believe.

Frankel and Snyder (1978) demonstrated this strategy in a laboratory study. Subjects who had previously worked on unsolvable problems (and thus had "failed") subsequently worked harder on a second set of problems when they were described as highly rather than moderately difficult. This counterintuitive finding is understandable if we assume that it is more threatening to one's self-esteem to fail to solve moderately difficult than very difficult tasks. Why should it bother someone to fail a task that is so difficult that virtually everyone else fails it too? Thus, it is likely that subjects who worked on what they thought were moderately difficult problems withheld full effort so that they could attribute possible failure to low effort. When the problems were described as very difficult, they could try harder because there was no threat of trying, but failing to solve, very difficult problems.

In a study of this effect outside of the laboratory, Rhodewalt, Saltzman, and Wittmer (1984) administered to members of Princeton University's men's swim team a scale that measured their propensity to self-handicap. They found that, whereas swimmers who scored low on the self-handicapping scale increased the amount they practiced prior to important meets, high self-handicappers did not. There were no differences in the practices of low and high self-handicappers prior to unimportant meets. Apparently, swimmers who tended to self-handicap withheld maximal effort before important meets in order to have a plausible, non-ability-related excuse for failure.

In summary, laboratory and field investigations show that people threatened by possible failure sometimes arrange situations such that self-created impediments may be blamed for their difficulties. Although self-handicapping strategies make success more difficult, they reduce the degree to which the individual must accept personal responsibility for failure.

Self-handicapping and maladaptive behavior. Unfortunately, little research has been conducted on the role of self-handicapping in real-world behavioral problems. Still, it is likely that people sometimes do engage in self-defeating actions as a way of preserving self-esteem. For example, many of the laboratory studies discussed above used paradigms in which subjects chose to ingest drugs or alcohol, which they assumed would debilitate their performances. Results of these studies suggest that some instances of drug and alcohol abuse may serve a self-handicapping function. As Jones and Berglas (1978) suggested, one of the reinforcing properties of alcohol may be its widespread reputation for reducing one's responsibility for one's actions while under its influence. Individuals may thus use alcohol and other drugs as self-handicaps that decrease their personal accountability for ego-threatening performances. This is not to say that self-handicapping is the only or even the most important cause of problem drinking. Still, the role of self-esteem maintenance should be considered in cases in which people chronically drink or take drugs in ego-threatening situations.

The second arena in which self-handicapping may operate is suggested by the studies that show that people who fear the self-relevant implications of failure withhold full effort on threatening tasks (e.g., Frankel & Snyder, 1978). It is possible that chronic underachievers—individuals who never seem to live up to their potential—may be self-handicapping (Jones & Berglas, 1978). By failing to "apply themselves," such individuals protect themselves from self-deflating evidence that they are incompetent, while allowing them to maintain that they *could* accomplish great things if they ever decided to really apply themselves. Although underachievement invites ascriptions of laziness, lack of motivation, or disinterest, these self-characterizations may be much preferred over the label "incompetent."

In sum, self-defeating actions often may be traced to individuals' attempts to obscure the meaning of self-relevant feedback. As long as the person subtly, yet deliberately sabotages his or her efforts, self-esteem is insulated from the implications of failure.

Self-Reported Handicaps

In the cases of self-handicapping discussed above, people create actual impediments to success when possible failure threatens their self-esteem. In other instances, people confronted by threats to self-esteem may simply *report* that their performance is handicapped by some factor that is beyond their control. For example, people may announce physical or psychological symptoms, such as illness or anxiety, as an indirect way of accounting for past or potential failure.

The term *self-handicapping* has sometimes been applied to these verbal reports of handicaps, as well as to the creation of actual impediments that we have already discussed. However, it is more accurate to refer to the use of self-reported symptoms and disabilities as "self-reported handicaps" because one is not actually inhibiting future performance, just excusing it (Leary & Shepperd, in press). The difference between real self-handicaps and self-reported handicaps may be clarified by an example. If, on the day before an important track meet, a runner intentionally drops a cement block on his foot in order to have an excuse for losing a race, we would say that this individual has *self-handicapped*. If, however, the runner simply claims that his foot hurts (and it has been either accidentally injured or is not really hurt at all), he is simply *reporting a handicap* and has not self-handicapped at all.

The self-reported handicaps studied in much recent research (see Snyder & Smith, 1982) are a subclass of self-serving attributions, explanations in which people attribute their successes to themselves but ascribe their failures to events beyond their control (Weary Bradley, 1978). Self-serving attributions generally are used to explain the quality of past performances, however, whereas self-reported handicaps may be mentioned prior to evaluative events.

Reports of physical handicaps. People sometimes report the presence of a physical condition that may excuse their poor performance. As in the old line, "What do you expect out of a man with a wooden leg?" people sometimes use their physical conditions to absolve themselves of responsibility for their actions. Common examples include the student who stresses that she "feels a cold coming on" before an important test or weekend athletes who enumerate their various handicaps prior to playing their favorite sport (e.g., "I haven't played in six weeks," "I have a sore tendon," or "I'm exhausted from a hard week at work").

Although most people report handicapping symptoms occasionally, chronic use of such strategies is likely to be dysfunctional. A case in point involves hypochondriacs, who regularly proclaim the impact that their frail health has upon their lives. Smith, Snyder, and Perkins (1983) demonstrated that hypochondriacs strategically report symptoms in a manner that protects their self-esteem. Smith et al. recruited undergraduate women who had scored either low or high on the Minnesota Multiphasic Personality Inventory's Hypochondriasis scale and gave them a test that the subjects believed was either a valid measure of "social intelligence" (thereby creating a threat of evaluation) or an innocuous measure being pilot-tested for future research. Further, some subjects were told that their physical health was unlikely to affect their test performance (thereby eliminating the use of symptoms as an excuse for poor performance), whereas others were given no information about the effects of health on test scores.

When subjects were subsequently asked about their physical health, hypochondriacal subjects threatened by the test of social intelligence reported a sizable number of symptoms, but only when those symptoms could serve as a reasonable excuse for poor performance. At its core, hypochondriasis may reflect the tendency to use illness-based excuses for real and potential failure as a way of absolving oneself of responsibility for one's shortcomings.

Reports of psychological handicaps. In a similar fashion, people may report adverse psychological states or symptoms in the face of esteem-threatening failure, claiming that debilitating psychological conditions (such as anxiety, depression, grief, or job stress) may interfere with their ability to perform normally. Although the use of symptoms in the maintenance of self-esteem has been recognized for many years (e.g., Adler, 1930; Artiss, 1959; Carson, 1969), this topic has been studied experimentally only recently.

Just as hypochondriacs report being ill when threatened by possible failure, students high in test anxiety report being anxious when they think anxiety will be a plausible explanation for poor performance on an intelligence test (Smith, Snyder, & Handelsman, 1982). Similarly, shy males report feeling more nervous when a high level of anxiety can explain poor social performance under threatening interpersonal conditions (Snyder, Smith, Augelli, & Ingram, 1985). Such individuals may in fact be anxious, but it is clear that their reports of anxiety are embellished to provide a self-protective attribution for poor academic or social performance.

One result of the mass popularization of psychology is that many laypersons believe that their current difficulties can be traced to events occurring earlier in their lives. Thus, people sometimes report events from their past as a way of accounting for current problems. Research by DeGree and Snyder (1985) shows that people who face an esteem-threatening evaluation report traumatic events from their pasts that they think will excuse possible failure (see also Leary, Barnes, & Griebel, in press).

From a clinical standpoint, these data suggest that clients' reports of their past experiences may be constructed in ways that help them preserve self-esteem and/or save face. Because clients generally find themselves in therapy because of personal difficulties and shortcomings, they may overemphasize the role of life events that provide a plausible, self-serving explanation of their problems. When the causes of one's difficulties are not obvious, clients' self-reports may be biased in ways that preserve self-esteem.

Self-Esteem Maintenance or Impression Management?

Most researchers who have studied self-handicapping and self-reported handicapping have assumed that the motive of preserving one's self-esteem underlies these self-defeating behaviors (Berglas & Jones, 1978; Jones &

Berglas, 1978; Snyder & Smith, 1982). However, most of the data are as easily interpreted within an impression management framework. People may self-handicap not so much to preserve their self-image as to maintain a desirable image in others' eyes (see chapter 5).

In the only study that clearly tests these competing explanations of self-handicapping, Kolditz and Arkin (1982) reasoned that, in order for self-handicapping to be successful as an impression management strategy, it is necessary for others to know that the handicapping condition exists. That is, the procurement of a handicap will allow and individual to save face in others' eyes only if those others are aware of the handicap. From a self-esteem perspective, whether others know about the handicap is irrelevant; the individual's self-esteem should be protected by handicapping factors of which only he or she is aware.

In Kolditz and Arkin's study, subjects who had previously received non-contingent success feedback (cf. Berglas & Jones, 1978) were given the opportunity to self-handicap by taking a performance-debilitating drug before a second test. However, half of the subjects believed that their choice of a debilitating or facilitating drug would be private—the experimenter would not know which they had chosen—whereas the others believed their choice would be public. Consistent with an impression management explanation, subjects in the noncontingent success condition chose to take debilitating drugs primarily when their choice of drugs was public.

Although these results do not indicate that people never self-handicap as a way of protecting self-esteem, they show that self-handicapping probably also serves an interpersonal, impression management function.

Summary

There is considerable evidence that people's attempts to maintain their self-esteem sometimes lead them to behave in ways that work against their own best interests. They may avoid situations in which their self-esteem may be threatened, and thereby miss the many rewards that come from tackling and accomplishing difficult tasks. They may also self-handicap, stacking the cards against themselves to avoid possibly deflating feedback. In other instances, they may simply claim that they are handicapped by adverse physical or psychological factors. Although it is quite normal to prefer ego-enhancing over ego-deflating feedback, chronic efforts to avoid diagnostic information about oneself can result in a variety of maladaptive responses.

Self-Awareness

As hard as they might try, people cannot always avoid information that threatens their self-esteem, and are confronted regularly by indications that they are not as intelligent, astute, talented, skilled, socially adept, attractive, or in control of their lives as they would like to believe. No empirical verification is required to demonstrate that these blows to people's self-images are nearly always unpleasant.

Self-Awareness Theory

Negative reactions to events that threaten self-esteem are heightened when the individual is in a state of self-focused attention, or self-awareness. According to self-awareness theory (Duval & Wicklund, 1972; Wicklund, 1975), the objects and events upon which people focus their conscious attention may be dichotomized into those that are "external" and those that are "internal" to the individual. The complete theory details the conditions that promote internal, self-focused attention and describes the consequences of self-awareness; however, we will focus here only on the portion of the theory that deals with one's reactions to discrepancies between one's personal standards and one's actual behavior—discrepancies that usually involve threats to self-esteem.

The theory posits that whenever people are self-focused (i.e., consciously thinking about themselves), their thoughts are directed toward whatever aspect of the self is most salient. For example, if an individual has just been shunned by another person, becoming self-aware will induce the individual to contemplate the rejection (Fenigstein, 1979). However, if the individual has just won a contest, self-awareness will stimulate thoughts about the accomplishment.

Further, the theory suggests that self-awareness results in negative emotional reactions when people attend to behavior they find unsatisfactory. In Carver's (1979) terminology, the self-aware individual may perceive a discrepancy between his or her behavior and relevant internal standards, such as goals, morals, values, or standards of performance. The perception of such a discrepancy results in a discomfort that is proportional to the size of the discrepancy and the amount of time the individual attends to those aspects of self that are deficient. Phrased another way, events that threaten self-esteem produce negative affect to the degree that the individual is in a state of self-awareness and is consciously thinking about them.

When people are self-focused and perceive a discrepancy between their behavior and their standards, two general consequences may occur. First, they may attempt to reduce the discrepancy. For example, they may work harder to attain their goals, rationalize away their shortcomings, or change their internal standards. In each case, the discrepancy between the person's standards and objective reality is minimized, and the consequent negative affect is reduced or eliminated.

Avoidance of Self-Awareness

Importantly, if people are unable to reduce the discrepancy between their behavior and their standards, they may be motivated to avoid the state of self-awareness. Stated simply, people do things to take their minds off of behaviors that fail to meet their personal standards.

One way in which people do this is by avoiding situations that cause them to think about themselves. To the extent that certain situations elicit more self-reflection than others, people who have failed to meet their standards should seek situations that minimize self-awareness. In a study by Duval, Wicklund, and Fine (reported in Duval & Wicklund, 1972), subjects who perceived a large discrepancy between their behavior and their standards left a room in which a self-awareness-evoking stimulus (a mirror) was present more quickly than did subjects who did not perceive a distressing discrepancy.

However, Steenbarger and Aderman (1979) found that the tendency to avoid self-awareness occurs only when the discrepancy is unlikely to change. In this study, when subjects anticipated possible improvement in discrepancies between their standards and their behavior, neither negative affect nor avoidance of self-awareness occurred. Thus, people appear to avoid self-reflection only when they do not expect to resolve the discrepancy in the near future.

Extrapolating from the laboratory to the real world, self-awareness theory suggests that when people are confronted with a discrepancy between their behavior and their standards and think they are unable to reduce the discrepancy, they are likely to engage in behaviors that reduce self-awareness. These actions may range from innocuous diversions such as excessive TV watching or increased working to more dysfunctional responses.

Alcohol Use as Avoidance of Self-Awareness

Hull (1981) suggested that the desire to reduce self-awareness in the face of failures to meet one's own standards may underlie many instances of problem drinking. People who experience distressing discrepancies between their behavior and their standards may try to reduce their awareness of the discrepancies (and, thereby, their negative emotional state) by ingesting drugs, such as alcohol, that reduce self-awareness.

In two experimental studies, Hull, Levenson, Young, and Sher (1983) demonstrated that alcohol consumption reduces self-awareness. Further, a third study showed that alcohol produces this effect by interfering with the drinker's ability to encode information in terms of its self-relevance (see Hull & Levy, 1979). By decreasing self-focused thought, alcohol not only reduces the aversiveness of discrepancies between standards and behavior, but also lowers the degree to which the drinker adheres to his or her standards. One consequence of lowered self-awareness is a decreased reliance on one's internal standards, which may result in lowered inhibitions and increased deindividuation (see Diener, 1979).

The studies by Hull et al. (1983) show that alcohol reduces self-awareness, but is there any reason to believe that people drink *in order to* render themselves less self-aware? Research by Hull and Young (1983) indicates that there is. In their study, male social drinkers were given bogus feedback indicating that they had performed either very well or very poorly on an IQ test. Then, under the guise of a second study that involved wine tasting, subjects were allowed to drink as much of several kinds of wine as they desired in the process of rating the wines. As predicted, subjects who were highly self-reflective (i.e., those who scored high on the Self-Consciousness Scale [Fenigstein, Scheier, & Buss, 1975]) consumed significantly more wine when they had received failure rather than success feedback on the test. Presumably, these subjects were motivated to reduce their level of self-awareness after failure, but not after success, as self-awareness theory predicts. The drinking of subjects who were not generally self-reflective (i.e., those who scored low on the Self-Consciousness Scale) was not affected by the feedback they received. Not being particularly self-aware in the first place, they apparently were not motivated to reduce their level of self-awareness by consuming alcohol after failure.

The results obtained in this laboratory study were conceptually replicated in a field study involving men who had recently completed an alcohol detoxification program (Hull & Young, 1983). These men completed the Self-Consciousness Scale (Fenigstein et al., 1975) and a measure of recent stressful life events. If problem drinking serves to reduce self-awareness in the face of threatening self-relevant events, we would expect to find that recovering alcoholics who had experienced a large number of stressful events would relapse at a higher rate than those who were under less stress. Further, this effect would presumably be most pronounced for subjects who are dispositionally high in their tendency to be self-attentive (i.e., highly self-conscious). The results of 3- and 6-month follow-ups after subjects' discharge from the program supported these predictions.

After 3 months, 70% of the highly self-conscious subjects who had experienced predominantly negative life events had relapsed, compared to only 14% of the self-conscious subjects who had experienced positive life events. Further, subjects low in dispositional self-consciousness were unaffected by the quality of life events; approximately 40% of these individuals relapsed regardless of the nature of the events they had experienced. At the end of 6 months, the same pattern of results was obtained, although, of course, a higher percentage of individuals in all groups had relapsed.

Although more research on this topic is needed, it seems clear that part of alcohol's appeal is as an agent that reduces self-awareness and, thus, reduces the negative emotional reactions that accompany personal failures to meet one's standards. We should stress that alcohol consumption has many determinants, and this model is not meant to explain all instances of either social or problem drinking. Nevertheless, the link between alcohol and self-awareness reduction is provocative and suggests a useful new model of drug and alcohol abuse.

The Deleterious Effects of Self-Preoccupation

According to self-awareness theory, self-directed attention is necessary for goal-directed behavior. Only when people are self-aware (and, thus, thinking about their internal standards) are they consciously oriented toward the accomplishment of goals and guided by personal standards regarding acceptable behavior. Thus, competent, moral, and efficient behavior generally requires some degree of self-reflection. However, self-reflection may also have detrimental effects. As seen in the previous section, self-awareness may attune people to their own deficiencies and result in dysfunctional behaviors that help them avoid the unpleasant self-confrontation that accompanies self-reflection after failure.

Further, in many instances, self-attention has deleterious effects on the performance of certain behaviors, particularly if the individual's self-attention is inappropriate or excessive. When people are preoccupied with themselves, two processes may interfere with the execution of behavior. First, because conscious attention may be focused on only one stimulus at a time (Buss, 1980; Carver, 1979; Duval & Wicklund, 1972), self-preoccupation makes it difficult to devote sufficient attention to other stimuli in the immediate environment, including ongoing tasks. For example, several researchers have suggested that test anxiety interferes with test performance because the anxious individual is overly self-focused (e.g., Dusek, Kermis, & Mergler, 1975; Sarason, 1980; Wine, 1971, 1980). Instead of devoting their full attention to the test itself (as people low in test anxiety apparently do), test-anxious individuals ruminate about possible failure, chastise themselves for their lack of knowledge or preparation, and think about the dire consequences that will occur if they fail the test. Excessive self-preoccupation monopolizes cognitive processes that should be devoted to the test.

Similarly, Brenner (1973) demonstrated that, when people must wait to "perform" in a predetermined order, they have difficulty recalling the contributions of individuals who immediately precede them; this phenomenon Brenner termed the "next in line effect." Thinking about one's own upcoming performance draws the individual's attention away from the people who immediately precede him or her, and this interferes with the encoding of information (Bond, 1985).

A second way in which self-awareness can be dysfunctional is in making habitual and overlearned responses conscious. Much behavior that is normally performed "mindlessly," without conscious awareness, is disrupted when people focus conscious attention on themselves and their behavior (Langer & Weinman, 1981). A skilled pianist who usually performs a well-learned piece with little conscious thought may have his performance severely disrupted if he begins to think about what he is doing as he plays. Similarly, paying close attention to one's own voice as one talks can be so disruptive that it causes stuttering (Kamhi & McOsker, 1982). Baumeister

(1984) demonstrated that "choking under pressure" (performance decrements under conditions that increase the importance of a performance) results when an individual's conscious attention is focused on the process of performing. Finally, recent work by Cheek and Melchior (1985) shows that dispositionally shy individuals are characterized by a high level of self-absorption. Their anxious self-preoccupation not only contributes to their shyness (Buss, 1980), but may interfere with their ability to interact adroitly, resulting in awkward and stilted interactions (Leary, 1983b, 1986a).

In short, dysfunction may result either from the defensive avoidance of self-awareness or from excessive preoccupation with the self. When such tendencies become chronic—as in test anxiety or shyness, for example—the resulting behavioral disturbances may be quite significant.

Conclusions

What people think about themselves has both facilitative and debilitating effects upon behavior. Attempts to evaluate oneself positively may result in the avoidance of potentially esteem-deflating information through self-handicapping or the use of self-reported handicaps that allow the attribution of one's shortcomings to factors other than one's (lack of) ability. Further, people may attempt to avoid the negative reactions that accompany failure by minimizing the degree to which they are self-aware, using drugs and other diversions to do so. The motive to maintain one's self-esteem is a potent one. Indeed, people sometimes engage in actions that are otherwise self-destructive in order to avoid confronting their own imperfections and inadequacies.

Chapter 5
Self-Presentational Aspects of Maladaptive Behavior

The impressions others form of us substantially determine how they treat us in social encounters. A man who is thought to be friendly, open, and honest, for example, is treated much differently than one who is viewed as dishonest, narcissistic, and cold. A woman whom others see as strong and competent receives quite different reactions than does a woman who is perceived as weak and ineffectual. Teachers react quite differently to a student who appears to be interested and motivated than to one who seems bored and unmotivated. Moreover, whether the impressions others hold of us are accurate is, in a sense, beside the point. Veridical or not, their impressions mediate much of their behavior toward us. As a result, social psychologists have long been interested in the processes involved in forming impressions of other people (see Harvey & Weary, 1982; Nisbett & Ross, 1980; Schneider, Hastorf, & Ellsworth, 1979).

Because interpersonal judgments are so important, it is understandable that people are interested in how others perceive them and often try to control the impressions others form, in a process termed *self-presentation* or *impression management* (Goffman, 1959; Schlenker, 1980). By selectively conveying certain images of themselves, people can influence how others perceive and evaluate them and thereby affect how others treat them. Through impression management, one can subtly elicit from others the responses one desires (Schlenker, 1980).

An Introduction to Self-Presentation

A number of studies over the past 25 years have explored both the determinants of self-presentation and the tactics people use to present themselves to others (for reviews, see Baumeister, 1982; Jones & Pittman, 1982; Schlenker, 1980; and Tedeschi, 1981). The nature of the impressions people try to foster depends upon a variety of factors, including their goals in the interaction, the characteristics of others who are present, the nature and extent of others' knowledge about them, their own self-concepts, and the role they are playing in the encounter (e.g., Baumeister & Jones, 1978; Leary, Robertson, Barnes, & Miller, in press; Schlenker, 1975a; Schneider, 1969).

Virtually any behavior can be used to convey information about oneself to others. Nonverbal behaviors, expressions of one's attitudes, disclosures of personal information, public explanations of one's behavior, and the conspicuous use of certain possessions (e.g., jewelry, books, cars) can all serve a self-presentational function, selectively and often strategically revealing oneself to others. Not all public behaviors are attempts to manage one's impressions, however. Actions are considered self-presentational only if one of the individual's goals in performing the action is to affect the inferences others draw about him or her (Jones & Pittman, 1982).

The notion that people manage the impressions others form of them does not imply that they go through life trying to deceive others into forming impressions that are not factually accurate. People do sometimes lie about themselves, attempting to claim characteristics they know they do not really possess, and these instances reflect one class of impression management strategies. However, such dissimulation is risky, and in most instances self-presentation involves choosing an *accurate* self-image for projection to others from a larger set of potential images. The impressions that are fostered are strategically chosen for a particular "audience" and social setting, but the images conveyed usually reflect the individual's true personal attributes as he or she sees them (Schlenker, 1980). Thus, there is nothing inherent in the concept of self-presentation that implies dissimulation.

As noted above, the specific impressions that people try to foster are determined, in part, by their goals in an interaction and by the nature of the impressions they believe are most likely to accomplish those goals. In many, if not most instances, the primary goal is to be regarded favorably by others and to elicit positive responses from them. Thus, people generally desire to make good rather than bad impressions, however "good" and "bad" are judged in a specific social context. For example, as a rule, people would rather be viewed as attractive, bright, and interesting than as unattractive, stupid, and boring. In most contexts, making a good impression is more likely to lead to valued social and personal outcomes for the individual, such as friendship, positive feedback, assistance, and so on.

Because people usually want to make good rather than bad impressions, self-presentation sometimes has been erroneously regarded solely as a strategy for gaining others' acceptance and approval. This view of self-presentation misses the point that impression management often is used to achieve goals that have nothing to do with being liked or accepted. In a taxonomy of self-presentational strategies, Jones and Pittman (1982) identified five different classes of self-presentation that differ according to the inferences the individual wishes others to draw. Three of these represent attempts to make a socially desirable impression by appearing likable (ingratiation), competent (self-promotion), or morally worthy (exemplification).

By contrast, the other two strategies, *intimidation* and *supplication,* reflect attempts to be perceived as dangerous or helpless, respectively, usually at the risk of making a socially undesirable impression. Through intimidating self-presentations, people demonstrate that they are able and willing to inflict stress, pain, or other aversive outcomes upon those who do not do their bidding. For example, a boss may want his employees to perceive him as critical, stern, and uncompromising in order to exert greater control over them. He is not interested in being liked; rather, his primary goal is to exert power over his employees, and he manages the impressions he conveys in a manner that makes his threats credible. In the case of supplication, people convey the impression that they are weak and dependent in order to elicit support and nurturance from others. For example, a woman may exaggerate her exhaustion at the end of a hard day at work in order to get her husband and children to do the household chores. As in the case of intimidation, the woman's goal is to control others' reactions rather than to be liked.

Nearly everyone engages in supplicating and intimidating self-presentations from time to time. There are occasions when it is clearly to one's advantage to appear helpless or threatening. However, habitual use of these strategies results in behavior that is, in the long run, maladaptive. The link between impression management and dysfunctional behavior should now be clear. When people believe that conveying impressions of themselves as hostile, out of control, helpless, or irrational will result in desired outcomes for them, dysfunctional behaviors may result. In this chapter, we examine dysfunctional phenomena that reflect the use of socially undesirable self-presentations.

Impression Management and Mental Illness

Since ancient times it has been recognized that otherwise normal people may manage their impressions in ways that make them appear "crazy" when it is to their benefit to do so. In *The Odyssey,* for example, Odysseus pretends to be crazy by yoking an ass and an ox to a plow and sowing a field with salt in order to avoid serving in the war with Troy. (Palamedes exposes the ruse by placing Odysseus' only son in front of the plow, leading Odysseus to turn the plow aside and expose his sanity.) In *King Lear,* Edgar disguises himself as a madman in order to hide from men sent by his father to kill him. More recently, it is never quite clear whether Jack Nicholson's character in the movie *One Flew Over the Cuckoo's Nest* is in fact mentally disturbed or merely faking mental illness to avoid prison (although the viewer suspects the latter). Corporal Klinger's motives on the television show *M*A*S*H* are more transparent as he dresses in women's clothing in an attempt to be discharged from the army. In a real-life case of feigned mental illness, Son of Sam killer David Berkowitz maintained that he had been ordered to kill by a neighbor's demon-possessed dog, but later he admitted that he fabricated the story as an excuse for his actions ("Berkowitz admits," 1979). Highly publicized cases in which accused criminals plead "guilty by reason of insanity" have sensitized both the courts and the public to the use of impression management that involves portrayals of mental illness.

However, both psychologists and the lay public draw a sharp distinction between "normal" people who pretend to mentally ill and individuals who are truly psychologically disturbed. Traditionally, it has been assumed that people who consistently behave in an illogical, irrational, self-defeating, or bizarre manner with no apparent ulterior motive for doing so are really mentally ill, the unfortunate victims of biochemical, environmental, or unconscious forces over which they have no control. Their bizarre behavior is interpreted in terms of underlying psychopathology. However, as will soon become clear, the distinction between real and contrived cases of mental disorder is much less clear-cut than we often assume.

Self-Presentational Aspects of Schizophrenia

Since the early 1960s there have been continuing attacks on the traditional conception of mental illness (Sarbin & Mancuso, 1980; Scheff, 1966; Szasz, 1961). To discuss these controversies would take us far afield, but one facet of these criticisms is pertinent. Specifically, the critics have argued that, rather from stemming from intrapsychic processes of various sorts, psychological difficulties are largely interpersonal in nature, emerging from problems in human relationships (see, for example, Carson, 1969). Further, it has been argued that many classic psychotic and neurotic symptoms may be regarded as interpersonal, self-presentational strategies designed, like all self-presentational behaviors, to achieve certain reactions from other people and to accomplish certain social and personal goals. The thesis to be examined in this section is that many individuals who manifest behaviors traditionally regarded as indicative of psychopathology, even those who are so severely impaired that they are confined to a mental institution, may be managing their impressions in order to appear psychologically disturbed.

To those of us who have been consistently rewarded for appearing sensible, competent, and well-adjusted, it may be difficult to understand why someone might want others to think he or she is psychologically disturbed. The best answer is that psychological disturbance frees the individual from many of the responsibilities and pressures of work, family, and social life. Society does not expect disturbed individuals to be self-sufficient, responsible, or productive citizens. On a more familiar and less extreme level, we can imagine a man exaggerating the stressfulness of his job in order to stop his wife from complaining about his failure to do his share of the domestic chores. By appearing to be exhausted, frazzled, and under stress when he gets home from work, he is able to avoid responsibilities he regards as unpleasant and prompt his wife to cater to his needs.

A similar desire to escape the responsibilities and hardships of life may underlie the psychological "symptoms" of many individuals who reside in mental institutions (Braginsky, Braginsky, & Ring, 1982). Most long-term residents of mental hospitals come from the lowest rungs of the socioeconomic ladder and tend to be poor, undereducated, and unemployed. In comparison to the overcrowded, dilapidated, unpleasant, and dangerous settings in which poverty-stricken individuals usually live, the prospect of residing in a mental hospital, either temporarily or permanently, may be an attractive alternative. In the hospital, they find asylum from the hardships of poverty within an institution that caters to their needs and expects little from them.

Braginsky et al. (1982) have gone so far as to suggest that some people from very poor backgrounds use the mental hospital for much the same reasons that wealthy people patronize a resort. Like a resort, the mental institution provides an escape from the normal demands of living, furnishes recreational facilities and social activities, and does not expect its residents to be productive. The idea of the resortlike function of mental institutions is reflected in the title of their provocative book, *Methods of Madness: The Mental Hospital as a Last Resort.*

Because people cannot live in mental hospitals unless they are, in one way or another, certified as mentally ill, people may manage their impressions in ways that make them appear appropriate for institutionalization. This is a very controversial thesis, one at odds with the dominant views of mental illness in psychiatry and psychology.

Before examining evidence that bears upon this notion, we should make a couple of important points. First, the idea that some mental patients manage their impressions does not imply that dysfunctional behavior is "nothing but" impression management. Many people do experience severe emotional and behavioral problems over which they have little, if any, control. Thus, we should not be misunderstood to be saying that all so-called mental illness reflects supplicating self-presentations of one sort or another. Nor do we mean to imply that the people who reside in mental institutions, even those who manage their impressions in order to appear disturbed, do not have psychological or social problems. An individual who maintains the image of being psychologically troubled in order to live in an institution clearly has difficulty living effectively in his or her normal environment. However, a self-presentational perspective does suggest that the nature of such individuals' problems is sometimes different than that traditionally identified by psychologists and psychiatrists.

Research Evidence

The use of impression management among hospitalized psychiatric patients has been investigated in several studies. In one of the first, Braginsky,

Grosse, and Ring (1966) reasoned that the longer a person resides in a mental institution, the greater his or her motivation to remain there. Not only may prolonged institutionalization be a direct result of the patient's wish to stay in the hospital, but long-term residents may increasingly come to doubt their ability to function in the outside world. If this assumption is true, we should find that, compared to new patients, long-term residents manage their impressions in ways that make them appear too disturbed to be released.

To test this hypothesis, the researchers administered a set of true-false items taken from the MMPI to a group of mental patients. Some of the patients were recent arrivals, having been in the hospital less than 3 months, whereas others were long-term residents. Before completing the test, the patients were told either that answering most of the questions "true" indicated that they were severely disturbed and should be hospitalized or that "true" responses indicated that they were not particularly disturbed and, thus, might be released soon. Consistent with the hypothesis, long-term residents answered more questions "true" when they thought "true" responses showed they were psychologically disturbed than when they thought "true" indicated a low degree of psychopathology. Newcomers showed the opposite pattern, answering more questions "true" when they thought "true" showed that they were relatively well adjusted. Thus, the overall impression created by old-timers was one of mental illness whereas that created by newcomers was one of mental health.

Of course, not all residents of mental hospitals want to stay there or to appear psychologically disturbed. Fontana, Klein, Lewis, and Levine (1968) used items from the Edwards Social Desirability Scale to distinguish between what they called "healthy" and "sick presenters." Healthy presenters are patients who are motivated to appear mentally competent; sick presenters are those who are motivated to appear incompetent. Presumably, sick presenters want to remain in the hospital to a greater degree than healthy presenters and manage their impressions in order to look too disturbed for release. In studies involving nearly 250 patients, Fontana et al. found that, compared to healthy presenters, sick presenters were less certain they could function outside of the hospital, thought they would be institutionalized for a longer period of time, and were rated by the medical staff as having more negative attitudes toward being discharged.

The two studies just described portray long-term residents and sick presenters, respectively, as motivated to remain hospitalized and as engaging in impression management to achieve that goal. However, an alternative interpretation of the results is that long-term residents and sick presenters are *really* more disturbed than newcomers and healthy presenters, or at least believe themselves to be. Long-term residents and sick presenters may have responded in ways that reflected how they truly saw themselves, as severely disturbed, rather than appearing maladjusted in order to remain in the hospital.

Although plausible, this explanation is discounted by other research. In a classic study by Braginsky and Braginsky (1967), 30 long-term schizophrenics were told that they would be interviewed by a staff psychologist and were given one of three different reasons for the interview. In the *open-ward* condition, patients were told that they were being interviewed to determine whether they should be placed on an open or a closed ward. Given that open wards are more pleasant places to live, being reserved for the least disturbed patients and allowing greater freedom, patients in this condition should want to appear as well adjusted as possible in order to remain on the open ward. In the *discharge* condition, patients were told that their suitability for release from the hospital was being assessed during the interview. If, as Braginsky et al. (1982) suggested, many long-term residents want to stay in the hospital, patients in this condition should try to give the impression that they are too disturbed to be released. The remaining third of the patients were told only that the psychologist wanted to see how they were getting along in the hospital (*mental status* condition); this information would be expected to have about the same effects on patients' self-presentations as the discharge condition. Three psychiatrists, blind to the experimental hypotheses, listened to tape recordings of the interviews and rated each patient according to the degree of psychopathology exhibited.

The data supported the hypothesis that patients would manage their impressions in order to remain hospitalized, yet avoid the closed ward. Patients in the open-ward condition displayed significantly fewer indications of having psychological problems than those in the other two conditions; they described themselves more positively to the interviewer and reported significantly fewer physical and mental problems. (In fact, no patient in the open-ward condition reported having any severe problems, whereas half of those in the other conditions did so.) Further, those patients who thought their suitability for an open ward was being assessed were judged as requiring less control and as exhibiting less psychopathology.

These findings were conceptually replicated in subsequent studies. Fontana and Gessner (1969) told psychotic and nonpsychotic patients that they were being tested for one of three reasons: for research purposes, to assess their suitability for discharge, or to determine whether they should be transferred to an older, larger, and less desirable institution that housed more severe cases. Patients threatened by the possibility of transfer appeared least disturbed on all measures taken, and this pattern was obtained for both psychotic and nonpsychotic patients (see also Fontana & Klein, 1968; Wilcox & Krasnoff, 1967).

Watson (1972) was unable to replicate these results in psychiatric interviews, although he obtained effects of open-ward versus discharge instructions on patients' responses on questionnaires. Interestingly, Watson's subjects who were threatened by discharge tended to use self-presentations that can best be described as neurotic rather than psychotic in nature. He suggested that it may be easier to convey the impression of being neurotic than of being psychotic.

Altogether, these findings suggest that, whatever the reasons for their initial hospitalization, some patients selectively display symptoms in order to influence others' judgments of them. Moreover, their self-presentations may serve instrumental ends. Although the causes of their problems are many and complex, and although their behaviors may be profoundly disturbed, some of those who are diagnosed as mentally ill can, like anyone else, employ principles of impression management to get what they want. Indeed, in some instances, abnormal behavior may be as much a product of strategic self-presentation as of any underlying psychopathology.

Case Studies

The psychiatric literature also includes mention of contrived psychiatric symptoms, although they are not discussed within the context of self-presentation per se. For example, Sadow and Suslick (1961) described several cases in which former mental patients consciously simulated their previous psychotic states when they subsequently found themselves under stress. In one case, a 32-year-old man exhibiting bizarre behavior was readmitted to a hospital 4 years after his release from the same hospital. Suspicious of the symptoms he reported, his physicians reminded him of the high financial cost of hospitalization. (He had left the hospital after his previous admission because of the cost.) At that point his symptoms disappeared, and he admitted he had faked psychosis in order to be admitted. He said that he had had impulses to hurt his wife and saw involuntary hospitalization as a way of preventing possibly violent behavior. Although this man clearly had other problems, his "psychosis" was a self-presentational ploy designed to gain admission to the hospital. It is interesting that, in psychiatric discussions of this sort of case, the patient's attempts to appear "crazy" are interpreted as further evidence of existing psychopathology rather than as reflecting a somewhat rational interpersonal influence strategy given the limited social and personal resources of a troubled individual (Braginsky et al., 1982). We return to this point later in the chapter.

In a discussion of borderline children, Cain (1964) observed that such children sometimes "play crazy." He suggested that they may pretend to be disturbed for a number of reasons. First, by consciously pretending to be disturbed, the child is able to achieve a sense of control over his or her frightening behaviors. In addition, playing crazy can become a source of social identity for the child. Through playing such a role, the child can gain attention and recognition as, in Cain's words, a "full-fledged odd one" instead of being a "nobody" within the family and peer group. Some children learn that fostering the impression of being out of touch can occasionally have its social and personal rewards.

Similarly, many adult patients adopt some salient aspect of their difficulties as a "trademark" that becomes a central aspect of their social identity. Just as normal individuals might foster the trademarks of being athletes, religious devotees, intellectuals, or jet-setters, a mental patient may capitalize on a single manifestation of his or her difficulties and become known as "the boy who kills dogs" or "the man with no feelings." Even though the trademark may reflect a real problem, it is used for self-presentational purposes as a way of identifying and characterizing oneself to others.

Dysfunctional Self-Presentations in Everyday Life

Despite the evidence just reviewed, the notion that people sometimes manage their impressions in order to appear psychologically disturbed may still strike some as difficult to understand, if not downright unbelievable. Indeed, the idea has been challenged by some psychologists (e.g., Arieti, 1959; Rosenbaum, 1969; Watson, 1972, 1975). This strategy of impression management may be more understandable if we provide a few examples of its use by people whom we would regard as normal.

In everyday life outside the mental institution, otherwise well-adjusted individuals sometimes try to convey the impression that they are experiencing psychological difficulties. Unlike the mental patients discussed above, most people limit their supplicating self-presentations to relatively minor and, usually, transitory psychological conditions, such as stress, fatigue, worry, overwork, grief, depression, intoxication, and confusion. In some situations, individuals' reports of their internal states may be quite accurate, whereas in others the reports are fabricated. In either case, the reported psychological difficulties may serve self-presentational goals. This is not to say that people who report negative emotional states are always engaging in impression management, only that they often are doing so.

Whether accurate or contrived, self-reports of psychological difficulties in everyday life serve roughly the same functions as the more severe claims of hospitalized schizophrenics. Claiming to be stressed, tired, anxious, grief-stricken, or whatever can free the individual from normal responsibilities. These negative emotional states serve as an acceptable reason to avoid social commitments (e.g., "I'm too upset to go to the party tonight") and shirk unpleasant responsibilities (e.g., "I'm so tired and uptight when I get home from work that I just *can't* help with the housework"). Further, people sometimes attribute undesirable actions to their mental state (e.g., "I lost my temper because I'm under a lot of stress") and excuse poor performances by bringing up their personal problems (e.g., "I failed the test because I was too depressed to study"). When such accounts are offered prior to events that threaten the individual's self- or social esteem, they represent instances of self-reported handicapping (see chapter 4).

In addition to serving as excuses, the use of supplicating self-presentations may prompt others to offer their support. For example, in an examination of depression, Bohime (1960) portrayed depressive behavior as a mode of interaction that elicits emotionally comforting responses from other people. Similarly, Coyne (1976b, pp. 34–35) suggested that the depressed individual "finds that by displaying symptoms [of depression] he can manipulate his environment so that it will provide sympathy and reassurance." This is not to say that people are never really depressed, but it does point out that depressive behavior can serve a self-presentational function by conveying the individual's inner distress to others and eliciting supportive reactions.

One last example of supplicating self-presentations in everyday life deserves mention: "playing dumb." The example easily called to mind is the woman who feels compelled to hide her achievements, feign ignorance on certain topics, and allow men to win at games because of her concern that men are threatened by highly competent women. Early research emphasized women's tendency to "play dumb" (Komarovsky, 1946; Wallin, 1950), but recent studies show that men are as likely as women to underplay their knowledge and competence. However, the situations in which men and women tend to use this strategy differ (Dean, Braito, Powers, & Brant, 1975; Gove, Hughes, & Geerken, 1980). Women are more likely to play dumb with their husbands than husbands are to play dumb with their wives, but men are more likely than women to play dumb with their bosses and co-workers. Although the actual incidence of playing dumb is relatively low, it is clear that people sometimes assume that it is to their advantage not to appear as knowledgeable or as competent as they believe themselves to be.

Self-Presentation of Psychological Problems: Conclusion

In summary, supplicating self-presentations that emphasize weakness, incompetence, ignorance, and psychological difficulties are used occasionally by virtually everyone. In extreme cases, individuals may manage the impression of being so severely disturbed that they require institutionalization and derive their social identity from their status as a mental patient. We should reemphasize that this does not imply that all psychological disturbances are reducible to impression management or that all people who appear to be suffering from problems are managing their impressions. But studies do show that people sometimes try to appear weak, ineffectual, or disturbed, and that the presence of psychological "symptoms" cannot necessarily be taken as indicative of underlying problems, even when displayed by people diagnosed as chronic schizophrenics.

One question often raised is whether impression management is conscious. Do mental patients and others consciously and intentionally control how they are perceived by others, fully aware of what they are doing and their reasons for doing so? As Schlenker (1980) pointed out, self-presentation may be either a conscious or a nonconscious act. On the one hand, people sometimes consciously portray themselves in particular ways, quite aware of what they are doing and why. On the other hand, self-presentation is often a habitual and nonconscious action. Behavior that is undertaken without conscious planning may still have the goal of creating a particular impression and, thus, would be considered self-presentational (Jones & Pittman, 1982). For example, most people do not consciously comb their hair each morning in order to make a good impression on others, but combing their hair is nonetheless a purposive self-presentational behavior. In the same way, the self-presentations of mental patients may occur without conscious deliberation and planning, reflecting habitual ways of presenting themselves in certain contexts.

There is the possibility, too, that once-conscious strategies of self-presentation can become habitual and nonconscious as the images one portrays are gradually integrated into one's self-concept. Jones, Rhodewalt, Berglas, and Skelton (1981) have shown that successfully conveying certain impressions (i.e., having others accept them and react to the individual in terms of them) can reshape the presenter's own image of himself or herself. Subjects who were instructed to convey positive impressions of themselves to another person subsequently showed higher levels of self-esteem than subjects who were instructed to be self-deprecating. The research of Jones et al. suggests that people who adopt supplicating self-presentational strategies may, over time, come to view themselves as weak and ineffectual.

Behind everything that has been said about impression management and mental illness in this section is a more provocative conclusion. Traditionally, the prototypic schizophrenic has been regarded as severely impaired. Not only is schizophrenia typically characterized by disordered thinking and bizarre behavior, but the schizophrenic is portrayed as out of touch with reality and socially ineffectual (e.g., Schooler & Parkel, 1966). The body of research discussed above questions this depiction. As Braginsky et al. (1982) noted, the mental patients they observed "did not appear to us to be the disoriented, dependent, and socially inept creatures that textbooks described" (p. 29). Whatever their psychological and social problems, a significant proportion of these individuals are sufficiently in tune with their social worlds to engage in the complex cognitions required for successful self-presentation. They are able to take others' perspectives, draw accurate inferences regarding other's reactions to various self-presentations, develop goals and plans regarding how those goals may be achieved, and implement those plans in interpersonal encounters (cf. Shaver et al., 1984).

The few studies that have explicitly studied the self-presentational ability of hospitalized schizophrenics show that they are quite adept at managing their impressions on demand (Kelly, Farina, & Mosher, 1971; Sherman, Trief, & Sprafkin, 1975). As Ludwig and Farrelly (1967, p. 740) observed, schizophrenics are "more expert at producing certain reactions on the part of the staff, the family, and society at large than the latter are at evoking desired patient responses." Clearly, research on self-presentation and mental disturbance provides further evidence that undermines traditional views of schizophrenia (Braginsky et al., 1982; Sarbin & Mancuso, 1980; Scheff, 1966; Szasz, 1961).

Self-Presentations of Physical Illness

Few readers can claim that they have never "played sick" either to get out of something they did not want to do (such as going to school or going on a date with the school buffoon) or to account for undesirable behavior (such as failing a test or playing a sport poorly). People often report they do not feel well when appearing to be in less-than-perfect health has benefits for them. In American society three classic examples come easily to mind: the child who plays sick in order to stay home from school, the malingerer who feigns illness or injury to avoid military duty, and the unwilling sexual partner who claims to have a headache. Of course, in many instances, people really do not feel well, but in others their report of physical illness is fabricated. Either way, reporting one's ill health to others can serve self-presentational functions.

Underlying self-presentations of illness are culturally shared assumptions regarding the sick role. In his seminal treatment of the topic, Parsons (1951), the noted sociologist, observed that Western society holds several assumptions about people who are ill. Among these is the assumption that the sick individual is exempt from normal social obligations for the duration of the illness. We seldom expect people who are ill to engage in their normal range of activities or to perform them with characteristic skill or energy. In addition, implicit societal assumptions maintain that sick individuals have a right to expect others to care for them to some degree (Gordon, 1966). Given these culturally shared assumptions regarding the sick role, there are clearly advantages to being, or at least appearing to be, ill.

Twaddle (1979) made the interesting observation that, at any given time, most people have something physically wrong with them. In most instances, people's physical complaints are minor ones, such as sore muscles, indigestion, headaches, allergies, and minor aches. On other occasions their complaints are more severe, as in the case of serious illnesses and injuries. Given the pervasiveness of physical maladies of various sorts, why do people report their physical condition to others only occasionally? Although there is no research that addresses this question, it is reasonable to suggest that people are increasingly likely to express their ailments as the perceived rewards of appearing to be ill or injured increase. That is, the act of communicating one's physical discomfort to others can serve a self-presentational function.

Thus, many people occasionally use physical symptoms to elicit desired reactions from others, whether to avoid undesirable responsibilities, to excuse undesirable behaviors, or to elicit supportive and care-taking behavior from others. However, some people use these types of supplicating self-presentations as a preferred way of influencing others' behavior toward them. Indeed, some people adopt a social identity defined in terms of illness.

Their ill health becomes a defining characteristic that governs most of their encounters with others. Viewed from an impression management perspective, hypochondriacs may be regarded as individuals who characteristically use self-presentations that emphasize poor physical health. Their obsession with their health is such that others cannot help but respond to them except in terms of their illnesses and frailties.

In many instances, the self-serving nature of the hypochondriac's reported symptoms is quite obvious (Snyder & Smith, 1982). Chapter 4 discussed research showing that hypochondriacs are particularly likely to mention their ill health when threatened by the prospect of failure. Although Smith et al. (1982) interpreted this finding in terms of a self-esteem maintenance model (see chapter 4), it is as easily interpreted within a self-presentational framework. Hypochondriacs may use physical symptoms as a way of influencing how others regard and treat them.

Because of the possibility of malingering, society often requires some degree of validation of the individual's illness (Gordon, 1966). The best validation seems to be legitimization by a physician; a doctor's excuse is widely accepted as evidence that the person is truly ill. In fact, just a visit to a physician may provide legitimization, because seeing a doctor demonstrates that the individual is concerned enough about his or her health to seek professional help, whether or not the physician finds anything wrong. This legitimizing function of seeking medical advice may explain hypochondriacs' incessant trips to the doctor; visits to a physician serve a self-presentational function, as people who go to a doctor are perceived to be more ill than those who only report various symptoms and stay home. (In an analogous fashion, visits to a psychologist may lend legitimacy to claims of psychological distress.)

The presence of observable symptoms also serves to validate illnesses. As a result, the individual who wishes to show others, truthfully or untruthfully, that he or she is ill often behaves in ways that overtly convey the impression of being ill or injured. People may adopt a weak or tired countenance, grimace, rub injured or diseased portions of their bodies, move more slowly or carefully than usual, and engage in other actions that indicate they are experiencing the symptoms they claim. Moreover, people may use these sorts of nonverbal self-presentations even when they are really ill if there is reason to think that others doubt the veracity of their reports or underestimate the extent of their distress.

In summary, people sometimes try to convey the impression that they are physically ill or injured. Although everyone does this from time to time, there is evidence that some individuals chronically use self-presentations of ill health. Many cases of hypochondriasis may be traced to a consistent use of illness-related impression management. A great deal more research is needed that examines the self-presentational functions of hypochondriasis and other illness behaviors.

Aggression and Criminality

In this section we explore the role of impression management in aggressive, antisocial, and criminal behavior.

Self-Presentation and Aggression

In the same way that appearing disturbed, weak, incompetent, or ill helps some individuals achieve their personal and social goals, intimidating self-presentations lead to desired outcomes for others (Jones & Pittman, 1982). Thus, antisocial behavior sometimes occurs because individuals *want* to be regarded as aggressive or reckless.

Intimidating self-presentations can serve three major functions for the individual who uses them. First, fostering an image of aggressiveness is often effective in getting others to comply with one's wishes. As a result, people may manage their impressions in a way that makes them appear threatening to induce others to do their bidding (Felson, 1978; Tedeschi, Smith, & Brown, 1974). For such a self-presentational strategy to be effective, the individual must occasionally carry through on his or her threats, thereby validating the hostile image. Much seemingly senseless violence may serve this self-presentational purpose.

Another function of aggression is to preserve one's social image in the face of physical or verbal attacks. Retaliatory aggression does this by demonstrating to the offending individual and others present that one is not to be trifled with. For example, an experiment by Brown (1968) showed that adolescent males were more likely to retaliate against an opponent when they were told that observers thought the opponent had exploited them and made them look foolish. In fact, Brown's subjects saved face through retaliation even when it cost them real monetary profits they could have received by continuing to be cooperative; the impression the observers formed of them seemed to be more important than cold, hard cash.

Outside of the lab, a study of 50 episodes of violence between street gangs showed that the most common precipitating factor was a perceived insult or affront to the honor of a gang or one of its members (Horowitz & Schwartz, 1974). The purpose of the violence appeared to be to reinforce the offended gang's reputation and restore its honor in the eyes of the other gangs. In essence, aggression resulted from events that threatened the public image of a gang or its members.

Third, self-presentations of aggressiveness are often directly reinforced by certain societal subgroups. For example, many street gangs openly admire members who display a hostile, brazen, and reckless image (Bandura, 1973). Taken to the extreme, in some circles individuals are socially rewarded for aggressive behavior such as attacks upon out-groups (Short & Strodtbeck, 1963). Among these groups, the valued image of being an aggressive individual is achieved partly through overtly aggressive acts.

People use intimidating self-presentations primarily when they do not think that more positive social images will achieve their personal and interpersonal goals. This may explain why aggressive self-presentations (including overtly aggressive behavior) are more prevalent among members of lower socioeconomic groups (Felson, 1978). People who are poor, uneducated, and unemployed have fewer socially desirable activities upon which to base a positive social identity. As Sarbin (1982, p. 117) put it, "instances of dangerous conduct follow from practices that transform a man's social identity downward and leave no room for substitute identities." Sarbin argued that the dehumanizing treatment of aggressive criminals in prison compounds the likelihood of aggression by stripping them of alternative, prosocial identities. Penal systems may create institutional cultures in which the self-presentational use of aggression is strongly rewarded.

Criminal Behavior

Hogan and Jones (1983) suggested that even nonaggressive criminal behavior can serve self-presentational functions. They maintained that habitual criminals differ from noncriminals chiefly in the degree to which their parents and peer groups reward antisocial rather than conventional identities. When the attention, respect, and approval of one's parents and peers are contingent upon the impression of being tough and antisocial, people will manage their impressions so as to be viewed as "criminal." These self-presentational strategies range from mere antisocial posturing to outright criminal behavior. Even among otherwise law-abiding citizens, the desire to be regarded as a risk-taker or a "good sport" or as willing to go along with the group occasionally leads to illegal behavior.

As Hogan and Jones pointed out, this view of criminal behavior has important implications for the rehabilitation of many criminals. To the extent that one's social identity is based upon appearances of criminality, rehabilitation must focus on creating a new social identity for the individual, one that includes a new self-image, a new reference group, and new self-presentational strategies. Programs that fail to take criminals' social motives into account neglect an important determinant of their illegal actions.

Theoretical Integrations

The research discussed in this chapter demonstrates that the desire to achieve and/or avoid certain outcomes sometimes leads people to project images of themselves that include undesirable or dysfunctional characteristics. In this section we examine a theory of self-presentation that helps account for the use of socially undesirable self-presentations.

In any given situation, people have a large but finite set of impressions that they can potentially create. For example, let us imagine a woman who is on her first date with a man whom she likes. She has a variety of self-presentational options from which to choose. She could try to appear athletic, religious, intellectual, humorous, liberal, sophisticated, profeminist, serious, seductive, apolitical, ambitious, clever, or nurturant, to suggest just a few of the possibilities. These different images are not necessarily mutually exclusive, but in practice she must choose a relatively small number to emphasize during the evening. Nor are any of these images necessarily false or deceitful. Although some may describe her better than others, they all may represent true aspects of her personality. Given these possibilities, which image or images will the woman try to project to her date?

According to Schlenker (1980), she will choose to convey those images of herself that she thinks will have the *highest value when claimed*. The expected value of a potential image is a function of three things: First, the more valuable the outcomes one expects to receive for being perceived in a particular fashion, the higher the expected value of that image, all other things being equal. People recognize that certain impressions are more likely to achieve their goals or to result in desired outcomes than other impressions. The higher the expected rewards and the lower the expected costs of successfully making a particular impression, the higher its expected value and the more likely the person is to attempt that impression. Thus, if the woman thinks her date admires women who are athletic, but is unimpressed by those who are intelligent, she is more likely to emphasize her athletic qualities, all other things being equal.

However, people also consider the fact that it is easier for them to manage some impressions than others. People's self-presentations are held in check by their views of themselves and by their assessment of the risks involved in trying to make certain impressions. Thus, the expected value of an image is also dependent upon the likelihood of successfully claiming the image and the potential costs of attempting to make that particular impression but failing. Trying to impress her date with her athleticism would only make the woman look foolish and deceitful, for example, if she is not in good shape and knows little about sports.

In brief, people tend to claim those images that have the highest expected value when successfully claimed. The expected value of an image is a function of (1) the value of outcomes assumed to be contingent upon achieving the impression, (2) the probability of achieving the impression, and (3) the sanctions involved for trying but failing to manage the impression successfully.

Applying this model to the use of the supplicating and intimidating self-presentations discussed in this chapter highlights the causes of dysfunctional impression management. First, the model makes it clear that the social desirability of an image (i.e., the degree to which it makes a good rather than a bad impression) is not in itself a consideration in choosing among impression management options. Although socially desirable impressions are, on the average, more likely to result in the outcomes people desire, there are instances in which socially undesirable impressions are more likely to accomplish one's objectives. In such situations, people should claim those less desirable images, even at the risk of making "bad" impressions. In all of the examples discussed in this chapter, supplicating and intimidating self-presentation occurs because the individual believes that the use of those types of impressions is most likely to have the desired effects.

Second, undesirable self-presentations may be chosen over desirable ones because the likelihood of achieving undesirable impressions is usually higher. It is often easier to make a bad than a good impression if one desires to do so. In light of this, people may forgo positive self-presentations (even ones with a high expected payoff) when they do not think they can successfully sustain such images, and opt instead for a more easily attainable, but less desirable social identity. For example, the mental patients studied by Braginsky et al. (1982) may have believed, perhaps accurately, that they could not achieve a satisfactory life-style by impressing others with their competence, intelligence, and social skill. In light of this assessment, they had the choice of forgoing a comfortable life or resorting to less desirable self-presentations in order to achieve it. Similarly, we noted earlier that intimidating self-presentations seem to be more common among those who have fewer positive activities upon which to base an acceptable social identity (Felson, 1978; Sarbin, 1982).

Thus, a person's self-presentation of belligerence, impulsivity, illness, abnormality, weakness, or even psychosis may not be as unlikely or as counterproductive as one might assume. Such impressions may at times be intentionally managed as a fairly rational way of maximizing their (perhaps limited) personal and social outcomes.

Conclusions

Much dysfunctional behavior may be traced to individuals' attempts to influence others' reactions to them. Maladaptive behaviors that spring from impression management motives do not reflect intrapsychic disturbances, as traditional models of abnormal behavior suggest. Rather, they represent interpersonal self-presentational strategies used when other, more acceptable modes of interpersonal influence are not likely to be effective.

In light of this, treatment of dysfunctional patterns of behavior stemming from self-presentational processes must focus on helping individuals develop alternative, socially desirable identities that will be effective in accomplishing their goals. It is noteworthy that social-skills training has been shown to be effective in reducing a variety of maladaptive responses, including those discussed in this chapter (Bellack & Hersen, 1979). Unlike many other treatments, social-skills training teaches clients how to interact more effectively with others in achieving their interpersonal goals. From an impression management perspective, the process of teaching social skills also improves clients' self-presentational abilities, leading them to have greater confidence that they will be regarded favorably by others and reducing their need for intimidating and supplicating self-presentations.

Chapter 6

Anxiety and Inhibition in Interpersonal Relations

Although the characteristics that describe the "well-adjusted" individual are always open to debate, few would argue that the ability to interact with others in a confident, skilled, and open manner is not among them. People who are not able to interact comfortably are at a distinct disadvantage as they go through life, being less likely to have rewarding interpersonal relationships and being plagued by anxiety and insecurity in their dealings with others.

Unfortunately, many people are troubled by feelings of social inadequacy. Although virtually everybody becomes nervous and uncertain in certain social situations, many people regularly find their interactions with others derailed by intense feelings of anxiety accompanied by a debilitating tendency to act in an inhibited, awkward, and reticent fashion. In fact, 40% of Americans label themselves as "shy," and 4% indicate that they feel shy almost all of the time (Zimbardo, 1977). Similarly, about a quarter of all college students report that they are uncomfortable dating or interacting with members of the other sex (Arkowitz, Hinton, Perl, & Himadi, 1978; Borkovec, Stone, O'Brien, & Kaloupek, 1974; Glass, Gottman, & Shmurak, 1976). Situations in which people speak before audiences are particularly likely to make them uncertain and anxious; the fear of public speaking is a very common fear (Bruskin Associates, 1973; Bryant & Trower, 1974; Geer, 1965), with at least 20% of American college students suffering from a dysfunctionally high level of apprehension about speaking in public (McCroskey, 1977).

Whether experienced on dates, during job interviews, while speaking in public, or while engaged in everyday conversations, social anxiety is a common, often debilitating reaction to interpersonal encounters. Given the importance of interpersonal relations to happiness and adjustment, behavioral scientists have devoted a great deal of attention in recent years to the problem of anxiety and inhibition in interpersonal encounters (see Buss, 1980; Jones, Cheek, & Briggs, 1986; Leary, 1983b).

In this chapter we examine portions of this literature. We first introduce three models of social anxiety that have guided most research and treatment in the area. We then turn our attention to a newer social psychological theory that provides an alternative explanation for these sorts of social difficulties and encompasses all three of the earlier perspectives. We then discuss the behavioral difficulties that arise when people become nervous in interpersonal encounters, and we explore implications of theory and research for treating clients who experience excessive social anxiety.

Theories of Social Anxiety

Why do people often become nervous when they interact with others? What is it about even mundane conversations that makes so many people awkward and uncomfortable? Most explanations of social anxiety fall roughly into one of three theoretical perspectives, each of which we will discuss briefly.

Classical Conditioning

Most students of psychology are familiar with the story of "little Albert," a young boy who was the subject of John Watson's research on conditioning (Watson & Rayner, 1920). Using Albert as a subject, Watson showed that fears can be learned by pairing aversive, fear-producing stimuli with otherwise innocuous neutral objects. Watson conditioned little Albert to become afraid of a white rat (which initially he did not fear) by banging loudly on a steel bar with a hammer whenever Albert tried to touch the animal. After several pairings of the rat and the clanging bar, Albert reacted fearfully whenever the rat was present, even though Watson no longer banged on his noisemaker. In the terminology of classical conditioning, the rat had become a conditioned stimulus capable of evoking the conditioned response of fear.

Since this early demonstration, a great deal of research has shown that potent fears may be learned in such a fashion by both animals and humans (see Bandura, 1969, for a review). Although, for obvious ethical reasons, no research has attempted to condition socially based anxieties, it seems clear that people may begin to experience anxiety in certain social situations after having suffered aversive consequences in those situations in the past. For example, a man who previously had not been anxious about speaking in public may develop severe speech anxiety after giving one particularly terrible speech. Or a girl may become nervous in her dealings with boys after a traumatic incident in which a group of boys taunts her in front of her friends. Indeed, Zimbardo (1977) reported than many shy people are able to trace the onset of their anxiety and inhibition to a particular traumatic social event.

If social anxiety is conditioned when aversive experiences are paired with certain social stimuli, we would expect to be able to decondition social anxiety by pairing the threatening social stimuli with pleasant, favorable consequences. In fact, much research has shown that chronic social anxiousness is reduced by treatments based on conditioning procedures such as systematic desensitization (Bander, Steinke, Allen & Mosher, 1975; Bandura, 1969; Curran, 1975; Curran & Gilbert, 1975; Kanter & Goldfried, 1979; Kondas, 1967; Meichenbaum, Gilmore, & Fedoravicius, 1971; Paul, 1966). In systematic desensitization, anxious clients are taught to associate relaxation responses with the threatening interpersonal stimuli so that the link between the stimulus and the anxiety is reduced. Although the effectiveness of systematic desensitization was originally explained in terms of behavioristic, nonmentalistic learning principles, there is growing agreement that desensitization is mediated by cognitive processes (Bandura, 1969, 1977; Bandura & Adams, 1977; Goldfried, 1979; Murray & Jacobsen, 1971).

Importantly, the effectiveness of systematic desensitization in reducing social anxiety does not imply that social anxiety is necessarily classically conditioned. There is no logical connection between the cause and the treatment of a particular problem. Just as the effectiveness of radiation therapy for certain kinds of cancer does not indicate that cancer develops because of insufficient radiation, the effectiveness of systematic desensitization does not prove that social anxiety develops through classical conditioning. We are not arguing that social anxiety is not classically conditioned in some cases, but we want to note that the effectiveness of desensitization is, at best, only weak evidence for this model.

In brief, then, one explanation of social anxiety suggests that the reaction is classically conditioned, and, although the evidence is indirect, the effectiveness of systematic desensitization as a treatment for social anxiousness lends some support to this model.

Social-Skills Deficits

For social interactions to proceed smoothly, the interactants must generally behave in an appropriate, facilitative, socially skilled manner. Conversations quickly become awkward when one or more participants use nonverbal cues inappropriately, engage in inappropriate or annoying behaviors, fail to hold up their ends of conversations, or otherwise mismanage their portion of the interaction.

According to the social-skills deficit model, social anxiety occurs when people lack important social skills and thus create aversive, anxiety-producing situations when they interact with others (Bellack & Hersen, 1979; Curran, 1977). Not only do social-skills deficits result in less-than-favorable reactions from others (Arkowitz et al., 1978) and create awkward situations, but they lead the unskilled individual to perceive himself or herself as socially inadequate. Such consequences are understandably anxiety producing.

In support of the social-skills model of social anxiety, studies have shown that socially anxious individuals are rated as less socially skilled than less anxious individuals (Arkowitz, Lichtenstein, McGovern, & Hines, 1975; Bellack & Hersen, 1979; Curran, 1977; Twentyman & McFall, 1975). However, it has been difficult to identify *specific* skill deficits among socially anxious people, though they may involve, in part, behaviors related to timing and turn-taking during conversations (Fischetti, Curran, & Wessberg, 1977; Peterson, Fischetti, Curran, & Arland, 1981).

Therapists who subscribe to the social-skills deficit explanation use one of several variations of social-skills training for socially anxious clients. In social-skills training, clients are taught through modeling, direct instruction, and practice how to interact more adroitly. Research has shown that skills training is quite effective in reducing high levels of social anxiety (Bellack & Hersen, 1979; Curran, 1975; Curran & Gilbert, 1975; Fremouw & Zitter, 1978; Glass et al., 1976), although it is not clear whether skills training is effective because it reduces the probability that people will mismanage their interactions with others or because it increases their self-confidence in social encounters (Bandura, 1977). Either way, there is a clear link between social-skills difficulties and social anxiety. However, the processes by which skill deficits lead to anxiety and inhibition are not completely understood.

Cognitive Approaches

A third set of explanations of social anxiety adopt a cognitive approach, emphasizing the role of people's beliefs about themselves, other people, and social relationships. Three related but distinct themes can be identified in this literature.

First, there is evidence that social anxiety is associated with unfavorable self-evaluations. As Clark and Arkowitz (1975, p. 212) noted, "the behaviors of the socially anxious individuals may be reasonably adequate by external standards but evaluated as inadequate by the socially anxious individual." In support of this position, several studies have shown that socially anxious people generate more negative thoughts about themselves both before and during social interactions than less anxious people do (Cacioppo, Glass & Merluzzi, 1979; Clark & Arkowitz, 1975; Glasgow & Arkowitz, 1975). They also tend to have lower self-esteem (Leary, 1983c) and expect to perform more poorly in social encounters (Cacioppo et al., 1979; Efran & Korn, 1969). Although there is no way to show that negative self-thoughts *cause* people to be socially anxious, the association between self-derogation and nervousness in social situations is undisputed.

A second set of cognitive models may be traced to Ellis' (1962) emphasis on irrational beliefs. According to Ellis, many people hold the "irrational" belief that it is important to be loved and approved of by nearly everyone and that less than full acceptance by others indicates that one is worthless as a person. Ellis called these beliefs irrational because they represent goals that are unattainable and that result in unnecessary unhappiness and insecurity.

The relationship between a desire for social approval and social anxiety has been supported by several studies, including one showing that the belief that it is necessary to be liked by everyone correlates positively with anxiety in both interpersonal and public-speaking situations (Goldfried and Sobocinski, 1975).

A third cognitive model focuses on the effects of excessively high standards on social anxiety. As Bandura (1969, p. 37) noted, many people who seek professional help "are neither incompetent nor anxiously inhibited, but they experience a great deal of personal distress stemming from excessively high standards for self-evaluation, often supported by unfavorable comparisons with models noted for their extraordinary accomplishments." In other words, when people expect too much of themselves in social life, they are likely to experience social anxiety.

A variety of treatments for chronic social anxiousness have emerged from these cognitive theories of social anxiety. Although differing in specifics, they share a common emphasis on changing clients' beliefs about themselves and their social relationships. For example, Meichenbaum's (1977) cognitive restructuring techniques teach clients to recognize the dysfunctional effects of their negative self-thoughts and to substitute more facilitative, coping self-statements when they catch themselves falling into self-disparagement. Similarly, Ellis' (1962) rational-emotive therapy attempts to convince clients of the irrationality of a high need for social approval and to help them set more realistic interpersonal goals for themselves. Counseling research attests that these sorts of cognitively based therapies are effective in reducing problematic social anxiety (Fremouw & Zitter, 1978; Glass et al., 1976; Kanter & Goldfried, 1979; Malkiewich & Merluzzi, 1980; Meichenbaum et al., 1971; Rehm & Marston, 1968; see Goldfried, 1979, for a review).

Self-Presentation Theory

The classical conditioning, social-skills deficit, and cognitive models discussed above have each contributed to our understanding of social anxiety and provided treatment models for clinical work with socially anxious individuals. However, none of these approaches successfully accounts for all of the known antecedents and consequences of social anxiety (Leary, 1983b).

Schlenker and Leary (1982, 1985; Leary, 1980, 1983b; Leary & Schlenker, 1981) have proposed a social psychological theory of social anxiety that is somewhat broader than the approaches described above. By specifying the necessary and sufficient conditions for all instances in which people become socially anxious, and by accounting for both situational and dispositional antecedents of social anxiety, their model subsumes each of the other approaches, offering a more general framework for understanding and treating social anxiety.

This theory, which is rooted in a self-presentational analysis of social behavior (see chapter 5), is based on the assumption that people often desire to control the impressions others form of them—a process called self-presentation or impression management (Goffman, 1959; Schlenker, 1980). By monitoring and controlling the impressions they convey to others, people can subtly influence others to treat them as they desire. Simply stated, making a "good" impression often results in desired reactions from others, whereas making a "bad" impression is likely to result in undesirable responses.

According to Schlenker and Leary (1982), people experience social anxiety when they become concerned about the kinds of impressions others are forming of them. More specifically, they suggest that people become socially anxious when they are motivated to make particular impressions on others but doubt that they will do so.

Self-Presentational Motivation

According to this theory, people will not experience social anxiety unless they first are motivated to make a particular impression on others. People may have a number of goals when they interact with others—to obtain information, to make a business contact, to have fun, to attract a sexual partner, to humiliate an opponent, and so on—but one key goal may be to foster certain impressions in other's eyes. People are not always motivated to control how others see them, but when they are not, social anxiety will not occur.

An examination of the factors that tend to make people nervous in social situations reveals that many of them have their effects by increasing the degree to which people are motivated to control the impressions others form (see Leary, 1983b; Schlenker & Leary, 1982). For example, most people are more nervous when interacting with those who are attractive, prestigious, and powerful than they are in dealing with people who are less attractive or of low status. This may be because people are more motivated to make a good impression upon those who are attractive and powerful. Likewise, people are particularly prone to be nervous when they meet someone for the first time; because they recognize that first impressions are particularly important, they are more concerned with how they come across during an initial encounter and feel more anxious as a result. Research also suggests that situations that lead people to focus on and think about public aspects of themselves make them more concerned with others' reactions (Fenigstein, 1979) and heighten social anxiety (Buss, 1980). As these examples show, situational factors that increase people's concerns with the impressions others form of them increase social anxiety.

Similarly, people who possess personality characteristics that predispose them to be highly motivated to manage their impressions are particularly likely to become nervous in social situations (Schlenker & Leary, 1982). For example, people who have a high need for social approval (Crowne &

Marlowe, 1964), who worry about being evaluated negatively by others (Leary, 1983e; Watson & Friend, 1969), or who endorse the irrational belief described by Ellis (1962) regarding the importance of being loved by everyone are highly motivated to manage their impressions and frequently experience social anxiety (Leary, 1983b). Such individuals are likely to be among those who seek professional help for their high degree of interpersonal anxiety.

In brief, the theory states that any situational or dispositional factor that elicits self-presentational motives also increases the likelihood that people will become socially anxious, and the available research evidence is consistent with this proposition (Leary, 1983b).

Perceived Probability of Self-Presentational Success

The Schlenker-Leary model posits that, for social anxiety to occur, people must not only be motivated to make certain impressions, but also harbor doubts that they will do so. This implies that any situational or dispositional variable that lowers people's expectancies that they can successfully convey a desired impression should increase social anxiety (Leary, in press-b).

Leary and Atherton (1986) suggested that people may doubt their chances of self-presentational success for two distinct reasons (see also Maddux, Norton, & Leary, in press): On the one hand, an individual may hold low *self-presentational efficacy expectations,* doubting that he or she can adequately execute the behaviors needed to make the impression. For example, a man may find that his date, whom he wants to like him, is attracted to men who are athletic, energetic, robust, and interested in outdoor activities. He, however, detests exercise, sunburns quickly when outdoors, and is frail. Under such circumstances, he is likely to doubt his ability to create a desired impression, and he may feel socially anxious. Similarly, a woman may become anxious in a job interview when she wants to create the impression that she thinks well on her feet, but privately knows that she does not.

In other instances, people may have full confidence in their interpersonal (and self-presentational) abilities, yet still expect not to make a good impression. In such cases, people may perceive that, because of the nature of the encounter or the characteristics of other interactants, there is nothing they (or anyone else) can do to make a good impression. In such a case, the difficulty lies not in one's social ability but in the encounter itself, and the person may have high self-efficacy expectations (believing he or she can perform behaviors that would normally make good impressions) yet hold low *self-presentational outcome expectations.* For example, a socially confident man may perceive that his date is characteristically snobbish, disinterested, and very hard to please, or a woman may know she is a competent and successful employee, yet worry about the evaluations of her sexist, hypercritical boss.

As noted above, the self-presentation approach easily encompasses the three earlier explanations. For example, people may doubt they can make desired impressions in those social situations that have caused them problems in the past, thereby accounting for conditioning processes. The self-presentation theory also accounts for the fact that socially anxious people tend to be low in self-esteem (Leary, 1983c). To the degree that people with low self-esteem believe that others will detect their real or imagined deficiencies, they may doubt they will make a good impression in a variety of encounters and feel anxious as a result. Thus, it is not low self-esteem per se that contributes to social anxiety, but the fact that people with low self-esteem expect to make unsatisfactory impressions on others that causes trouble. In the same way, people who lack important social skills may experience social anxiety, not because of their social-skill problems per se, but because their perceived deficiencies lead them to doubt that others will form positive impressions of them.

The most aversive, traumatic, and discombobulating instances of social anxiety involve situations in which a person who is very concerned with making a good impression behaves in a way that makes him or her appear incompetent, immoral, foolish, or otherwise undesirable. These sorts of incidents, termed self-presentational predicaments, generate a great deal of anxiety popularly known as embarrassment (Goffman, 1955; Miller, 1986; Schlenker, 1980). According to the self-presentation theory, such occurrences are so distressing because the individual wishes to make a good impression, but has behaved in way that has mortally wounded the image he or she wished to create.

In summary, the self-presentation theory assumes that social anxiety occurs when people desire to make certain impressions upon others, but do not think that they will do so. Social anxiety is thus precipitated and exacerbated by factors that motivate people to manage their impressions and/or that lead them to believe they will not do so successfully.

Inhibited and Avoidant Behavior

Whatever their precise determinants, episodes of social anxiety are often accompanied by changes in the way people act (Leary, 1983b; Leary & Dobbins, 1983). The most obvious indication that a person feels nervous in a social encounter is that he or she does not participate fully in the ongoing conversation (Zimbardo, 1977). Compared to those who are not anxious, socially anxious people initiate fewer conversations with others, speak less frequently during the interaction, talk a lower percentage of the time, take longer to respond when it is their turn to speak, and break silences in the conversation less often (Arkowitz et al., 1975; Cheek & Buss, 1981; Glasgow & Arkowitz, 1975; Leary, Knight, & Johnson, in press; Pilkonis, 1977).

Despite a burgeoning research literature dealing with social anxiety, shyness, and communication avoidance (see Daly & McCroskey, 1984; Jones et al., 1986; Leary, 1983b), there is no consensus of opinion regarding why social anxiety is accompanied by inhibited and avoidant behavior. Although it is tempting simply to conclude that anxiety "causes" people to become inhibited, this explanation is disputed by Schachter's (1959) classic research on fear and affiliation. Schachter showed that when people are anxious for nonsocial reasons, such as when they believe they are to receive an electric shock, they tend to affiliate *more* than when they are not anxious. Thus, anxiety per se bears no necessary relationship to inhibition or disaffiliation. People become quiet and inhibited only when the source of their anxiety lies in their interactions with others (Leary, 1983b, 1983d).

Why do people tend to disaffiliate and adopt a passive style of interacting when they feel socially anxious? This question has a number of possible answers, each of which has some degree of support. It should not be assumed that these explanations of the relationship between social anxiety and inhibition are mutually exclusive. Rather, they may work together to lead socially anxious individuals to withdraw from social contacts.

Reinforcement of Withdrawal Behaviors

First, people may interact less when anxious in order to reduce or escape the experience of anxiety. If interaction is aversive, withdrawing from interaction may reduce one's anxiety and thus be negatively reinforcing. As a result, behaviors that increase anxiety (such as talking) decline in frequency, whereas those that reduce anxiety (such as quietness or withdrawal) increase in frequency.

Learned Helplessness

In addition, people may respond passively when they are socially anxious because they experience learned helplessness. As we saw in chapter 3, people may stop trying to achieve their goals and display learned helplessness when they perceive that their outcomes are unaffected by their behavior. According to the attributional version of learned helplessness theory (Abramson et al., 1978), people's expectancies of achieving their goals are affected by the attributions they make about the noncontingency between their behavior and outcomes. If they attribute their inability to achieve the desired outcome to transient states, particularly those that may be overcome by volition, they should expect to regain control of the situation; helplessness, if it occurs at all, should be minimal and brief. On the other hand, if an individual believes that the noncontingency is due to factors that are unchangeable, he or she will not expect to regain control, and helplessness will result.

Thus, whether people become inhibited when anxious may depend upon the attributions they make for their interpersonal difficulties. If people attribute their social difficulties to transient, unstable characteristics of themselves or the situation, they should hold a reasonable expectation of eventually achieving their goals and should not behave in a helpless fashion. For example, a woman may feel uncertain and anxious at a party, but attribute her reaction to the fact that she has not yet learned enough about the other partygoers or has not hit upon the right interpersonal strategy. Under these conditions, she should continue to interact rather than withdraw, because she believes that success is likely in time. However, if socially anxious individuals attribute their difficulties to stable, uncontrollable factors, they will hold a low expectation of achieving social rewards and will manifest learned helplessness. For example, if the woman at the party thought her nervousness resulted from her own ineptitude, she would be more likely to withdraw.

In a relevant study, Anderson (1983a) asked subjects to solicit blood donors and led them to attribute failures to obtain donors either to stable factors (ability and trait factors) or to unstable (strategy and effort) factors. As predicted by an attributional, learned helplessness model, subjects who attributed their failures to insufficient effort or inappropriate persuasive strategies expected to improve with practice, were more motivated to solicit donors, and performed better at the solicitation task than subjects who made ability and trait attributions (see Goetz & Dweck, 1980, for a similar study on children). Thus, inhibition and withdrawal may reflect learned helplessness in the social encounter.

Self-Efficacy

Bandura (1977) suggested that "efficacy expectations are a major determinant of people's choice of activities, how much effort they will expend, and of how long they will sustain effort in dealing with stressful situations" (p. 194). Extended to settings that elicit social anxiety, a self-efficacy analysis concludes that people will exert minimal effort and, perhaps, withdraw from encounters in which they feel incapable of making the impressions they want to make (Leary & Atherton, 1986; Maddux et al., in press).

Further, according to self-efficacy theory, people infer their self-efficacy from a number of sources, one of which involves their subjective experience of arousal or anxiety. People use their arousal as an index of how well they are handling stressful situations: High anxiety implies low self-efficacy, whereas low anxiety implies high self-efficacy. Thus, the more anxious people feel in a social encounter, the more likely they are to assume that they are handling the situation poorly, and the more likely they are to withdraw.

Of course, the attributions people make regarding *why* they feel nervous mediate their sense of efficacy and, thus, their interpersonal behavior when nervous. A study by Leary, Atherton, Hill, and Hur (in press) showed that people who attribute their feelings of social anxiety to stable characteristics of themselves (such as low social ability or their predisposition to get nervous) are more likely to avoid social encounters than people who attribute their anxiety to unstable characteristics of themselves (such as the specific behavioral strategy they used) or the nature of the situation and other interactants. Thus, when attributed to characterological factors, subjective anxiety may serve as a "low self-efficacy indicator" that leads socially anxious people to adopt defensive interpersonal strategies such as inhibition and avoidance (Bandura, 1977; Leary & Atherton, 1986; Leary, Atherton, Hill, & Hur, in press).

Self Presentation

A fourth explanation of withdrawal under conditions of social anxiety is suggested by the self-presentation theory (Schlenker & Leary, 1982, 1985). Instead of representing a lack of control and/or self-efficacy, avoidant behavior may be an active strategy of cutting one's perceived social losses. To the extent that socially anxious people think they are not making good impressions on others, they are likely to assume that continued participation in the encounter will further erode their fragile social images. As a result, they may withdraw as a way of protecting what remains of their social identity. Thus, reticence and inhibition may represent a meta-self-presentational strategy, one that is designed to avoid further damage to one's social image (Leary, 1985; Leary, Barnes, & Griebel, in press; Leary, Knight, & Johnson, in press).

Of course, when people fail to participate fully in an encounter, they run the risk of being perceived as aloof, disinterested, or socially inept. Thus, the tendency for socially anxious people to remain silent is opposed by social pressures to converse. Research suggests that anxious individuals often balance these competing pressures by adopting a passive interaction style that allows them to hold up their end of the conversation while participating as little as possible and maintaining an innocuously sociable image. Such a tack represents a protective self-presentational style—a strategy intended to avoid making a bad impression (Arkin, 1981; Arkin, Lake, & Baumgardner, 1986; Baumgardner & Arkin, 1985; Leary, in press-b).

For example, when socially anxious, people ask proportionally more questions per utterance, a tactic that conveys interest in others and that keeps the spotlight off themselves (Leary, Knight, & Johnson, 1986). Similarly, socially anxious interactants use more back-channel responses, which are the vocalizations a person makes to indicate that he or she is listening to another, such as "uh-huh" (Leary, Knight, & Johnson, in press; Natale, Entin, & Jaffe, 1979). Socially anxious people are also more likely to smile and express agreement with others; this also serves to convey a pleasant image while remaining passive (Cheek & Buss, 1981; Pilkonis, 1977). In brief, inhibition and withdrawal may help the individual who is worried about others' impressions or him or her to maintain a low profile in the interaction and not risk further losses of social esteem.

Altogether, then, the self-presentational model suggests that inhibited, avoidant behavior may be people's *preferred* response to situations in which they fear they will be regarded less favorably than they desire. Given that avoidance and inhibition in anxiety-arousing situations appear to be multiply determined (by reinforcement, helplessness, self-efficacy, and self-presentational processes), it is little wonder that social anxiety is so often accompanied by social withdrawal.

Implications for Treatment

Although nearly everyone experiences social anxiety occasionally, many individuals are bothered enough by the frequency and/or intensity of their nervousness that they seek professional help. Schlenker and Leary's (1982) theory has several implications for the treatment of highly socially anxious clients that go beyond the recommendations of the conditioning, social-skills, and cognitive approaches.

Most importantly, the model suggests that radically different treatment approaches should be used with different socially anxious clients (Leary, 1983b, in press-c). Although the model maintains that all instances of social anxiety may be traced to self-presentational concerns, it also suggests that people may be habitually anxious in social situations for a variety of specific reasons.

Some people may be chronically socially anxious because they are overly motivated to make good impressions on others in order to obtain social approval. These clients would benefit most from treatments designed to reduce excessive need for approval, such as those based on rational-emotive therapy (Ellis, 1962). Other people, however, may be anxious a great deal of the time, not because they are overly concerned with others' impressions of them, but because they know they lack important social skills and come across very poorly in many social situations. These clients would benefit most from social-skills training designed to improve their interpersonal adeptness (Bellack & Hersen, 1979; Curran, 1977). Still other anxious individuals may be highly anxious because they have low self-esteem and thus assume that other people do not regard them favorably. These individuals require a treatment approach that focuses on modifying their negative self-image (see Haemmerlie & Montgomery, 1982, 1984).

If the self-presentation model is valid, all cases of problematic social anxiety evolve from self-presentational concerns. However, the specific precipitating factors may be quite idiosyncratic. Attempting to use a single strategy, whether it be systematic desensitization, social-skills training, cognitive restructuring, or whatever for all socially anxious clients ignores these important differences. The bottom line is that counselors and psychotherapists who deal with socially anxious clients should be alert to the fact that a single treatment is unlikely to be maximally effective for all clients (see Leary, in press-c, for a detailed discussion of client-specific treatments for social anxiety based upon the self-presentation approach).

Conclusions

Social anxiety ranks with depression and loneliness as one of the most common psychological difficulties faced by the average person. Unfortunately, the self-presentational theory suggests that a certain amount of social anxiety is an unavoidable consequence of the fact that interpersonal interactions are mediated partly by the impressions that people form of one another. How people perceive and evaluate one another has a strong impact on how they react, and as a result, people often are concerned with making the sorts of impressions that will facilitate the accomplishment of their social goals. Viewed from this perspective, a certain amount of social anxiety is quite natural. Only when the individual is distressed much of the time would we regard the experience as requiring remediation. When treatment is needed, a variety of approaches may be useful, because chronic social anxiousness may be precipitated either by exaggerated desires to impress others or by doubts in one's ability to do so.

Chapter 7

Troubled Relationships

One's interpersonal relationships substantially affect one's well-being. Indeed, clinicians and counselors have long recognized that a person's social relations are central to normal adjustment (e.g., Henderson, 1977; Sullivan, 1953). In his investigation of happiness, Freedman (1978) suggested that:

> there is no simple recipe for producing happiness, but all of the research indicates that for almost everyone one necessary ingredient is some kind of satisfying, intimate relationship . . . people who are lucky enough to be happy in love, sex, and marriage are more likely to be happy with life in general than any other people. (p. 48)

Beyond mere unhappiness, argued Duck and Gilmour (1981), "the disturbed interpersonal context of the lives of many sorts of persons can be a crucial influence on their tendency to commit violent crime, to experience clinical depression, or to resort to abuse of alcohol or drugs" (p. viii). The experiences of separation and divorce are clearly correlated with psychopathology (Bloom, Asher, & White, 1978). Even physical health problems can be traced to the breakdown of relationships (House, Robbins, & Metzner, 1982; Lynch, 1977; Stroebe & Stroebe, 1983).

Thus, it is promising that after years of studying attraction between strangers (e.g., Byrne, 1971), social psychologists have begun intensive study of ongoing close relationships (e.g., Brehm, 1985; Duck, 1982, 1984; Gilmour & Duck, 1986; Ickes, 1985a, Kelley et al., 1983; in addition, a new *Journal of Social and Personal Relationships* began publication in 1984). This chapter surveys this new specialty, examining factors of both social and clinical relevance that help determine the quality of people's relationships. We examine three different components of troubled relationships: 1) personal dysfunctions that afflict one member of a dyad; 2) interactive dysfunctions that debilitate the moment-to-moment interactions of a particular couple; and 3) relationship dysfunctions inherent in the long-term transactions of a couple. Our survey will touch upon interpersonal communication, power, serious individual problems, role conflict, emotional affection, and attractions to alternative relationships (such as extramarital affairs); these are six of the nine areas judged by marital therapists to have the most damaging effect on marital relationships (Geiss & O'Leary, 1981).

Personal Dysfunctions

Our concern here is with those problems in relationships that trouble an individual without necessarily affecting his or her partners. The complaints we address—jealousy, loneliness, and depression—are of particular interest because they can both result from and cause troubled relationships (see Duck, 1980). As we are about to see, for example, jealous men often behave in ways that endanger the relationships they fear they are losing.

Jealousy

Jealousy seems to be a universal experience; in a survey of more than 100 San Francisco residents, Pines and Aronson (1983) found that all of them had experienced jealousy. Some people are more prone to jealousy than others (Greenberg & Pysczynski, 1985); in particular, a strong desire for sexual exclusivity with one's partner (Buunk, 1982; White, 1981a) and a traditional gender-role orientation (Hansen, 1985; White, 1981a) put one at risk. However, jealousy largely depends upon the nature of the relationship we share with our partners, and anyone can become jealous. Whenever people feel inadequate and incapable of satisfying their partners (White, 1981a, 1981b) and/or feel dependent on the relationship, thinking it irreplaceable (Berscheid & Fei, 1977; Buunk, 1982; Hansen, 1985), jealousy becomes more likely.

The basis for jealousy, of course, is the fear that a valued relationship may be usurped by a rival. Jealousy is the reaction that follows a threat to one's self-esteem and/or to the quality of a relationship "when those threats are generated by the perception of a real or potential romantic attraction between one's partner and a (perhaps imaginary) rival" (White, 1981b, p. 296). However, it is not just the simple fact that a relationship is threatened that induces jealousy, but our perception of *why* the threat exists that causes us pain. White (1981c) asked college undergraduates to list reasons why their boyfriends or girlfriends might become romantically involved with someone else and found that some motives were likely to cause a partner jealousy whereas others were not. Four broad motives emerged: The subjects believed a partner might leave them because of 1) dissatisfaction with the current relationship, 2) a desire for sexual variety, 3) the general attractiveness of the other person, or 4) a desire for greater commitment than the present relationship provides. White then obtained ratings of these motives and of jealousy from 300 respondents. For both men and women, the perception of dissatisfaction in a partner was a strong predictor of jealousy, with the need for sexual variety somewhat less so. The attractiveness of a rival induced jealousy in women but not in men, and a partner's search for more commitment was not related to jealousy in either sex. Thus, if a partner's interest in another person reflects discontent with us or a desire for more or better sex, it hurts. By contrast, if the partner seeks something we choose not to provide, jealousy is unlikely.

White's (1981c) findings were extended by Buunk (1984) in a provocative study assessing subjects' attributions for their spouses' actual extramarital affairs. Buunk found that males' jealousy was highest when they perceived a desire for sexual variety in their wives, whereas females were most jealous when they believed their husbands were dissatisfied. Again, jealousy depended on the subjects' interpretations of the situations they faced. Mathes, Adams, and Davies (1985) also found this to be true, determining that losing a partner to accidental death, a job transfer to a distant city, or even outright rejection (i.e., "he [she] does not love you anymore") all created less jealousy than losing a partner to a rival.

Two particular gender differences in jealousy are noteworthy. First, females more often than males report *trying* to induce jealousy in their partners in order to "test the relationship" or to get more attention (White, 1980). This seems a dangerous strategy, however, because the sexes respond differently to jealousy when it occurs. When shown a jealousy-evoking videotape of a same-sex target unexpectedly finding her (or his) current partner embracing an old flame, females usually said that in such a situation they would feign indifference and try to make themselves more attractive to their partners (Shettel-Neuber, Bryson, & Young, 1978). Women, then, generally react to jealousy by trying harder, concentrating on repairing a damaged relationship. Men, on the other hand, try to repair their egos. Males reported that they would threaten the rival, get drunk, and start chasing other women. Thus, a woman who intentionally induces jealousy in her partner in the hope that he will pay her more attention may be sorely mistaken.

The fact that anyone would try to induce jealousy suggests that the experience of jealousy does not necessarily damage a relationship; because partners can "prove their love" (i.e., demonstrate their insecurity and dependency) by becoming jealous, people sometimes find jealousy desirable (Pines & Aronson, 1983). However, jealousy is commonly found by clinicians to have destructive effects on relationships (e.g., Clanton & Smith, 1977; Docherty & Ellis, 1976), often serving as an early warning signal that something is wrong (Constantine, 1977). Attempts to alleviate troublesome jealousy can focus on three different domains: First, the situation facing a jealous person can be changed. Jacobson and Margolin (1979) argued that if a threat to the relationship is real, it should be minimized as soon as possible; couples in marital therapy, for instance, should suspend any extramarital affairs. Similarly, both Ard (1977) and Constantine (1977) feel that clear communication about the appropriate limits partners wish to place on one another's behavior can clear up misunderstandings and help prevent jealousy in the first place.

A second domain of intervention addresses a partner's appraisal of the threat to the relationship. Ellis (1977b) distinguished between rational and irrational jealousy, suggesting that it is reasonable to be concerned by a real threat but that it is silly and unrealistic to allow catastrophizing cognition to blow one's fears out of proportion. Finally, the emotional and behavioral components of jealousy can be directly treated, desensitizing the sufferer and rewarding calm and poise (Jacobson & Margolin, 1979).

Loneliness

Jealous people at least have valued relationships that they stand to lose. Another personal dysfunction, loneliness, afflicts those who feel that the relationships they have are not enough. Loneliness occurs when one's network of intimate and social relationships is smaller or less satisfying than desired, that is, when there is "a discrepancy between one's desired and achieved levels of social relations" (Perlman & Peplau, 1981, p. 32). It is an aversive experience, routinely involving desperation, impatient boredom, self-deprecation, and depression (Rubenstein, Shaver, & Peplau, 1979). Unfortunately, it is a common experience (Rubenstein & Shaver, 1982). A person's social network can be constricted suddenly by situational forces beyond that person's control, and any such change may precipitate loneliness. Thus, the end of a marriage through death or divorce, or the physical separation that accompanies a graduation or career move, can put one at risk (Cutrona, 1982; Weiss, 1973). Even getting married can cause unanticipated shrinkage of one's network, particularly among women (Fischer & Phillips, 1982; Milardo, Johnson, & Huston, 1983). Any adverse change in one's opportunities for interaction can bring on loneliness, and once it exists, it can be regrettably persistent.

When people are lonely, their social behaviors differ from those of the nonlonely in three broad respects. First, lonely subjects report a *negative outlook* toward themselves and other people (Jones, Freemon, & Goswick, 1981; Jones, Sansone, & Helm, 1983). When Jones et al. (1983) placed lonely college students in brief "get acquainted" conversations with other students, the lonely subjects believed that their partners did not like them much—a belief that was generally unfounded. Furthermore, lonely subjects liked their partners less than nonlonely students did. When people are lonely they consider themselves relatively unlikeable people surrounded by unlikeable people; they interact with others expecting rejection and blame themselves for their troubles (Anderson & Arnoult, 1985; see chapter 2).

Second, lonely people exhibit *social-skills deficits*. When Jones, Hobbs, and Hockenbury (1982) examined the conversational behaviors of lonely subjects, they found an interactive style that was relatively self-absorbed, unresponsive, and inattentive. Compared to nonlonely subjects, lonely people talked more about themselves, asked fewer questions of their partners, arbitrarily changed the topic more often, and responded more slowly to their partners. Their relative lack of social skill was obvious; Jones (1982) reported that, when one nonlonely male ventured the observation that he liked girls from Colorado, his lonely female partner scornfully replied, "Colorado girls, huh, is that because they have frosted tits?" The lonely are also more likely to be unassertive, shy, and self-conscious in interaction (Jones et al., 1981).

A final characteristic of the social behavior of lonely people is its *superficiality*. Sloan and Solano (1984) have found that lonely males are more inhibited and less intimate in their conversations with both strangers and roommates than are other men. In fact, most studies that investigate the issue find loneliness to be associated with low self-disclosure (for instance, Solano, Batten, & Parish, 1982). As a result, lonely subjects do not report having fewer "best friends" than nonlonely people, but the perceived level of intimacy in those relationships is lower, a perception with which the "best friends" agree (Williams & Solano, 1983). Similarly, when Jones (1981) asked students to keep a diary record of their daily interactions, he found that, although the total amount of time spent interacting with others was similar for the lonely and nonlonely, lonely subjects reported more time spent with strangers and acquaintances, and less time with family and friends (cf. Stokes, 1985). Overall, it seems that lonely people chronically act in a less intimate and less satisfying style than other people do (Wheeler, Reis, & Nezlek, 1983), and they are less likely to concentrate their energies on developing a few close friends.

Loneliness is thus a key example of how personal dysfunction can contribute to troubled relationships. Lonely people are usually surrounded by others, but are dissatisfied—at least temporarily—with their social networks; this dissatisfaction is manifested in a pessimistic, inept, superficial style of interaction that is likely to prolong the loneliness. How does such a problem ever go away? Cutrona (1982) tracked 162 college freshman over 7 months and found that those who overcame initial loneliness did so by "gradually making friends" with the people around them. Importantly, they did this mainly by changing their evaluations of the friendships they already had; the nature of their interactions did not change particularly much, but their outlook toward their relationships did. By contrast, Cutrona reported, "students who remained lonely throughout the school year most often said that 'finding a boyfriend/girlfriend' was the only way they would ever get over their loneliness" (p. 298). Insisting on a close attachment to another person is likely to keep a lonely person dissatisfied.

Thus, it appears that any of us can be plunged into loneliness by upheaval in our lives, but that individual aspirations and outlooks have much to do with how quickly we recover. When people are lonely, can they be helped? Let us briefly consider another individual dysfunction before targeting treatments for loneliness.

Depression

Loneliness and depression are different constructs that are not causally related to one another, but they are correlated and have much in common (Weeks, Michela, Peplau, & Bragg, 1980). Like the lonely, depressives engage in pessimistic, negativistic cognition (e.g., Beck et al., 1979) and often exhibit impaired social skills (e.g., Libet & Lewinsohn, 1973). However, studies of depression have examined an important issue not yet addressed by loneliness researchers, namely, how other people react to interactions with depressed partners.

In a classic study, Coyne (1976a) arranged 20-minute telephone conversations between college women and depressed female outpatients, and then assessed the resulting moods of the normal participants. In this and other studies, "depressed persons induced hostility, depression, and anxiety in others and got rejected" (Strack & Coyne, 1983, p. 803). Although this effect does not always occur (e.g., King & Heller, 1984), depressives can induce negative affect in others that impedes rewarding, mutually satisfactory interaction. As a semester proceeds, for instance, the roommates of depressed college students gradually become more depressed themselves (Howes, Hokanson, & Loewenstein, 1985). Thus, it may be useful to consider depression a "self-perpetuating interpersonal system" (Coyne, 1976b) in which the individual's dysfunction creates a deficient social environment that keeps the problem in place.

Viewed in this light, the social inadequacy of several clinical groups—schizophrenics, neurotics, and alcoholics, for example—may influence the persistence of their disorders (Argyle, 1981; Haley, 1985; Kazdin, 1979). Deficient personal skills that make a person an unrewarding partner can cut that person off from the essential social reinforcements that most of us enjoy. Even among normals, skill in constructing and maintaining relationships may be essential if one is to benefit from a supportive social environment (Hansson, Jones, & Carpenter, 1984). For instance, it may be the quality, not the quantity, of social interaction we enjoy that mediates the relation between social support and good health (Reis, Wheeler, Kernis, Spiegel, & Nezlek, 1985).

Thus, personal dysfunctions that contribute to troubled relationships are no small matter. There are a variety of therapeutic strategies that may help alleviate loneliness or depression, but many therapists suggest that efforts to modify both a client's cognition and his or her social skills may be necessary (e.g., Rook & Peplau, 1982). Conjoint therapy with a spouse or other intimate partner may be valuable (Dryden, 1981). Situational interventions that provide a person new opportunities for social contact may also be desirable, particularly for loneliness (Rook, 1984). It may even be possible to prevent some cases of loneliness through education and family training with high-risk groups (i.e., the young, unmarried, or unemployed), although the effectiveness of such interventions has yet to be determined (Rook, 1984).

In sum, personal dysfunctions can have impactful, debilitating effects on relationships. Jealousy, loneliness, and depression are particularly interesting because they can both result from and cause troubled relationships. However, there may be a more widespread personal dysfunction that, in its lasting effects, is even more important than those we have mentioned thus far: *being male*. Alas, consideration of that daring assertion must await the introduction of other, interactive dysfunctions in troubled relationships.

Interactive Dysfunctions

Our concern in this section is with components of interaction that are not of themselves necessarily dysfunctional—and that do not cause individuals distress—but that do cause problems for particular couples. The seemingly average attributes of two normal people can combine to create awkward, unsatisfying interactions that are unique to that dyad. A dysfunctional, troubled relationship can thus emerge from the interactive joint contributions of two people who have no apparent personal dysfunctions and who can (and do) enjoy satisfactory relationships with others. In this sense, the dysfunction can be said to lie not in the individuals but in their interaction or "interpersonal situations" (Kelley, 1984), entities that can be conceptually distinguished from the persons themselves. Our first example addresses a couple's ability to communicate well nonverbally.

Nonverbal Communication

The patterns of our physical movements, expressions, and spacings from one another, in combination with the vocal characteristics of our spoken words (such as the loudness, pitch, rate, and intonation of our speech), underlie and regulate our interactions with others. The directions of our gaze, the expressions on our faces, the orientations of our bodies, the gestures we perform all constitute a nonverbal language that is a fundamental component of our social relationships. Patterson (1983) suggested that nonverbal communication serves five major functions: First, nonverbal exchanges *provide information* that influences our perceptions of a person's mood, disposition, or meaning. The paralinguistic cues of how something is said, for example, communicate whether or not it was meant to be sarcastic. Second, nonverbal exchanges *regulate interaction;* turn-taking in a conversation is facilitated by postural and voice cues between speaker and listener, for example (e.g., Duncan, 1972; Thomas & Bull, 1981). Third, nonverbal behaviors *express intimacy*, helping to define a relationship. For example, mutual gazing and touching is characteristic of romantic involvement (e.g., Rubin, 1970). A fourth function is the exercise of *social control*, the expression of status and dominance (through the use of gaze and nonreciprocal touch, for instance) and attempts at persuasion (Edinger & Patterson, 1983).

Finally, a *service-task* function permits intimate, but impersonal and socially meaningless contact between physician and patient, barber and customer.

Thus, it is evident that nonverbal communication is an integral part of interpersonal interaction. Indeed, Noller (1984) described the "impossibility of not communicating"; even our best efforts at sending no message (or at being deceptive) may leak clear signals that can be read by others (DePaulo, Stone, & Lassiter, 1985). In addition, when the verbal and nonverbal components of a communication do not match, we usually give more weight to the nonverbal part (Argyle, 1975). With this in mind, let us note that two people who have difficulty communicating nonverbally are likely to encounter frequent misunderstandings, irritation, and conflict, and that nonverbal deficiencies may underlie troubled relationships.

For instance, comparisons of distressed and nondistressed married couples consistently find that unhappy couples communicate more negative, and less positive, affect to one another than do satisfied couples (e.g., Gottman, 1979; Margolin & Wampold, 1981; Noller, 1985). Moreover, "negative affect reciprocity" is characteristic of distressed couples (e.g., Levenson & Gottman, 1983); they match each other frown for frown, and snarl for snarl, whereas happier couples are less likely to become enmeshed in tit-for-tat displays of distaste.

However, the most compelling evidence of a link between nonverbal communication and satisfaction in relationships comes from studies of communication accuracy in married couples. Nonverbal exchanges may fail because of errors in either encoding or decoding: The sender may not make his or her message clearly recognizable, or the receiver may fail to correctly interpret a message that is clear to anyone else. In general, women are both better encoders and more astute decoders than men are (Hall, 1984), but in an unhappy marriage both spouses may communicate poorly.

The independent contributions to nonverbal accuracy of the encoding and decoding of both husband and wife can be assessed by asking each spouse in turn to send a specific standardized nonverbal message that is then decoded by the spouse's partner. If a group of impartial judges cannot accurately read the message, then it is assumed to have been poorly encoded; however, if the judges can read the message but the spouse's partner cannot, the partner's decoding skill is implicated. The messages used in such studies are usually adapted from Kahn's (1970) Marital Communication Scale, a group of verbal statements (e.g., "I'm cold, aren't you?") that can have several different meanings depending on how they are nonverbally enacted (e.g., "Come warm me, darling" versus "Turn up the damn heat").

In the first ingenious study of this sort, Noller (1980) compared spouses high in marital adjustment to others with less happy marriages and found that the high-adjustment spouses communicated better with one another. Interestingly, their success seemed to be linked more to the talents of the husbands than of the wives. Husbands in the high-adjustment group sent clearer messages and made fewer decoding errors than husbands in the low-adjustment group, but there were no such differences among the wives. The poorer communication of the distressed couples, therefore, appeared to be the husbands' fault. Compared to happily married men, for instance, husbands in distressed marriages were more likely to misunderstand communications from their wives that were clearly interpretable by total strangers. Similar results were obtained by Gottman and Porterfield (1981).

Importantly, the communication deficits identified in the husbands are interactive dysfunctions that appear to be specific to their marital relationships. The men appear to be capable of accurate nonverbal communication but fail to perform well with their wives (Gottman & Porterfield, 1981). In a second study, Noller (1981) compared the ability of spouses to decode their partner's nonverbal messages with their ability to decode strangers' communications. In low-adjustment couples, both husband and wife were able to read strangers more accurately than they read their spouses. Moreover, the poorer a couple's adjustment, the greater the disparity between the spouses' skill in reading strangers and their performances in decoding their partners. Unhappy husbands and wives may fail to read one another adequately even though each is capable of accurate nonverbal communication.

Further, spouses in troubled relationships may confuse each other by sending ambiguous messages that can be decoded as either criticism or praise. Noller (1982) found that both husbands and wives in low-adjustment couples send discrepant messages (in which the encoder's nonverbal behavior conflicts with what he or she is saying) more often than do well-adjusted spouses. It is possible, of course, that such nonverbal deficiencies follow from prior dissatisfaction with the relationship and do not precipitate poor adjustment. The available evidence suggests that nonverbal dysfunction does lead to dissatisfaction, however, and that dissatisfaction further impairs nonverbal performance (Brehm, 1985).

Thus, two individually skilled partners can contribute to an interactive, nonverbal dysfunction that undermines their relationship. Therapy can teach a variety of useful communication skills to a couple (see Noller, 1984, for a review), but if the partners already possess valuable skills that they are not using, skills training is unlikely to be effective. In that case, therapy needs to identify the problems that discourage clear communication. When skill deficits do exist, both partners may be blameworthy, though husbands' generally poorer nonverbal skills are almost always suspect. Naturally, finding one important gender difference like this leads one to ask if there are others, and in fact, differences in male and female sex roles can also be potent determinants of interactive dysfunction.

Gender Differences in Instrumentality and Expressiveness

Ickes (1985b) provided an instructive fable about "Felicia Femme" and "Michael Manley," a traditional woman and man who marry thinking they are perfect for each other. Michael seems a strong, ambitious man who will be a good provider, while Felicia appears to be a warm, caring woman who will be a terrific mother. Everyone considers them a wonderful match. Ten years later, however, there's trouble. Felicia feels that she lives in an emotional wasteland with a man who is married to his work; her marriage is 90% sex and 10% love, and she'd be happier if it were the other way around. Michael can't understand what her problem is; he *is* a good provider, and he makes love to her all the time. What more, he wonders, does she want? Both Felicia and Michael feel they made the wrong decision when they decided to marry.

Perhaps they did. A man who fits traditional notions of masculine behavior possesses predominantly instrumental traits; he is likely to be ambitious, independent, competitive, self-confident, and assertive, but not particularly sensitive, kind, tender, or gentle. By contrast, a traditionally feminine woman is everything the traditional man is not: sensitive, nurturant, and emotionally expressive. Although these traditional, gender-related stereotypes may be increasingly outdated, many men and women nevertheless develop very different behavioral characteristics (Bem & Lenney, 1976). This is unfortunate, for instead of making men and women more compatible, these gender differences "may actually be responsible for much of the *incompatibility* upon which divorce statistics are based" (Ickes, 1985b, p. 188).

Two surveys of married respondents have found that traditional women who have traditional husbands are generally among those who are *least* satisfied with their marriages (Antill, 1983; Shaver, Pullis, & Olds, 1980, cited in Ickes, 1985b). By comparison, women (and men) who have either androgynous spouses—that is, partners who are skilled at both instrumental and expressive behaviors—or just "feminine," emotionally expressive spouses tend to be the most content and happily married. Ironically, whatever their own sex-role orientations, women married to nontraditional, sensitive, expressive men consistently report greater marital satisfaction than women who are married to men who fit our traditional notions of what men should be.

A provocative study by Ickes and Barnes (1978) provides a concrete example of how pairings of traditional men and women can be disadvantageous. Ickes and Barnes randomly assigned male and female subjects to mixed-sex dyads in which 1) both participants were traditionally sex-typed (i.e., pairing a "masculine" male with a "feminine" female), 2) both were androgynous, or 3) one was traditionally sex-typed while the other was androgynous. After establishing that the members of each couple had never met, the researchers simply left them alone together in a waiting room for 5 minutes and covertly audio- and videotaped their interaction. The results were striking. The traditional dyads shared interactions that were significantly less involving and rewarding than those couples in which at least one person transcended tradition. The traditional dyads talked less, looked at each other less, laughed and smiled less, and afterward reported that they liked each other much less than any other type of couple. Masculine men and feminine women simply do not get along with each other especially well at first meeting, and the marital surveys suggest that their long-term interactions hardly improve.

Traditional sex roles create other impediments to satisfying cross-sex interaction as well. Check and Malamuth (1983) argued that such roles cast men as sexual aggressors who are expected to ignore women when they say they don't want sex; after all, the men may believe feminine women are supposed to say no delicately without really meaning it. In fact, Check and Malamuth found that the more traditional a man's sex-role orientation, the more closely his attitudes and arousal in response to a rape depiction duplicated those of known rapists. Traditional men were also more likely to believe that women responded favorably to coerced sex, and to indicate some likelihood that they might rape a woman, than were nontraditional men. Furthermore, Abbey (1982) found that men are more likely than women to read sexual overtones into an innocuous interaction; they perceive women as flirtatious, promiscuous, and seductive when the women do not intend to be, and they are likely to misinterpret friendliness as a sign of sexual interest. Check and Malamuth concluded that "traditional sex roles socialize . . . men to be [sexual] offenders and women to be victims" (p. 354).

Traditional men and women also seem to put more stock in the physical attractiveness of their partners than nontraditional people do. Andersen and Bem (1981) found that sex-typed subjects were more responsive, interested, and involved in phone conversations when they believed their partner was good-looking than when the partner was said to be plain. Androgynous subjects did not treat others differently according to their looks. What is more, Coleman and Ganong (1985) reported that androgynous people are more loving than sex-typed individuals; they are more aware of their feelings and more willing to express them, and better able to tolerate their partner's faults. Overall, asserted Coleman and Ganong, "sex typed persons are less able to love" (p. 174).

Social behaviors like these, coupled with the rigid, sex-typed division of labor in a traditional household (Atkinson & Huston, 1984), portray masculine men and feminine women more as adversaries than as collaborators. However, we should note that traditional gender differences are not always an interactive liability. For instance, the interactions of two sex-typed masculine men, although lacking in intimacy, are nevertheless smooth, natural, and relaxed (Ickes, Schermer, & Steeno, 1979); two such men are similar to one another, and interaction flows easily. However, sex-linked differentiation of social skills contributes to awkward *heterosexual* interaction, and that, of course, is what can make traditional sex roles dysfunctional. The interactions of traditional men and women are simply less satisfying than those of couples with more behavioral flexibility, and, over time, that relative dissatisfaction can lead to troubled relationships.

There seem to be independent advantages of both instrumentality and expressiveness, and by specializing in one or the other, masculine or feminine people close themselves off from certain valuable skills. For instance, the instrumental talents of masculine and androgynous people are associated with low neuroticism and high self-esteem; purely feminine people score more poorly on these dimensions (Spence, Helmreich, & Holahan, 1979). However, femininity is linked to the intimacy and rewardingness of one's interactions (Fischer & Narus, 1981; Reis, 1986), and it is for this reason that we daringly suggested that, with regard to relationships, being male was dysfunctional.

Reis and his colleagues (1986; Wheeler, Reis, & Nezlek, 1983) have tracked the interactions of men and women by asking them to record their reactions to each of their interactions (of 10 minutes or more duration) over a 2-week period. They have found that interactions among men are generally less supportive or meaningful than interactions that include women. Among themselves, most men disclose less about themselves, elicit less self-disclosure from others, and share interactions that are less intimate, pleasant, and satisfying than those they share with women. This is no small matter in that most interactions are with those of one's own sex; the social lives of men are thus chronically more superficial and less rewarding than those of women. As a result, men are more likely than women to be lonely (Borys & Perlman, 1985) and are generally dependent on women for the meaningful interactions that can keep them from becoming lonely.

For both sexes, the more time a person spends interacting with a woman, the less lonely that person is likely to be; by contrast, the amount of time one spends with men does not seem to affect one's loneliness (Wheeler et al., 1983). As a result, it is particularly valuable to a man, but not to a woman, to have an opposite-sex romantic partner; women with and without romantic attachments report similar loneliness scores, but men with a partner are substantially less lonely than men without one (Reis, 1986). There are some men, of course, who do engage in "meaningful" interactions with other men (and who also spend more time socializing with women than most other men), but they are not traditionally masculine fellows. Such men, who are rarely lonely, tend to have more "feminine," expressive abilities than the typical, sex-typed man, and from Antill's (1983) data, we can assume they have happier marriages, too.

Thus, a fairer statement of our assertion is that it is not being male, but merely being masculine (i.e., highly instrumental but emotionally inexpressive) that is dysfunctional in relationships. Such men (most, though not all, "masculine" people are men) have more superficial interactions, are more likely to be lonely, interact stiffly with feminine women, are hung up on sex and good looks, have dissatisfied wives, and are probably among those men who fail to communicate well nonverbally. By comparison, androgynous and feminine men are much better off socially, and such is the influence of sex roles on relationships. Curiously, however, most men apparently engage in nonintimate same-sex interaction by choice, not through any lack of ability (Reis, Senchak, & Solomon, 1985). When urged to do so in laboratory studies, men are capable of interacting as intimately with each other as with women. Such reluctance may be more amenable to change than is a lack of skill, and so our tolerance of those who try to transcend socially prescribed sex roles becomes all the more important.

Attributional Processes

We have already given attributional processes a great deal of attention (in chapters 2 and 3), but we would be remiss if we did not briefly mention their recent application to the study of relationships. As Sillars (1985) noted, attributions for events within a relationship may be especially complex because each partner may be the other's "most knowledgeable *and* least objective observer" (p. 280). Relationships are characterized by interdependence and emotionality, and both may complicate one's judgments of causality; interdependence may mean that both partners are partially responsible for some event, whereas strong emotions may accentuate negative events and exacerbate each partner's self-serving perspective. Further, attributions are particularly important within relationships in that they can be used to *communicate* feelings about the relationship to one's partner (Forsyth, 1980; Orvis, Kelley, & Butler, 1976). In this way, they are a barometer of the health of a relationship (Harvey, 1985) and can either help maintain or destroy one.

Three broad themes emerge from recent studies of relational attributions. First, partners are affected by robust actor-observer biases despite their intimate knowledge of one another (Orvis et al., 1976; Passer, Kelley, & Michela, 1978). Although both partners may be acutely aware of the situational influences that have directed their own behavior, each tends to ignore how such circumstances affect the partner, attributing the partner's behavior to his or her intentions and personality. This leads both partners to overlook how they may provoke the behavior they observe in their partner. During an argument, for instance, if one partner thinks, "She infuriates me so when she acts that way," the other is likely to be thinking, "He is so temperamental and has so little self-control." What is more, the two partners are unlikely to be aware of the discrepancies in their attributions, each person believing that the other sees things his or her way (Harvey, Wells, & Alvarez, 1978).

A second theme addresses partners' egotistic or self-serving biases. Even in close relationships, both partners are likely to overestimate their own responsibility for positive events while denying their blame for negative outcomes. For example, husbands and wives both claim more credit for keeping their marriages going than they deserve (Ross & Sicoly, 1979; Thompson & Kelley, 1981). Together, the actor-observer and self-serving biases suggest that when conflict occurs, both partners are likely to see it as the other person's fault, a notion supported by Sillars (1981).

Finally, several recent studies have found that a couple's attributions are linked to their satisfaction with their relationship. In general, it appears that happily married partners give each other credit for their positive actions and kindnesses, perceiving them as intentional, habitual, and deliberate; happy partners also tend to excuse one another's transgressions, seeing them as accidental, unusual, and circumstantial (Fincham, 1985; Fincham & O'Leary, 1983; Jacobson, McDonald, Follette, & Berley, 1985). In comparison, the attributions of distressed couples are mirror opposites. They see each other's negative actions as deliberate and routine, and kindnesses as accidental. Distressed partners are also more self-serving than those who are satisfied (Fichten, 1984). Thus, the attributions of distressed couples are of a sort that are likely to keep them dissatisfied, regardless of how the partner behaves. When distressed spouses are nice to one another, each is likely to write off the other's kindness as a temporary, uncharacteristic lull in the negative routine (Holtzworth-Munroe & Jacobson, 1985; Jacobson et al., 1985). When kindnesses seem accidental and hurts seem deliberate, satisfaction must be hard to come by.

In sum, both partners' idiosyncratic perspectives allow them to have better excuses for their mistakes than their partner has, to cast the partner as the source of most disagreements and conflict, and to claim more credit than the partner would allow for how hard they work to maintain the relationship. These egocentric judgments may be adaptive for the individual, but they are hardly adaptive for the relationship, and particularly in distressed couples such attributions help cause and maintain trouble in the relationship. Thus, attributions are another example of interactive dysfunction, a fact duly recognized by some marital therapists (Berley & Jacobson, 1984; Warner, Parker, & Calhoun, 1984). Several interventions specifically aimed at changing spouses' perceptions of one another's behavior have become a standard part of cognitive-behavioral marital therapy (see Berley & Jacobson, 1984).

Relationship Dysfunctions

With personal and interactive dysfunctions in hand, one broad source of troubled relationships remains. Over time, a relationship may fail because a couple's interactions simply fail to be routinely rewarding enough for one or both of the participants. Both partners may be free of personal dysfunction, and together they may be capable of smooth, errorless interaction, but in the long run they may still be discontented. In this case, the locus of disorder may be the pattern and type of their long-term transactions (i.e., their relationship itself). Perhaps the partners have gotten so used to each other that they no longer find pleasure in each other's company, perhaps other people now seem more attractive and are drawing them away, or perhaps one partner is exploiting the other and the relationship seems unfair. Whatever the particulars, such concerns can doom a relationship. We discuss two major types of such dysfunction, dealing in turn with partners' desires to maximize reward and to be treated fairly.

Social Exchange in Relationships

"Exchange" theorists suggest that two people seek interaction with one another only insofar as it is to their advantage to do so. The exchange perspective is essentially an economic one that holds that people are aware of their rewards and costs in an interaction, that they seek to maximize their rewards and minimize their costs, and that they continue only those relationships that remain rewarding enough. A couple must be able to "exchange" with one another rewards that are adequate for both partners, or interaction is unlikely to continue. Several different versions of exchange theory are based on these assumptions, but the concepts of Thibaut and Kelley (1959) are most often used by social psychologists, and we employ them here.

There are two key criteria by which we evaluate our relationships. The first one assesses whether we consider our outcomes satisfactory. There exists for each of us an idiosyncratic *comparison level* (CL), which is the value of the outcomes that we believe we deserve in our dealings with others. Our CLs are based on our past experiences, but whatever they are, when the outcomes we receive rise above our CLs, we are satisfied—we are getting more than we expected. However, if our outcomes fall below our CLs, we are dissatisfied, even if we are still doing better than most other people. A popular, spoiled movie star, for example, may have an unusually high CL and be rather dissatisfied with a partner who bedazzles the rest of us.

Importantly, however, Thibaut and Kelley (1959) asserted that simple satisfaction is not the only, or even major, factor that determines whether relationships last. Whether or not we are happy with what we have, we use a *comparison level for alternatives* (CL$_{alt}$) to determine whether we could do even better with someone else. Formally, the CL$_{alt}$ is the lowest outcome an interactant will accept "in light of the available alternative opportunities" (Thibaut & Kelley, 1959, p. 21). If new potential partners promise better outcomes than we currently receive, we are likely to pursue those new partners even if we are satisfied with what we already have. Conversely, even if we are dissatisfied with our current relationship we are unlikely to leave it unless a better alternative presents itself. Our CL$_{alt}$s, then, determine our dependency on our relationships; whether or not we are satisfied, if we believe that we already have the most rewarding relationships available to us, we are dependent on those relationships and unlikely to leave them. Moreover, the greater the gap between our current outcomes and our poorer alternatives, the more dependent we are.

This portrayal of people as hedonistic, uncommitted reward seekers sits poorly with some critics who feel that it is inappropriate to apply exchange principles to close, intimate relationships. For instance, Mills and Clark

(1982; Clark, 1985) distinguished between *exchange* relationships, to which the assumptions of social exchange pertain, and closer *communal* relationships with kin, romantic partners, and friends. In a communal relationship, partners are thought to care enough for each other that they reward one another whether or not the favor is returned. However, recent extensions of exchange theory (Kelley, 1979, 1984) suggest much the same thing. Long-term partners are unlikely to be concerned with immediate tit-for-tat reciprocity because they know that, over time, the relationship is likely to be mutually profitable. Moreover, in an interdependent relationship, the continued satisfaction of one's partner becomes increasingly important to one's own continued reward and thus enters into each partner's calculations (Kelley, 1979, 1984; Levinger, 1979). In fact, merely anticipating interaction with someone else is enough to get most people to take the other's (potential) outcomes into consideration (Berg, Blaylock, Camarillo, & Steck, 1985).

Furthermore, exchange principles may not seem to describe intimate relationships because such relationships, when they are healthy, enjoy an "economy of surplus" (Levinger, 1979, p. 177). Both partners are receiving satisfactory outcomes that are presumably the best available to them, and there is little need to explicitly quantify one's investments and outcomes. If the relationship begins to deteriorate, however, both partners may again become concerned with the processes of exchange, with their feelings about the relationship depending on the quality of their last transaction. This, in fact, occurs (Jacobson, Follette, & McDonald, 1982; Jacobson, Waldron, & Moore, 1980). Distressed couples are characterized by the exchange of non-rewarding or even punishing behaviors, as exchange theory would suggest (Birchler, Weiss, & Vincent, 1975; Gottman, 1979). In addition, romantic relationships often end when the attractiveness of a partner's alternatives rises and social and economic barriers to separation decline, or, in short, when a partner's CL_{alt} goes up (Edwards & Saunders, 1981; Levinger, 1979). In fact, the better a person's alternatives, the less loyal he or she is to a relationship, and the more likely that person is to leave the relationship when dissatisfied (Johnson, Rusbult, & Morrow, 1983).

Implications of exchange theory. Thus, the basic precepts of exchange theory hold up to empirical scrutiny fairly well. The greater importance of the exchange perspective, however, lies in the nonobvious predictions it makes about subtleties in relationships. For instance, consider that one's CL, being based on experience, "tends to move to the level of outcomes currently being obtained. In other words, the person adapts to the presently experienced levels: after shifting upward to a new level, the once longed-for outcomes gradually lose their attractiveness" (Thibaut & Kelley, 1959, p. 98). Through this process a once-rewarding relationship can become dissatisfying, even though (and perhaps because) nothing has changed. Once a partner begins to take for granted the relationship rewards that once seemed so special, it becomes more and more difficult to engage in mutually profitable exchange.

If dissatisfaction sets in, however, the relationship may still continue. Another instructive contribution of exchange theory is the suggestion that the continuance of a relationship is relatively independent of the participants' happiness in that relationship. The theory thus provides an explanation for those puzzling situations in which a miserable, perhaps abused partner clings to a broken, disastrous relationship. Such a person must believe that his or her next best alternative—including solitude—would be more disastrous still. The factors that might influence such a calculation are many, ranging from individual differences (e.g., low self-esteem) to situational variables (e.g., the economic entrapment of a nonworking spouse) to cultural, societal influences (e.g., religious sanctions against divorce). In any case, a low perceived CL_{alt} can make one dependent even on a hateful relationship. Studies of abused wives, for instance, find that the worse their prospects outside their marriages and the more they would lose by leaving, the less likely they are to escape their abusive relationships (Gelles, 1976; Strube & Barbour, 1983).

Power within relationships. Another useful application of exchange theory is its explanation of the power, or the ability to influence another's behavior, that relationship partners have. In an interdependent relationship, each partner desires the rewards the other partner can provide. By strategically manipulating the availability of such rewards, each partner can entice or induce the other to behave in desired ways. A person's use of power, of course, is limited by the partner's counterpower over that person, but in general each partner is able to subtly shape the other's behavior.

In many cases, however, one partner has more power than the other. Exchange theory suggests that one's power in a relationship is inversely related to one's dependency on the partner, so that the less dependent partner is more powerful. The "principle of least interest" states that "that person is able to dictate the conditions of association whose interest in the continuation of the affair is least" (Waller & Hill, 1951, p. 191). The person with less to lose by ending the relationship gets to call the shots. In fact, this principle seems to be accurate. Berman and Bennett (1982) assessed the interdependency of 200 couples and then observed them in a decision-making task, and found that the more involved partner won fewer arguments and directed fewer decisions. Indeed, the couples recognized this themselves, acknowledging that the partner with the lesser love for the other was the more dominant.

To improve our power, then, we can either work at improving our own alternatives so that we become less dependent, or strive to control more valuable rewards and resources so that our partners become more dependent on us. Unfortunately, when dominant partners begin to lose their superiority, one resource to which they sometimes turn is violence. Physical force has been called the "ultimate resource" that can augment a person's power when legitimate means of influencing others begin to fail (Goode, 1971).

Violence is, of course, aversive, but when used against someone who is unable or unwilling to escape, the user can demonstrate his or her power without ending the relationship.

In fact, some husbands and wives wreak terrible violence on their partners. Both sexes are targets of spouse abuse, but observers generally agree that the greatest damage is done by men, particularly among the poor (Gelles, 1980; Straus, 1980). As the exchange perspective suggests, these abusing men often use violence as a substitute for other sources of power that they cannot maintain (Gelles & Straus, 1979). They resort to force when their status within the couple is threatened, such as when they lose jobs or their wives start to work (Kahn, in press). The greater a husband's social status and other resources, the less is his use of physical violence (Allen & Straus, 1980).

Therapeutic applications. Altogether, then, social exchange theory provides a useful perspective with which to understand the processes of satisfaction, stability, and power in long-term relationships. Outcomes that chronically fall below a partner's expectations and alternative relationships that remain tempting too long lead to unsatisfying, unstable relationships and thus can constitute relationship dysfunctions. Moreover, the economic framework of exchange theory provides a conceptual base for several aspects of behavioral marital therapy that attempt to reestablish positive, mutually desirable exchanges between distressed spouses (e.g., Jacobson & Margolin, 1979; Stuart, 1980). For instance, such therapy may actually invite couples to draw up explicit contracts that specify what rewards will be exchanged and with what frequency. Interventions like these are often effective beginnings (Jacobson, Follette, & Elwood, 1984), but exchange theory also suggests that in truly satisfying relationships the partners have probably stopped counting and quantifying rewards. The ongoing challenge for therapy is to develop means of helping clients institute patterns of trusting, long-term, mutual reward that "move beyond the confines of literal exchange" (Levinger, 1979, p. 189), and recent efforts attempt to do just that (see Follette & Jacobson, 1985).

Equitable Relationships

It is one matter to ask whether a person is gaining satisfactory reward from a relationship, and another matter altogether to ask whether the available reward is being apportioned fairly between the two partners. "Equity" theorists build on the framework of social exchange to suggest that we are most satisfied with those relationships in which there is proportional justice, with each partner gaining benefits from the relationship that are in fair proportion to his or her contributions to it (Hatfield & Traupmann, 1980). Roughly, equity depends on the ratio of our outcomes to our inputs being similar to that of our partners, or when:

$$\frac{\text{our outcomes}}{\text{our inputs}} = \frac{\text{our partners' outcomes}}{\text{our partners' inputs}}.$$

Note that equity does not require that two partners gain equal rewards from their interaction; indeed, in many cases, equality would be inequitable. Instead, this perspective suggests that one should be rewarded relative to one's inputs and that the relative amounts of net profit the participants receive are just as important as their absolute amounts.

Another central assumption of equity theory is that it is distressing to find oneself in an inequitable relationship. When there is inequity, one partner is "underbenefited," receiving less than his or her fair share, and is thus likely to be angry and resentful; the other partner, then, is "overbenefited" and likely to be somewhat guilty. It is better to be over- than underbenefited, of course, but any departure from an equitable relationship is thought to cause at least some discomfort. When inequity exists, the distressed party has three options. First, actual equity can be restored through suitable manipulation of one's own (or one's partner's) outcomes and inputs. Failing that, psychological equity can be restored by changing one's perceptions of the relationship and deciding that the situation really is equitable. Finally, as a last resort, one can abandon the relationship to seek fairness elsewhere. Equity theory thus shares with social exchange the assumption that we seek to maximize our outcomes in our social relationships (in this case by treating each other fairly), and one may again wonder whether considerations like these actually pertain to close relationships. The evidence clearly shows that they do (Hatfield, Traupmann, Sprecher, Utne, & Hay, 1985).

Two broad hypotheses have guided recent study of equity in intimate relationships. The first predicts that equitable relationships should be more satisfying than inequitable relationships. This appears to be true, and among unmarried partners equitable relationships are more sexually intimate, too. Walster, Walster, and Traupmann (1978) interviewed 537 men and women in dating partnerships and, on the basis of the subjects' estimates of their own and their partners' inputs and outcomes, classified each of them as over-benefited, equitably treated, or underbenefited. Those in equitable relationships were most content, and were happier than—in order—the overbenefited and the underbenefited. In addition, equitable partners were likely to have engaged in sexual intercourse, whereas those in inequitable relationships tended to stop short of that much intimacy. In another study, Traupmann, Hatfield, and Wexler (1983) also showed that respondents in equitable dating relationships enjoyed more sexual satisfaction than those who felt underbenefited, although in this case the equitably treated were no better off then the overbenefited.

Equity enhances the satisfaction of married partners as well. Davidson (1984) assessed perceptions of equity and dyadic adjustment in 162 married couples and found that the happiest relationships were indeed those that both partners viewed as equitable. When both partners felt overbenefited, for example, adjustment scores were somewhat lower, and if both felt under-benefited adjustment was substantially reduced. Depression is also linked to equity concerns in married couples, occurring more often among the under- and overbenefited than among the equitably treated (Schafer & Keith, 1980). Moreover, people who feel underbenefited in their marriages are more eager to engage in extramarital affairs, and actually have one an average of 3 to 4 years sooner than those people who are overbenefited or equitably treated by their spouses (Walster, Traupmann, & Walster, 1978).

Equity thus appears to be linked to satisfaction in even the most intimate relationships. Are equitable partnerships more stable and lasting as a result? A second broad hypothesis suggests that they are, and the available evidence supports this prediction as well. Walster, Walster, and Traupmann (1978) found that equitable dating relationships were most likely to last over the 3½-month time span of their study, and Utne, Hatfield, Traupmann, and Greenberger (1984) reported that newlyweds in equitable marriages are the most certain that their marriages will last. In addition, we have already seen that partners in equitable marriages are as likely as anyone else (and more likely than some) to eschew extramarital affairs (Walster, Traupmann, & Walster, 1978). Despite the critics who feel that a concern for equity can actually harm a marriage (e.g., Murstein, MacDonald, & Cerreto, 1977), and "despite the popular notion that 'true love is unselfish,' for both men and women, the best kind of love relationship seems to be one in which everyone feels that he or she is getting what they deserve" (Utne et al., 1984, pp. 331–332).

Thus, chronic inequity is a relationship dysfunction that puts a partnership at some risk, even when the relationship is otherwise fairly rewarding. Importantly, equity theory alerts us that there can be some discomfort in being overbenefited as well as in being underbenefited—a reaction that may reflect our implicit understanding that inequity in any form is trouble. We do not know of any therapeutic interventions that specifically address inequity, but that is not surprising; it is probably either managed by the partners themselves or presents itself as part of a broader dysfunctional dissatisfaction with the relationship. Still, equity stands as a good example both of the remarkable complexity of contentment in long-term relationships and of social psychology's occasional abilty to defy common sense and still—it appears—be right.

Conclusions

We have identified several factors that contribute to troubled relationships, but our list is far from complete. We have barely touched on processes of conflict (e.g., Rands, Levinger, & Mellinger, 1981) and aggression (see chapter 12), and we have been unable to review the extensive literature addressing social support and systems of family relationships (see chapter

12). A comparative analysis of relationship therapies (i.e., Brehm, 1985) would be worthwhile but is also beyond the scope of this chapter. Still, we hope that we have been able to provide an indication of the enormous intricacy of happy relationships and of the number of levels at which they can break down. We identified personal, interactive, and relational sources of dysfunctional relationships but are reluctant to make too much of those distinctions; it is likely that dysfunctions at one level can precipitate problems at another, and that several of these problems—and dissatisfaction with the relationship itself—reciprocally cause one another. A feminine woman who becomes frustrated with the inexpressiveness of her masculine spouse may badger him to the point that he tunes her out and starts missing vital nonverbal information that he would have noticed before. This makes him a much less rewarding partner, leaving her with the impression that she gives too much for what she gets and alienating her further. And so it goes. We thus strongly agree with therapists like Whitaker (1975, p. 167) who consider therapy with couples the treatment of three different clients: "the husband is one patient, the wife is one patient, and the *relationship* is one patient" (italics added).

There are potential dangers in seeking intimacy with others (Hatfield, 1984): We may fear abandonment, exposure, or loss of control. For most of us, however, never enjoying intimacy would be more threatening still. Given the fundamental importance of close relationships in our lives, the understanding of the processes of both healthy and unhealthy relationships is an essential focus for the social-clinical-counseling interface.

Part II

Interpersonal Processes in the Diagnosis and Treatment of Psychological Problems

Chapter 8
Clinical Inference

Imagine that you learn of a 16-year-old girl who has begun inquiring "How many aspirin does it takes to kill somebody?" She is newly pregnant and has been deserted by her boyfriend, and is a member of a strict, authoritarian family in which the father drinks heavily. She is not an attractive girl, but she is a solid student. Is the girl really suicidal? Should she, or her entire family, be urged to seek psychological treatment? If so, what diagnosis applies and what treatment is appropriate? What criterion can gauge her progress, and when can therapy be stopped?

Clinicians and counselors are constantly asked to answer thorny questions like these, assessing the behavior and circumstances of other people and judging whether change is desirable or likely. In this, they are much like anyone else as they evaluate and interpret the behavior, intentions, and personalities of those they meet. The formal judgments of therapists usually have more impact than a layperson's casual observations, however, and errors are less allowable. It is thus particularly important to understand the *person perception* or interpersonal judgments of clinicians and counselors, and an extensive body of social psychological research is applicable here.

Unfortunately, the overriding lesson of studies of interpersonal perception is that we are much poorer judges of others than we believe ourselves to be. It has long been known, for instance, that we quickly form impressions of other people from only limited information about them, and that, once formed, those impressions are rather resistant to change. Early studies of person perception in general (Asch, 1946; Bruner & Tagiuri, 1954) and of therapists' judgments of clients in particular (Meehl, 1960; Rubin & Shontz, 1960) showed that impressions were rapidly formed and that the presentation of additional, even contradictory information often did little to change them. In recent years, however, both social and clinical psychologists have come to realize that the potential problems with our social judgments go far beyond mere haste and resiliency. We seem to select, weigh, and interpret information in ways that sustain our existing beliefs, practically guaranteeing that, whatever we think, we will seem to be right. We see patterns in behavior where no patterns exist, and we are confident of factual beliefs that in truth are quite wrong. Moreover, our *behavior* toward people is influenced by our beliefs about them, and even our erroneous predictions about others can become self-fulfilling as we create in others the responses we expect to find. In short, recent studies of social cognition have compiled a catalogue of faults and biases in human judgment that seem to be common, if not unavoidable, components of social thought (e.g., Nisbett & Ross, 1980).

For all of their expertise, cleverness, and wisdom, professional psychologists appear to be prone to some of these judgmental shortcomings, and in this chapter we examine those potential problems that seem to us to be most relevant to clinical practice. Our intent is not to belittle the processes of clinical inference, for its problems are pitfalls for us all, scientists and practitioners alike (Mahoney, 1976). As Wiggins (1981, p. 14) aptly noted, clinicians' errors are human errors, and we may all profit by understanding them better:

> Are the judgmental shortcomings and biases of clinicians distinctively different from those of other professional decision makers? That is, have these shortcomings been demonstrated in groups of stockbrokers, physicians, intelligence analysts, electrical engineers, etc.? (Answer: definitely yes.) . . . Given that all of us—laypersons, clinicians and other professionals—are in the same boat, how would you evaluate our characteristic judgmental and inferential strategies with reference to the formal canons of scientific inference? (Answer: C−).

Our challenge, of course, is to improve social judgment, not simply to criticize it, and the final section of this chapter examines possible strategies for improving that C− grade, focusing on potential means of improving human (e.g., clinical) inference.

Statistical Versus Intuitive Decision Making

The first shortcoming we examine is also one of the best known. In deciding on diagnoses or courses of treatments, clinicians must integrate information from a wide variety of sources: psychological tests, assessment interviews, demographics, self-reports, etc. This is often done by subjectively, impressionistically, and intuitively combining the data to yield an overall judgment of (it is hoped) high accuracy. Unfortunately, Meehl (1954) and a legion of followers (e.g., Goldberg, 1970; Mischel, 1968; Sawyer, 1966; Szucko & Kleinmuntz, 1981) have persuasively argued that decision makers would do better by pulling out hand calculators and combining their data in a mechanical, statistical way. In fact, say these observers, clinicians' faith in their ability to accurately integrate diverse date is misplaced, whatever their experience and expertise; a clerk with a calculator can do better.

This assertion has elicited a number of defensive reactions from wounded clinicians (e.g., Holt, 1970), but it surprises us that anyone would be seriously insulted by the statistical advocates. No one has ever suggested that clinical expertise is not essential to the *selection* of the data to be considered and the validation of assessment techniques; the superiority of statistical techniques lies merely in the *combination* of disparate, incomparable data, and computers are unquestionably better at that than are people. The best way to integrate such data is to construct a linear model, as in regression analysis, in which the diverse sources of data are individually weighted so as to maximize the correlation between the overall equation and the criterion one is trying to predict. It sounds impersonal, but it works: "in the entire literature [of nearly 50 years' time] there is no study that has shown informal judgment procedures to be superior to predictions made from a simple linear statistical model" (Wills, 1982, p. 9).

The distinction between the expert selection of data and its statistical integration was clearly illustrated by Einhorn (1972). He asked physicians to predict an outcome more definitive than those usually faced by psychologists (i.e., death) by interpreting biopsies of patients with Hodgkin's disease. The experts were totally unable to accurately predict the survival time of the patients, but the information selected for analysis by the doctors did predict survival time when used in a linear regression model. Results like these, which also apply to psychologists (e.g., Dawes, 1979), are so consistent that Wiggins (1981) noted that "the original issue of clinical versus statistical prediction (should multivariate input data be *combined* by a person or a computer?) now seems to most of us a rather odd topic to occupy the attention of serious scientists for 25 years" (p. 14).

Still, many clinicians remain reluctant to use statistical decision-making procedures, and this hesitancy seems to be grounded in two separate concerns (cf. Dawes, 1979, 1982). First, statistical approaches appear to ignore the unique qualities of individual clients, the idiosyncrasies that can only be appreciated by a human judge. "Reducing people to numbers" seems distasteful, and clinicians may be reluctant to forgo the fine-tuning of a diagnosis that seems to require a professional's intuition. It is probably something of a professional conceit, however, to assume that one's own subjective impressions should replace the results of a standardized assessment of proven validity. Instead, one's intuitive judgments should be added to the linear model to be combined statistically with other, more impersonal data. Professional judgments can and should be made, but the integration of those judgments with other disparate data should still be done through some formal procedure.

This all sounds quite complicated, and the time, equipment, and sophistication needed to do a regression analysis have also been imposing barriers to the use of statistical techniques. Although it is less exact, intuitive decision making is certainly simpler and quicker (Cantor, 1982). Remarkably, however, one need not do anything too complicated to improve on mere intuition. Simply guessing at how much each piece of data should be weighted does better than clinical intuition, provided that each weight is in the right (positive or negative) direction (Dawes, 1979). In fact, even treating all sources of data as equally valuable—that is, not differentially weighting them at all—standardizing them, and just adding them together works appreciably well (Dawes, 1982; Wainer, 1976). Sophistication is required in choosing the information one needs to know to make a diagnosis or select a treatment, but once the data are in hand their integration should be a simple mechanical task, not a test of professional wisdom. As Dawes and Corrigan (1974, p. 105) suggested, "the whole trick is to know what variables to look at and then to know how to add."

Caution in trusting our intuitive decisions is also advisable in that we are often not consciously aware of how we have been influenced by particular data. Information that we think important may not have influenced us at all, whereas data we have dismissed as trivial may have had a major impact.

The Limits of Introspection

It seems plausible to assume that we are usually aware of the manner in which certain information about a person affects our subsequent judgments about him or her. Studies of judgmental processes suggest, however, that we actually have quite poor insight into the origins of our judgments and that we often do not know why we think the way we do. For instance, Nisbett and his colleagues (Nisbett & Bellows, 1977; Nisbett & Wilson, 1977a, 1977b) have repeatedly demonstrated that college students often overlook stimuli that are influencing them, often deny that genuinely important stimuli had any impact at all, and often identify as critical stimuli that did not influence them a bit.

In studies of this sort, subjects are usually asked to form an impression of some target stimulus as the available information about the target is systematically manipulated; as they form their judgments, the subjects are asked to indicate how influential various pieces of information are. For example, Nisbett and Bellows (1977) asked their subjects to evaluate a lengthy job application that either described or did not mention the applicant's attractiveness, intelligence, recent clumsiness, car accident, and so forth. The subjects' perceptions of how these data affected their judgments of the applicant were in most cases quite unrelated to each datum's actual effects. The subjects simply did not know whence their judgments came.

In another study, Nisbett and Wilson (1977a) asked subjects to evaluate via videotaped interview a foreign professor who was introduced either as a warm, likable fellow or as a cold, autocratic martinet. The subjects reported their global liking for the professor and specifically evaluated his appearance, mannerisms, and accent (which, of course, were the same for all viewers). As one would expect, they liked the "warm" professor much better than the "cold" one, and those global evaluations affected their judgments of the target's characteristics, which were seen as endearing with the warm version, irritating with the cold. The subjects categorically denied that their (supposedly objective?) ratings of the three attributes had been influenced by their liking for the target, however, and some of them actually insisted that their disapproval of his mannerisms had led to their disliking him—a complete reversal of the true causal relationship! The subjects were apparently unable to disentangle their specific ratings of the target from their global like or dislike for him, but they nonetheless were completely certain that their judgments were unbiased, impartial, and objective.

Nisbett and Wilson (1977b) provided another particularly illuminating example of the limits of introspection. One of their studies asked shoppers to evaluate four identical pairs of nylon stockings and to pick the pair of the best quality. A serial position effect emerged, with the stockings on the far right being preferred over those on the far left by nearly a 4 : 1 ratio. When asked to explain their choice among equals, however, the shoppers conjured up imaginary differences in materials and manufacture as the reasons for their right-sided preference. Moreover, when specifically asked about a possible position effect, nearly all of them completely dismissed it, thinking it a silly idea. These good people did not know what had influenced their judgments and scoffed at one influential factor when it was presented to them.

Clinicians sometimes act the same way. Gauron and Dickinson (1966) asked psychiatrists to make tentative diagnoses and to rate their confidence in those diagnoses as a series of data were obtained about a client. A piece of information was designated as important if it substantially influenced a subject's final diagnosis or enhanced his confidence in his final judgment. The subjects' own estimates of the importance of each datum were totally unrelated to its true importance, however, and it again appeared that the subjects were largely unaware of the factors that had actually caused them to make the decisions they had made.

Findings like these unfortunately suggest that clinicians' inferences may be routinely affected by variables of which they are unaware, or worse, whose influence they consciously deny. Like the participants in Nisbett and Wilson's (1977a) study, for instance, clinicians seem to be influenced by their liking for a client. Attractive, likable clients may receive more help and greater effort (Doherty, 1971; Fehrenbach & O'Leary, 1982) and be judged as progressing more satisfactorily than less attractive clients (Brown, 1970; Shapiro, Struening, Shapiro, & Barten, 1976). As another example, clinicians may be led by clients' social class to interpret the same objective symptoms differently for clients of different classes (Abramowitz & Dokecki, 1977; Routh & King, 1972). Similarly, it may be hard for clinicians to make judgments that do not take a client's sex or race into account (cf. Zeldow, 1984).

In short, the certainty with which we identify the sources of our interpersonal judgments is often misplaced. We may feel objective and not be, and the reasons we announce may not be real. Feeling deliberate and impartial does not make us so.

Personalistic Biases in Judgment

A broad source of data that usually has *less* impact on our judgments than it should is the situational context in which a person behaves. We seem to be oriented toward assessing and understanding others' unique personalities and that orientation leads us to underestimate the extent to which others' behavior is influenced by the constraints and demands of the surrounding situation. In fact, our judgments are biased by a tendency to overestimate how much others' dispositions routinely influence their behavior. Indeed, this personalistic bias is so pervasive and robust that social psychologists have termed it the "fundamental attribution error" (Ross, 1977).

Some examples are in order here. In an early study of personalistic biases, Jones and Harris (1967) presented undergraduates with debaters' speeches supporting or attacking Fidel Castro. When the speeches were said to have been freely chosen by the debaters, the students reasonably assumed that the advocated positions reflected the speakers' private opinions. In another condition of the study, however, Jones and Harris forewarned subjects the positions had been arbitrarily assigned by the debate coach. Subjects in that condition generally ignored the fact that the speakers had had no choice of what to say and continued to believe that the advocated positions indicated the speakers' true beliefs.

In a similar study, Napolitan & Goethals (1979) had undergraduates talk with a counselor who behaved in a manner that was either warm and friendly or cool and aloof. The subjects were informed that the counselor's style was either spontaneous and genuine or prearranged and feigned for the purposes of the study. The subjects apparently found it difficult to believe that a person acting friendly (or unfriendly) wasn't really friendly (or unfriendly), however. They disregarded the possibility that the counselor's behavior had been influenced by the role she had been assigned and saw her behavior as a reflection of her personality in every case.

These and other studies (e.g., Ross, Amabile, & Steinmetz, 1977) demonstrate that we are likely to overlook or discount even obvious situational explanations for others' actions. "Behavior" seems to be synonymous with "personality" whatever the circumstances. Still, studies with naive undergraduates do not necessarily suggest that professional psychologists are also prone to a personalistic bias, and one may wonder whether these findings are generalizable to highly trained scientists.

Indeed they are. In a content analysis of the first 6 months of the 1970 *Psychological Abstracts,* Caplan and Nelson (1973) found that 82% of the research dealing with black Americans implicitly interpreted their difficulties in terms of "personal shortcomings," blaming blacks for their problems.

Moreover, Batson, O'Quin, and Pych (1982) have argued that trained helpers (e.g., clinicians and counselors) are especially likely to infer that "a client's problem lies with the client as a person even when it is really due to some aspect of the client's situation" (p. 60). Not only do trained helpers clearly employ more dispositional explanations for clients' problems than untrained observers do (Batson, 1975; Batson & Marz, 1979; Pelton, 1982), but Batson et al. also suggested that both the information available to helpers and their role as helpers virtually guarantee that personalistic biases will occur.

As observers, for instance, helpers' attention is focused on the client rather than the situation; moreover, the client may be seen in a therapeutic setting far removed from his or her normal environment. The client's dispositions are thus much more salient than the situational context, and because we tend to attribute causation to whatever seems salient (Storms, 1973; Taylor & Fiske, 1978), the person gets blamed. As helpers, clinicians and counselors are expected to help, and most of their resources are oriented toward changing the client, not the situation (cf. Batson, Jones, & Cochran, 1979). In addition, the training they receive may set the expectation that the person is the problem (Snyder, 1977). In short, it seems that merely being a helpful observer of other people's problems fosters a personalistic bias; undergraduates asked simply to play the role of peer counselor in mock counseling sessions adopt a more dispositional point of view than their "clients" do (Snyder, Shenkel, & Schmidt, 1976).

A tendency to discount situational determinants of clients' behavior may not always mean that clinicians' judgments are actually wrong (Batson et al., 1982; Harvey, Town, & Yarkin, 1981). However, there are two other potentially troubling sequelae of personalistic biases that should not be overlooked. First, by focusing on clients' personalities, clinicians adopt a perspective that differs from that of their clients, who are likely to attend to the situation surrounding them (Jones & Nisbett, 1971; Storms, 1973). This actor-observer discrepancy is predictable, but it may occasionally engender some dispute (see chapter 7).

More treacherous is the possibility that personalistic biases lead to undeservedly negative perceptions of clients. To the extent that clients are held personally, even solely, responsible for their various dysfunctions while the contributions of adverse situations are overlooked, they appear to be even more incapable than they really are. Wills (1978) reviewed several studies that found that trained helpers' perceptions of their clients are more negative and damning than those of lay observers or the clients themselves (even when the clients were normal!). Moreover, the more experienced a therapist is, the more negative his or her judgments are likely to be (Fehrenbach & O'Leary, 1982; Wills, 1978). Other factors probably contribute to these harsh perceptions—for instance, dissimilarities between therapist and client and exposure to the worst of a client's behavior—but personalistic biases are almost certainly involved (Wills, 1978).

It is thus often disadvantageous to underestimate, however unwittingly, situational determinants of a client's distress. Not only may important influences be overlooked, but unjustified blaming of the client may result. Personalistic biases are just one example, however, of the manner in which unspoken assumptions, perceptual perspectives, and preconceptions about the nature of a client's problems influence and direct a helper's interpretation of events.

The Constraints of Preconceptions

Thus far we have asserted that we should not trust our intuitions when integrating diverse data, that our decisions are often influenced by factors of which we are unaware, and that our person-centered perspectives often ignore how much others' behavior is influenced by situational pressure. Each of these concerns is important, but they all speak to the manner in which we form our tentative judgments and hypotheses. What happens once we have some initial judgments in mind?

This is a vital question that will occupy us for much of the remainder of this chapter. As we will see, the manner in which we are influenced by preconceptions and tentative hypotheses is a key concern because we interpret events in ways that are likely to support and sustain our preconceptions, whatever they are. Once we form a judgment, or adopt a particular theoretical perspective, our evaluation of subsequent data no longer seems to be impartial and detached. Instead, our perceptions of the world are molded and shaped to fit our existing beliefs (instead of the other way around).

In a striking demonstration of this process, Lord, Ross, and Lepper (1979) found groups of Stanford undergraduates who were either in favor of the death penalty (believing that it deterred crime) or opposed to it (thinking it ineffective). Lord et al. presented both groups with two research studies, one that suggested that capital punishment was a deterrent and another that showed it was not. In addition, the two studies employed different methodologies: Each subject found that one study used a cross-sectional design, the other a longitudinal technique, but each design supported the death penalty for half the subjects and opposed it for the other half. Subjects were thus confronted with mixed evidence that only partly supported their existing beliefs and logically cast doubts on the certainty of their positions. Did they accept the mixed data and moderate their stances? Hardly. They praised and accepted the study that supported their beliefs, but criticized and rejected the study that opposed their positions. This meant that when the cross-sectional design confirmed their beliefs it was judged to be the only reasonable way to study the issue, and when the longitudinal design supported them, *it* seemed to be the only sensible approach. Evidence with which they agreed was accepted at face value, but disconfirming data were severely criticized. The remarkable end result was that when the two opposing groups were given identical mixed information they each became more certain that they were right.

Our preconceptions clearly control our interpretations of incoming information, and other fascinating examples abound. Carreta and Moreland (1982) reminded us that during the U.S. Senate Watergate hearings in 1973, supporters of President Nixon were confronted with daily headlines that increasingly implicated Nixon in criminal activities. Most people who had voted for Nixon were largely unaffected by the bad news, however. Unlike McGovern supporters, whose attitudes toward Nixon became less and less favorable, believers in Nixon maintained their liking for him; they dismissed the headlines as liberal slander and shrugged off the burglaries as "politics as usual." Information that contradicted their beliefs was not believed.

One need not oppose a person's deeply held beliefs to show that preconceptions control interpretations, however. Even simple presuppositions structure our perceptions and judgments. For instance, Snyder and Frankel (1976) showed Dartmouth undergraduates a silent videotape of a woman being interviewed and told some of them that the conversation concerned sex, others that it pertained to politics. Those watching the "sex" interview perceived the woman to be considerably more anxious and ill at ease than those watching the "politics" interview, although everyone, of course, saw the same tape.

Finally, social psychological research suggests that preconceptions control interpretations in *subtle* ways; we don't make egregious errors that are easily noticed, but we make errors nonetheless. For instance, Darley and Gross (1983) showed Princeton undergraduates one of two videotapes that provided information about the social class of a young girl named "Hannah." Some subjects found that Hannah was rather poor, playing in a paved, deteriorating schoolyard and returning to a dingy, small home, whereas others found Hannah to be fairly well off, playing in expansive, grassy fields and living in a lovely house. On the basis of these demographic data alone, the subjects did not blindly assume that the upper-class target was doing better in school; they avoided such blatant stereotyping and guessed Hannah's academic achievement to be about average, regardless of her social class. However, when Darley and Gross then showed subjects an ambiguous tape of Hannah taking an aptitude test, her social status clearly affected their judgments (and in a manner of which they seemed to be totally unaware). The tape showed Hannah performing inconsistently, correctly answering some difficult questions but blowing some easy ones. All subjects saw the same tape, but they interpreted it very differently depending upon their beliefs about her social class. Subjects who thought Hannah was poor cited her many mistakes and judged her as performing *below* her average fourth-grade level; subjects who considered her well-to-do noted her many successes and rated her as *better* than average. These perceivers, then, did not leap to judgments about Hannah on the basis of stereotypes alone (thus making errors that might be easily noticed). They reserved judgment until they had more data but then interpreted her actions in a biased manner that was determined by their stereotypes. We can imagine the confidence they felt in their judgments, never realizing that other people with different preconceptions were witnessing the same test results and reaching completely contradictory conclusions (cf. Vallone, Ross, & Lepper, 1985).

Professionals' Preconceptions

As unlikely or threatening as it may seem, the preconceptions of scientists and therapists bias their judgments in just the same way (Mahoney, 1977). In particular, several studies show that clinicians' or counselors' theoretical orientations, their advance knowledge about a client, or even their knowledge of others' judgments influence the interpretations they form. In a renowned study, for example, Temerlin (1968) asked psychiatrists, clinical psychologists, and clinical graduate students to listen to a taped interview with a "prospective patient." Just before the tape was played, a prestigious, well-respected colleague mentioned either that the "patient" was "a very rare person, a perfectly healthy man," or interesting because he "looks neurotic, but actually is quite psychotic." When "healthy" was suggested to the therapists, they unanimously agreed that the target showed no signs of disturbance. By contrast, when disorder was suggested, 92% of the subjects diagnosed some dysfunction—60% of the psychiatrists considered him psychotic—although, again, all subjects had heard the same interview.

Clinical influence appears to be so complex a process (Cantor, 1982) that it is possible for professionals to disagree like this and never realize it. Indeed, the professional training a therapist receives may be a particularly important "preconception" that leads him or her to recognize different symptoms and to make different diagnoses (of the same behavior) than a colleague with another theoretical bent. For instance, Langer and Abelson (1974) asked both behaviorally oriented and psychodynamically oriented clinicians to evaluate a videotaped interview of a man who was described as either a "patient" or a "job applicant." Regardless of his label, the behaviorists found him to be fairly well adjusted, but the psychodynamicists considered the "patient" more disturbed than the "job seeker." Although reacting to the "patient" label this way is not necessarily unreasonable (Davis, 1979), a further study found that the psychodynamicists also believed the "patient's" problems to be more dispositional than the behaviorists did (Snyder, 1977). The biasing effects of professional orientation were also demonstrated by Allyon, Haughton, and Hughes (1965), who taught a schizophrenic, institutionalized for 20 years, to carry a broom by using cigarettes as reinforcements. They asked a psychoanalyst to evaluate her and were told that the broom was "(1) a child that gives her love and she gives him in return her devotion; (2) a phallic symbol, [or] (3) the sceptre of an omnipotent queen" (p. 3).

Thus, there seems to be little doubt that a therapist's professional perspective influences his or her interpretations of behavior (see also Bishop & Richards, 1984). Indeed, one reading of this literature suggests that the variability in clinical judgment from one observer to the next implies that "such judgments may be less informative about the patients they are meant to describe than about the clinician who makes them" (Grosz & Grossman, 1964, p. 112). Whatever the case, there are two further examples of the judgmental effects of preconceptions that deserve attention.

Anchoring

Preconceptions can function as cognitive "anchors," initial estimates that exert a disproportionate influence on final judgments. Anchoring effects occur when initial impressions are not thoroughly revised to accommodate new information; the result is that different preconceptions yield different judgments that remain biased toward the original estimates (Tversky & Kahneman, 1974). In one demonstration of this effect, subjects were provided a random estimate of some quantity (e.g., the percentage of African countries in the United Nations) by spinning a roulette wheel. When they were then asked to revise that "estimate" upward or downward to reflect the true value, subjects seemed reluctant to change that wholly arbitrary starting point, and their final estimates reflected the impact of the anchor. For instance, subjects starting with an "estimate" of 10% would revise upward to only 25%, whereas those starting with 65% would revise downward to only 45%; the difference in the two final judgments reflects an anchoring effect (Tversky & Kahneman, 1974).

Similar results have been obtained with psychologists, psychiatrists, and social workers by Friedlander and Stockman (1983). They asked their subjects to evaluate a case of anorexia nervosa by successively reading five detailed interviews, which varied according to when indications of pathology appeared in the sequence of information. Substantial anchoring occurred in that late-appearing pathology had less impact on clinical judgment; when the anorexia was mentioned early in the sequence of information the case was viewed as significantly more serious, although by the end of the study all subjects had the same body of information in hand (cf. Jones, Rock, Shaver, Goethals, & Ward, 1968). In fact, experienced counselors and clinicians may be especially likely to settle on a diagnosis prematurely (Friedlander & Phillips, 1984; Hirsch & Stone, 1983; Houts & Galante, 1985), although all of us, once we have made a diagnosis, tend not to notice new symptoms that are inconsistent with that diagnosis (Arkes & Harkness, 1980).

In short, even if we have no biasing preconceptions about a case, the initial impressions we form as information is received often carry considerably more weight than they deserve. Whether they are preconceptions or first impressions, we are reluctant to revise our opinions when new data become available. Indeed, as we will soon discover, we may even cling to beliefs that can be shown to have no basis whatsoever. Before we consider belief perseverance, however, there is one more important example of the constraints of preconceptions to address.

Labeling

When a diagnosis or any other widely understood label is attached to dysfunctional behavior, it can become a public preconception that influences the subsequent judgments of an entire professional community. Labels can channel the perceptions and interpretations of observers just as private preconceptions do, but they can have even greater impact: Because they are consensually shared, many observers are affected. Indeed, some sociologists feel that the societal stigmatization that accompanies the labeling of abnormal behavior perpetuates deviancy that would otherwise be transitory (e.g., Scheff, 1975). This "labeling theory of mental illness" suggests that labels often set in motion events that exacerbate, not minimize, deviancy and that "helpers who label people may often create as much harm as good by the very process of practicing their trade" (Rappaport & Cleary, 1980, p. 77).

The concept that labeling creates deviancy has been roundly criticized (e.g., Gove, 1975), but it does have the value of alerting us to the deleterious effects that labels can have. Labels are particularly consequential in our educational systems, for example, where they are widely used. Fogel and Nelson (1983) provided teachers with a diagnostic label for a special education student and then showed them a videotape of the child's behavior. The teachers' behavioral observations were not differentially affected by different labels, but their subjective evaluations of those behaviors were; the more severe the label, the more problematic the behavior seemed to be. Similarly, when Burdg and Graham (1984) informed some of their subjects that preschoolers whose intelligence they would test were "developmentally delayed," the children received lower ratings and actually got lower test scores than other children who had been labeled as "normal." The "delayed" label affected not only the examiners' judgments but, apparently, their behavior as well, since they failed to elicit optimal performance from the children who had been randomly assigned the pejorative label. Perhaps labels can create ostensible dysfunction that would otherwise not exist.

Clinicians and counselors use labels, too, and in a famous (or infamous) study, Rosenhan (1973) examined the results of labeling sane people as schizophrenic. He encouraged eight normal people to report to mental institutions on both the East and West Coasts complaining of vague auditory hallucinations. All but one of them were diagnosed as schizophrenic and admitted to psychiatric wards, but once this was done they dropped all pretense of abnormality and tried to convince the staff that their sanity had returned. This proved hard to do. With a variety of anecdotal observations

Rosenhan argued that "a psychiatric label has a life and influence of its own" (p. 253); once the pseudopatients were labeled schizophrenic, much of what they did, however normal, seemed indicative of schizophrenia. Average life histories were seen as pathogenic, ordinary behavior appeared maladjusted, and the only observers who seemed able to see through the ruse were other (real) patients. The pseudopatients were eventually released after stays that averaged 19 days, but their labels pursued them home; with the one exception, all of them were still presumed to have schizophrenia "in remission."

Rosenhan's suggestion that modern psychiatry is unable to distinguish sanity from insanity has been rejected by observers who argue that he tested no such thing (Farber, 1975; Millon, 1975; Spitzer, 1975; Weiner, 1975). Still, his investigation stands as a provocative reminder that we often see what we expect to see. Expectations, whether they be "preconceptions," "first impressions," or "labels," exert powerful channeling effects on our interpretation and judgment of others' behavior. Moreover, such preconceptions are not easily changed. Even when we are shown that the evidence we used to establish a belief is completely false, the groundless belief may still persist.

Belief Perseverance

We have already seen that once we form initial judgments, evidence that supports those beliefs is readily accepted whereas evidence that opposes those beliefs is denigrated (e.g., Lord et al., 1979). Another remarkable illustration of this tendency emerges from studies of belief perseverance that examine the manner in which people sometimes cling to an impression even "when the evidential basis for such a position is completely invalidated" (Jelalian & Miller, 1984, p. 29). In studies of this sort, subjects are usually provided information that straightforwardly leads to a particular judgment about themselves or others; they are allowed to formulate those judgments but are then shown that the original information was bogus and fictitious and utterly without diagnostic value. The common result is that the judgments persist although they are now without foundation.

The first such study was particularly relevant to social psychologists who deceive research participants and depend on a postexperimental debriefing to erase the subjects' misconceptions. Ross, Lepper, and Hubbard (1975) asked their undergraduate subjects to distinguish between authentic and fake suicide notes and provided them false feedback indicating that they had done very well, very poorly, or about average. Once this was done, however, the subjects were informed that the feedback was fake; they were assured it had nothing to do with them and were shown the experimenter's instruction sheet that had randomly assigned them to one of the three groups. The subjects were then asked to estimate how well they had actually done on the task and to predict their future performance on similar tasks.

Although the subjects understood that their feedback was randomly assigned to them, the judgments they had formed with that feedback tended to persist. Logically, none of the subjects had any valid knowledge whatsoever about their actual abilities, but the "success" subjects continued to believe that they were pretty good, the "average" group considered themselves mediocre, and the "failure" subjects felt that they were not particularly good at the task. Moreover, a second study by Ross et al. showed that belief perseverance also influenced observers who watched the procedure, hearing the false feedback and subsequent debriefing; they, too, continued to judge "successful" actors as much better at the task than their "failing" counterparts. Indeed, it was even harder to disabuse observers of their groundless judgments. Ross et al. found that it was possible to correct most of the belief perseverance of the actors by engaging them in an extensive discussion of the perseverance phenomenon and the harm it can do, but observers were largely unaffected by even this elaborate exposition. Once they had formed an impression of the actors—even one based on demonstrably fictitious information—it was remarkably resistant to change.

These findings are pertinent to cases like one recently in the news in which a schoolteacher was falsely accused (as it turned out) of child sexual abuse by a student bearing a grudge. We now know that the teacher is totally innocent, but having once associated him with a heinous crime, do we really like and trust him as much as we did before the incident? Erroneous impressions can persevere, and Wegner, Wenzlaff, Kerker, and Beattie (1981) have shown that innuendo can have the same lasting impact on our judgments of others that factual accusations do. Even headlines that exonerate the innocent (e.g., "Andrew Winters Not Connected to Bank Embezzlement") produce negative impressions of those involved, and the perseverance phenomenon suggests that those impressions, although inaccurate and unjustified, change only with difficulty.

Why do beliefs persevere when the evidence that supports them is discredited? Ross et al. (1975) speculated that, once a person creates a plausible rationale for why he or she is good at evaluating suicide notes, for instance, the rationale may still seem reasonable and likely even when the information on which it was based is overturned. Ross, Lepper, Strack, and Steinmetz (1977) found that providing explanations for hypothetical events made them seem much more likely to occur, and, using the belief perseverance paradigm, Anderson, Lepper, and Ross (1980) showed that inventing explanations for one's beliefs made them much more resistant to evidential discrediting. Anderson et al. provided subjects case histories that suggested that risk taking made one either a good or bad firefighter, and then asked half of the subjects to explain why this should be so. When they then learned that the case histories were totally fictitious, subjects who had engaged in the causal processing exhibited considerably more belief perseverance than those who had not; indeed, those who had invented a theory to explain their beliefs were virtually unaffected by learning that the data base for their theory was worthless. To some degree, then, belief perseverance is based on the ease with which causal explanations spring to mind (Anderson, 1983b; Anderson, New, & Speer, 1985). Whatever explanations are most salient or available in our memories are likely to seem the most plausible, even when there is no valid basis for them.

Studies of belief perseverance do not deny that beliefs often change in response to new evidence. These studies do indicate, however, that change occurs grudgingly and that overwhelming evidence will often be required to change beliefs that were quickly formed (Jelalian & Miller, 1984). In clinical inference, data about clients are received over a period of time, the validity of a client's self-report is sometimes uncertain, and judgment involves constant causal analyses and explanations. As a result, the unwarranted perseverance of outdated hypotheses is always a possibility. When new, reliable evidence contradicts a clinician's working hypothesis and the hypothesis should be revised, it may still be hard to let go of the idea. Coles (1973) described Sigmund Freud's analysis of Leonardo da Vinci's life and art based on Leonardo's early memory of a "vulture" coming down to him in his cradle and opening his mouth with its tail. Vultures were symbols for mothers in ancient Egypt and, with this revelation in hand, Freud showed how only a man with Leonardo's special relationship with his mother could have created the Mona Lisa. Unfortunately, Freud was misled by a bad translation of Leonardo's notes; what Freud assumed was a vulture was actually a kite. With the basis for Freud's analysis discredited, did he revise his explanation of Leonardo's behavior? Of course not.

Perseverance phenomena are thus found outside as well as within the laboratory (Jelalian & Miller, 1984; Jennings, Lepper, & Ross, 1981), and those whose profession it is to explain and judge others' behavior should beware. This is doubly true, in fact, when the judge is able to select what data are to be considered; there is always the possibility that we not only value, but preferentially seek out, information that supports our existing beliefs.

The Confirmatory Bias

As they engage in counseling and psychotherapy, clinicians and counselors are not simply the passive recipients of whatever information their clients wish to divulge. Rather, they actively seek certain information, integrate that information to form ideas about the client and his or her dysfunction, and seek to test their hunches by gathering yet more information. Unfortunately, research on social inference suggests that, once initial impressions are formed, it is difficult for people to test the accuracy of those inferences in an unbiased fashion. Clinicians' and counselors' efforts to test their clinical intuitions can lead to erroneous conclusions. For instance, Snyder (1981) and his colleagues have repeatedly shown that undergraduate subjects, when asked to determine whether a belief about another person is true or false, are more likely to pursue information that will confirm the belief than to inquire after data that will prove it wrong. They seem to employ a one-sided strategy of seeking only instances that support their hypotheses instead of evenhandedly seeking instances that both do and do not fit them. Thus, Snyder found that people are biased toward confirming their assumptions about others and, as a consequence, rarely obtain impartial, representative information about them.

For instance, Snyder and Swann (1978a) invited half of their subjects to determine whether a person they would soon interview was an introvert; other subjects were asked to assess the person's extraversion. All the subjects were then provided a list of "interview topic" questions with which to conduct the interview. The questions were either neutral (e.g., "What are the good and bad points of acting friendly and open?") or biased toward eliciting introverted (e.g., "What do you dislike about loud parties?") or extraverted (e.g., "What do you do when you want to liven things up at a party?") responses. In general, the subjects selected questions that were likely to elicit evidence in support of their preconceptions about the person. The two groups of subjects thus adopted two very different lines of investigation, with each group ensuring that their targets would report many of the behaviors they expected to find. Indeed, Snyder and Swann found that the interviews were so biased that judges listening to audiotapes of the interactions actually believed the targets to be fairly introverted or extraverted, depending on the interviewers' respective preconceptions.

An impersonal example may help the reader appreciate how biased such confirmatory hypothesis testing can be. Suppose you are asked to determine the numerical rule we have in mind that explains this sequence of numbers: 2, 4, 6 (Wason, 1960). If you are allowed to generate as many series of three numbers as you like to test your understanding of our rule, being told each time whether your examples do or do not fit the rule, how would you proceed? In our experience with hundreds of students, we have found, like Wason (1960), that nearly everyone tests only numbers that fit their hypotheses; virtually no one tests possibilities that would prove them wrong. If they guess the rule is "all even numbers" they try 8, 10, 12 (which fits our rule); if they believe the rule is "increments of two" they try 1, 3, 5 (which also fits our rule). Very few explore a possibility that would negate their hypotheses, like -3, 0, 147, (it, too, fits our rule!), and by seeking only confirming instances the vast majority convince themselves of an incorrect belief. Few persist long enough to uncover the actual rule, "three ascending numbers."

Importantly, Snyder and White (1981) found that people recognize the value of disconfirming evidence but are generally just unwilling to pursue it. Snyder and White showed that when subjects were asked to determine if a person was not an introvert (or extravert), they sought disconfirming data with the same single-mindedness with which they usually pursue confirming instances. Still, confirmatory hypothesis testing appears to be the norm. Snyder and Swann (1978a) found that subjects continued to use confirmatory strategies even when they knew the hypothesis they were testing was rather unlikely to be true, and again when they were given a $25 incentive for accuracy. And even when subjects were given competing hypotheses, being asked to determine whether a person was "more like an extravert or more like an introvert," they chose one possibility and tried to confirm it instead of adequately testing both hypotheses (Snyder & Swann, 1978b).

Do similar biases affect clinicians and counselors? To the extent that they do, psychological professionals may occasionally convince themselves of hypotheses about clients that are simply untrue. Snyder (1981) suggested, for example, that:

> the psychiatrist who believes (erroneously) that adult gay males had bad childhood relationships with their mothers may meticulously probe for re-called (or fabricated) signs of tensions between their gay clients and their mothers, but neglect to so carefully interrogate their heterosexual clients about their maternal relationships. (p. 294)

Such a practice would no doubt confirm the clinician's expectation, since nearly everyone could report significant conflict with his or her parents (and spouse, and children, and colleagues) if asked (Renaud & Estess, 1961).

In fact, several studies have examined clinicians' hypothesis-testing strategies, and when Snyder's (1981) method of asking subjects to choose their questions from a preset list is employed, even experienced professionals often lapse into a confirmatory approach (e.g., Dallas & Baron, 1985). When they are allowed to construct their own questions, however, the clinicians usually adopt a more evenhanded strategy, sampling both confirming and disconfirming data (Dallas & Baron, 1985; Strohmer & Chiodo, 1984; Strohmer & Newman, 1983). Overall, the less structured an interview situation is, the less likely confirmatory bias appears to be (Clark & Taylor, 1983; Trope & Bassok, 1982).

Thus, the confirmatory bias may play only a minimal role in clinical inference, but no one suggests that it should be casually dismissed; observers unanimously warn that, without a conscious effort to test one's assumptions in an unbiased manner, confirmatory tendencies can emerge (Dallas & Baron, 1985; Strohmer & Chiodo, 1984).

Illusory Correlations

We have seen that our preconceptions lead us to preferentially accept and, occasionally, seek out data that support our assumptions. A final example of the impact of preconceptions on judgment involves the tendency to perceive plausible associations between events that are in fact unrelated, or are related in the direction opposite to that we detect. These fictional associations are "illusory correlations" (Chapman & Chapman, 1967), and they have been widely observed in clinical judgment.

In a famous series of studies, Chapman and Chapman (1967, 1969) demonstrated that practicing clinicians often report noticing (and basing judgments on) associations between clients' responses to projective tests and their symptoms that have no empirical basis whatsoever. On the Draw-A-Person test, for instance, clinicians report that muscular drawings are associated with concern over one's masculinity, and unusual eyes are linked to suspicion of others; on the Rorschach, they note that various anal and feminine responses are associated with homosexuality. In reality, such associations do not exist, and the Chapmans were able to show that naïve undergraduates, given projective data in which these various responses were randomly paired with the various symptoms, nevertheless reported the same plausible but fictitious correlations the clinicians say they see. Moreover, the Chapmans (1969) found that both clinicians and naïve subjects generally failed to notice the real patterns in the Rorschach that link homosexuality to less stereotypical responses (e.g., seeing monsters on Card IV).

Not only are actual correlations overlooked, but subjects' erroneous perceptions of illusory correlations are often remarkably persistent. Chapman and Chapman (1967) built a huge negative correlation between symptoms and stereotypical projective responses into the data subjects were given and found that the subjects still insisted that the symptoms and responses were positively related (although the association between them did not seem as strong). Golding and Rorer (1972) repeatedly gave subjects an individual Rorschach response, asked them to predict what symptom would be associated with it, and then revealed the actual symptom, so that subjects received immediate feedback about the accuracy of their assumptions as they studied the data; strong illusory correlations were still obtained. Waller and Keeley (1978) went so far as to provide subjects with elaborate explanations of illusory correlation, complete with practice sessions in which true positive and negative correlations were demonstrated, but the subjects still reported patterns in Draw-A-Person data that were illusory (cf. Mowrey, Doherty, & Keeley, 1979; Starr & Katkin, 1969).

Results like these are certainly not unique to clinical judgments (e.g., Jennings, Amabile, & Ross, 1982). Hamilton (1981) has persuasively argued, for instance, that illusory correlations help perpetuate erroneous cultural stereotypes (e.g., "All those minorities do is collect welfare"). It simply appears that accurate assessment of covariation between events is much more complex than most people realize, necessitating consideration of far more than just the frequency with which the events jointly occur (Crocker, 1981; Nisbett & Ross, 1980).[1]

---

[1] At minimum, four sets of data are needed to detect covariation: instances in which events A and B jointly occur: instances in which A occurs but B does not;

The difficulty of these judgments allows peoples' expectations and pre-conceptions to have as much, if not more, influence on their judgments as do the objective data they face (Alloy & Tabachnik, 1984; Kayne & Alloy, in press). People's preconceptions can influence what they think they see in a set of data, and those preconceptions often "flourish in the face of evidence that would create grave doubts in any unbiased observer—certainly in any unbiased observer who owned a calculator, an introductory statistics text, and some conventional knowledge about how to use them" (Jennings et al., 1982, p. 227).

Overconfidence

As clinicians and counselors form their complex judgments, their tentative evaluations gradually become more certain, and they feel more sure those evaluations are correct. However, like most people, they are probably more sure of themselves than they should be. People are generally overconfident that their beliefs are correct, thinking themselves right more often than they really are. Perhaps this is not surprising, given that biased interpretations, confirmatory hypothesis testing, and illusory correlations all combine to shield them from facts that would disconfirm their beliefs. There are, how-ever, a handful of processes that we have not yet mentioned that contribute further to people's misplaced certainty, and in this section we consider additional reasons why we are often more sure of ourselves than is war-ranted.

First, some examples of overconfidence: Fischhoff, Slovic, and Lichten-stein (1977) have shown that when answering factual general-knowledge questions college students are wrong more often than they think. Fischhoff et al. confronted subjects with a wide variety of questions such as "Absinthe is (a) a liqueur or (b) a precious stone," and "Which magazine had the largest circulation in 1970, *Playboy* or *Time?*" and asked them to select an answer and to indicate how certain they were of their answers. The results showed that the subjects were consistently overconfident, choosing fewer correct answers than they had estimated they would. Moreover, they were sure enough of many of their wrong answers to wager money on them; they were poor bettors indeed, because they missed about 1 of every 8 questions they gave 50 : 1 odds were correct!

Oskamp (1965) demonstrated the same phenomenon among clincial psy-

---

instances in which B occurs alone; and instances in which neither occurs. In addi-tion, all these data must be adequately sampled, classified, estimated, recalled, and interpreted (Crocker, 1981). It is a tough judgment.

chologists. He provided his professional subjects with a case study broken into four segments and asked them to predict the characteristics and behavior of the client, and to rate their confidence in their judgments, after each segment. The clinicians' predictive accuracy quickly reached a maximum, but as they read more of the case study their confidence in their judgments continued to increase. Ultimately, with the entire case study in hand, the subjects felt that 53% of their judgments were likely to be correct, but only 28% actually were. The clinicians were thus overconfident, and Oskamp concluded that "a psychologist's increasing feelings of confidence as he works through a case are not a sure sign of increasing accuracy for his conclusions" (p. 265).

Along with the influence of our preconceptions on our selection and interpretation of data, what can explain such overconfidence? We can identify four factors.

Hindsight and the "I-Knew-It-All-Along" Effect

One way we can feel as if we know more than we do is to overestimate how smart we used to be. It is difficult for people not to let their current knowledge of events contaminate their recollections of their past knowledge, so that they consistently remember themselves as smarter and less fallible than they really were. Knowing how things have turned out leads most of us to "remember" that the eventual outcome seemed obvious to us all along; although we could not have predicted the outcome we nevertheless feel that we "knew it all along" (Wood, 1978).

Many readers are familiar with this tendency in players of Trivial Pursuit; someone may come up with several answers to a question that are nowhere near correct, but still exclaim when the right answer is announced, "Oh, I knew that!" Several more formal demonstrations of this phenomenon have been conducted by Fischhoff (1975, 1977) and his colleagues. For instance, Fischhoff and Beyth (1975) asked subjects on the eve of President Nixon's 1972 trip to China to estimate how likely various results of the trip were. After the trip, the subjects were asked to recall their predictions, but they did not do particularly well. They remembered forecasting those events that did occur as being more probable than they had really seemed to them at the time, and similarly they believed that those events that did not transpire had never seemed very likely.

Hindsight, then, clearly distorts our judgments of what we used to think and know, generally leaving us with the impression that we were (and are) more knowledgeable than we really were. This hindsight bias, or the "I-knew-it-all-along" effect, has now been demonstrated in several studies (Goggin & Range, 1985; Leary, 1981, 1982; Slovic & Fischhoff, 1977; Wood, 1978), and it apparently is not easy to avoid; Fischhoff (1977) found that forewarning subjects by telling them about the bias did not help them correct their judgments.

Importantly, the bias affects clinicians. Using a sample of clinical psychology interns and psychiatrists, Hood (1970) found that knowledge of a client's later suicide distorted the clinicians' judgments of the suicidal intent evident in a description of the case. Knowing how things turned out, they were sure they could have predicted them all along. Thus, with the hindsight bias in place, clinical inference may seem much less difficult than it really is; no matter what people do, we may feel that their actions are not surprising and that our ability to judge others is sound.

Reconstructive Memory

Hindsight studies suggest that our memories of what we used to know are often faulty. Indeed, rather than being faithful reproductions of actual past events, many of our memories are "reconstructive." In other words, we often selectively misremember certain events, invent details, and fill in gaps, revising our recollections to produce seamless memories that fit our current circumstances (Loftus & Loftus, 1980). To the extent that we constantly edit our pasts to fit our presents, we may produce selective histories that make us seem much more clever, intuitive, and knowledgeable than we really are.

For example, past complexities may be remembered as obvious simplicities. Snyder and Uranowitz (1978) provided their subjects an extensive biography of a woman named "Betty K." and then told them a week later either that Betty was a lesbian or that she was a heterosexual (or her sexual preference was not mentioned). The subjects' memories for the events of Betty's life were demonstrably affected by their current beliefs about her sexual orientation: Those who thought she was heterosexual remembered that she had dated often in high school, for instance, whereas those who considered her homosexual remembered that she had not had a steady boyfriend (both of which were true). The subjects literally found it hard to remember those facts that did not fit their current impressions.

Our selective memories also lead us to test our current beliefs in a biased fashion so that, again, we find support for them. Two days after reading about "Jane," Snyder and Cantor's (1979) subjects were asked to evaluate her for a job either as a librarian or as a salesperson. Remembering her introverted behaviors, half the subjects thought she would make a great librarian, whereas the other subjects, recalling her extraverted actions, thought she would be good in sales. In addition, each group of subjects considered her rather unsuited for the job for which the other group was recommending her.

Such reconstructive memory can lead to revisions of our personal histories as well. Conway and Ross (1984) showed that, in evaluating the success of a study-skills program, subjects remembered themselves as having started the program with poorer skills than they had really had. They also reported greater improvement in their skills than did a waiting-list control group, but their actual performances did not differ. In short, the subjects believed that the skills program had been quite effective when it had actually done very little. By misremembering the extent of their past problems, the subjects were able to avoid acknowledging that they had wasted their time. Moreover, had their therapist requested an evaluation of the program, they would have no doubt praised it highly. Clients are not always the most objective judges of a therapist's efforts.

Feedback From Clients

A great many studies have now shown that people usually accept uncritically groundless generalized descriptions of their personalities. They are particularly likely to accept vague personal evaluations that seem to be based on psychological tests and are delivered by a professional clinician (for a review, see Snyder, Shenkel, & Lowery, 1977). This gullible lack of discernment, known as the "Barnum effect," ensures that those of us in the business of giving psychological evaluations are likely to receive lots of acclaim for our prowess that, in truth, is substantially undeserved. We may recieve praise from clients even when very little is accomplished. As Snyder et al. warned, "in no sense . . . can such praise be interpreted as 'validation' of either the clinician's skill or assessment procedures" (p. 113).

Respecting Uniqueness: Making Exceptions

A final way in which we can become overconfident is to make exceptions for ourselves and for the decisions we make. Meehl (1973) described clinicians' occasional reluctance to apply actuarial data to the individual case; "After all," the argument goes, "we're concerned with the unique individual, not the group." The great fallacy of that argument, as Meehl observed, is that, although departures from normative decision rules are sometimes appropriate, a policy that allows frequent exceptions will ultimately allow many errors and is thus indefensible. A clinician who trusts his or her intuition over statistical probability, who too often believes "This is a unique case," will make too many mistakes.

   In terms of overconfidence, clinicians and counselors who see themselves as unique cases to whom this chapter's inferential cautions do not apply are probably much too sure of themselves. Indeed, it is probably a further symptom of characteristic overconfidence to assume that one is personally immune to the various biases we have discussed. Unwarranted certainty and misplaced faith in our own veracity appear to be hard to avoid (Einhorn & Hogarth, 1978) and are unrelated to one's intelligence (Lichtenstein & Fischhoff, 1977); however, we might argue, as social philosphers do, that there is something intelligent in knowing what it is we do not know, and admitting our faults.

The Behavioral Confirmation of Erroneous Inferences

None of the inferential errors we have considered would be so harmful if, eventually, truth won out and our various errors were corrected. Unfortunately, some of our most egregious errors are probably never discovered. By acting on mistaken judgments of others, we can elicit from them the behavior we expect to find, behavior that would not have occurred without our prompting. Interpersonal judgments can thus be self-fulfilling prophecies in which we get what we expect from others (which, in turn, further convinces us of our inferential skill). The manner in which our beliefs create their own realities, and the potentially therapeutic impact of this phenomenon, will be detailed in chapter 11; here we simply wish to illustrate how consequential errors in inference can be.

Snyder, Tanke, and Berscheid (1977) provided an elegant example. They recorded college males' first phone conversations with women whom they believed, on the basis of randomly manipulated photographs, were either physically attractive or unattractive. Judges' ratings of the conversations indicated that the men were much more interesting social partners when they thought they were talking to good-looking women; they were rated, for instance, as more sociable, warm, outgoing, interesting, bold, and socially adept. The men's (often erroneous) judgments of the women were clearly reflected in their behavior toward them. How did the women respond? Those who were presumed to be attractive really did sound more alluring, reacting to their obviously interested partners by sounding more appealing themselves. By comparison, the women who talked with the relatively detached men who thought they were unattractive sounded pretty drab. In both cases, the men got out of the women the behavior they expected, whether or not their judgments were sound.

Even more remarkable is the finding that the targets of our judgments may gradually come to see themselves as we do. Fazio, Effrein, and Falender (1981) examined what it is like to be the target of confirmatory hypothesis testing. As you may recall, when subjects test another's extraversion they often ask a very biased set of extraversion-eliciting questions (Snyder & Swann, 1978a). Fazio et al. found that, following such treatment, those asked the biased questions described themselves as more extraverted than they previously had. What is more, they behaved differently in subsequent interactions. When meeting a stranger, they were more likely to initiate a conversation, sit closer, talk more, and sound more extraverted on tape than those previously asked a set of "introversion" questions. Thus, we may not only get people to behave the way we think they will, but we may also slowly mold them into the people we think they are. Such is the power, and the peril, of clinical inference.

Improving Clinical Inference

Again, no fingers are being pointed here. The inferential problems we have discussed are problems in human judgment and are not peculiar to clinical or counseling psychology. (Indeed, researchers also commit such errors.) In fact, clinical judgment may not be as treacherous as this chapter suggests; Hogarth (1981) argued that most studies of decision making overestimate our problems by ignoring the corrective role of feedback in normal social judgments. On the other hand, the studies we have described may underestimate our problems, since they usually provided subjects with unambiguous, pre-packaged data and implicitly encouraged participants to do their best (Nisbett & Ross, 1980). In any case, it seems obvious that the potential for grave errors exists, and many clinicians join us in urging caution (e.g., Turk & Salovey, 1985, in press). It is important to do more than just point out the pitfalls, however; our goal should be to improve social judgment, not merely to derogate it (Wiggins, 1982). What, then, can be done?

Education

Because there are limits to our introspection and we do tend to be overconfident, a first hurdle is convincing decision makers that potential problems even exist (Nisbett & Ross, 1980). Admitting our fallibility is far from enough, however, because recognizing inferential errors does not usually make them go away. Recall that warning people about hindsight biases (Fischhoff, 1977) and illusory correlations (Waller & Keeley, 1978), for instance, did not help correct them. Extensive training may be required to allow us to fully appreciate the extent of our judgmental biases (Fischhoff, 1982).

Turk and Salovey (in press) suggested a "bias inoculation" procedure in which people are allowed to experience judgmental errors with subsequent opportunities for analysis and feedback. The point would be to actually make these various mistakes so that they could be thoroughly understood and better detected later on. Nisbett and Ross (1980) would agree that any such training should be as vivid and concrete as possible, and they advocated the use of memorable slogans to keep corrective principles in mind: "It's an empirical question," so use the facts, not your intuition; "Beware the fundamental attribution error," and consider situations before labeling dispositions. Educational approaches can be profitable; the "process debriefing" of Ross et al. (1975), in which subjects were invited to understand belief perseverance, speculate as to its origins, and list its potential costs, was fairly effective in reducing perseverance.

Using Statistics

For complex judgments such as assessments of covariation, experience with the problem may not be enough (Waller & Keeley, 1978); statistical calculations are often required. For some judgments (detecting covariation with a four-cell contingency table, for instance) the needed calculations are simple (Nisbett & Ross, 1980), whereas for others (formulating Bayesian probabilities, for example) they are rather complex (Arkes, 1981). Nevertheless, the use of statistics and the reasoning that follows from them can cure a great many ills (Dawes, 1979; Nisbett, Krantz, Jepson, & Fong, 1982).

Arkes (1981) provides a fascinating example of how an explicitly statistical approach can salvage wrongful intuition. Assume that you are tempted to make a diagnosis of multiple personality because the chances that a person who was not a multiple personality would present you with the symptoms you have observed are, say, 1 in 100. Such odds do not mean your diagnosis has a 99% chance of being correct. Because multiple personalities are exceedingly rare (let's assume, generously, that 1 in 100,000 persons qualifies), your chances of encountering one are quite remote, and the actual probability that your diagnosis is correct is a mere .1%. If that seems astonishing, you can appreciate the value of statistics in setting you straight.

Considering Alternatives

Several types of judgments appear to be improved by careful consideration of why we might be wrong. More specifically, inventing plausible explanations for opposing points of view seems to help reduce belief perseverance, overconfidence, and biased interpretation of data. For instance, in a hindsight study, Slovic and Fischhoff (1977) found that asking subjects to explain explicitly how alternative outcomes could have occurred reduced the hindsight tendency to assume a particular outcome was inevitable. Similarly, getting subjects to list specific reasons why they might be right and why they might be wrong in an overconfidence study reduced their tendency to overestimate their knowledge (Koriat, Lichtenstein, & Fischhoff, 1980). Misplaced beliefs are also less likely to persevere when subjects imagine contradictory causal possibilities (Anderson, 1982). In general, it appears that the more salient or cognitively "available" a given belief is, the more plausible it is (Anderson et al., 1985); intentionally creating explanations for alternative beliefs can thus help us evaluate a given belief more impartially.

Being Explicit

The more information we have to process (Lueger & Petzel, 1979) and the more we have to rely on our faulty memories (Arkes, 1981), the less accurate our judgments will be. Dawes (1982) encouraged being explicit in our decision making, listing all logical possibilities and systematically estimating as carefully as possible the likelihood of each. Turk and Salovey (in press) echoed that suggestion, urging us to "de-automize" our judgmental processes so that we become more aware of our own thinking. Critically evaluating our judgments in a step-by-step fashion through self-interrogation and thinking aloud may help block those fuzzy, intuitive leaps where biases lead us astray. In addition, accountability, or the feeling that we will have to justify our decisions to others, may be valuable; Tetlock (1983, 1985) has shown that warning subjects of their accountability reduces anchoring effects and personalistic biases (cf. Harkness, DeBono, & Borgida, 1985).

Delaying Judgment

Finally, there may be some wisdom in putting off our judgments as long as possible. We have seen that, as soon as first impressions are formed, they begin to influence our interpretation of subsequent data. It may improve our judgments, then, to resist the tendency to arrive at premature conclusions. In fact, Dailey (1952) showed that the final judgments of subjects who began to predict another person's behavior halfway through his self-description were less accurate than those of subjects who made no predictions until the end. Delaying judgment as long as possible may be a desirable strategy.

Withholding judgment is probably easier said than done, however, and is likely to require conscious effort. Indeed, all of the strategies considered in this section ask us to actively attend to the manner in which we arrive at our judgments of others. Our inferential habits are frequently faulty, and improving them will no doubt require careful vigilance. Acknowledging those faults is the place to begin.

Conclusions

Clinical inference is open to the same biases, distortions, and errors that cloud all social judgment, likely leading to a misplaced faith in clinicians' judgmental abilities. We are prone to ignore how others' circumstances influence their behavior, and we tend to seek out and preferentially value information that supports our existing beliefs. If no such information exists, we may perceive it anyway, and we may even cling to beliefs for which there is no longer any support whatsoever. We are generally unaware of these inferential pitfalls because it is hard for us to recognize how data influence our judgments. The net result is that we are more sure of ourselves than we should be, often trusting our intuitions over statistical probabilities. We are probably not unable to change most of these bad habits, but we need first to acknowledge our fallibility and then be ready to go to work.

Chapter 9

The Social Influence Model in Counseling and Psychotherapy

Having examined the processes involved in clinical judgment and diagnosis, we are now ready to turn our attention to the process of therapy itself. During the 1960s, several writers began to examine the process of counseling and psychotherapy from social psychological perspectives. Although differing in emphasis, these analyses shared two central assumptions: that therapy and counseling involve interpersonal processes in which the therapist influences the thoughts, feelings, and behavior of the client, and that therapeutic change can be understood only within the context of the interpersonal dynamics of the counseling setting (Frank, 1961; Goldstein, 1966; Goldstein, Heller, & Sechrest, 1966; Strong, 1968). In fact, Strong (1968, p. 101) went so far as to suggest that "psychotherapy can be viewed as a branch of applied social psychology."

The notion that counseling and psychotherapy involve social influence processes is regarded as self-evident by most psychologists today, but Strong (1982) observed that this perspective was not widely accepted among most counselors and psychotherapists 20 years ago. Even today, many practitioners, particularly those who subscribe to humanistic or client-centered approaches, argue that psychologists should not directly influence their clients, but rather should provide a supportive environment in which the client can mobilize his or her own change processes.

From a social psychological perspective, such a view of psychotherapy and counseling is untenable. All human relationships involve mutual influence as the individuals act and react to one another, adjust their behavior on the basis of one another's actions, respond emotionally to each other, modify their beliefs and opinions as a result of what the other individual says and does, and so on. Given that counseling involves a social encounter between two or more persons, it is unavoidable that therapist and client influence one another during the course of therapy. Indeed, a therapeutic relationship in which influence does not occur is not a relationship at all, but merely an instance of two individuals coacting independently in the same place at the same time. Explicitly or implicitly, purposefully or accidentally, the effective counselor influences clients to adopt certain therapeutic goals, to think about themselves and others in more adaptive ways, to learn new social competencies, to apply cognitive and behavioral principles learned in therapy to their everyday lives, and so on.

In short, we accept as self-evident the premise that counseling and psychotherapy involve a process of mutual social influence in which a therapist and a client modify one another's beliefs, emotions, and behavior. Questions then arise regarding how this influence occurs and whether it contributes to desired changes in the client. These questions are the focus of this chapter.[1]

Social Psychological Foundations

With the onset of World War II, social psychologists became intensely interested in social influence processes within the context of such topics as attitude change, brainwashing, propaganda, and leadership. Since then, influence has come to be regarded as a component of all social interaction and has taken a central place in the study of interpersonal behavior.

Strong (1968) was one of the first to apply the vast social psychological literature on influence to an understanding of what happens when an individual seeks help from a psychologist or other mental health professional. In what has become a landmark paper, Strong noted close parallels between a speaker attempting to influence an audience and a counselor trying to help a client. In both cases, a communicator attempts to influence another's attitudes and behavior through verbal communication. Given the strong parallel, Strong argued that social psychology's understanding of attitude change was directly relevant to the counseling process. He demonstrated the viability of his claim by reviewing research dealing with the impact of communicator and audience characteristics on the influence process and by applying this research to an analysis of counseling (see also Goldstein et al., 1966).

Since that time, a tremendous body of research has examined the manner in which therapists influence their clients. This literature is quite extensive, so our coverage of this area will be necessarily selective. In determining which material to cover, we chose to deal chiefly with the research based most directly on social psychological perspectives and with findings in which we have the most confidence. Other reviews of this literature may be found

---

[1] Although we recognize that the client and the therapist influence one another, the emphasis in this chapter is only on the processes through which the therapist influences the client.

in Strong (1968, 1982), Strong and Claiborn (1982), Corrigan, Dell, Lewis, and Schmidt (1980), and Maddux, Stoltenberg, and Rosenwein (in press).

Most research on influence in counseling and therapy may be traced directly or indirectly to Hovland, Janis, and Kelley's (1953) work on attitude change. In *Communication and Persuasion,* Hovland et al. (1953) provided an extensive review of the existing literature on variables that affect the influence process, classifying them into factors relevant to the *source* or communicator of a message, the *target* or audience of the communication, and characteristics of the *message* itself. This line of work has had a greater impact on research in counseling and psychotherapy than any other in social psychology. Building on the framework provided by Hovland et al., researchers in counseling and psychotherapy have studied characteristics of the counselor (source), client (target), and treatment (message) that affect therapeutic outcomes. It is to this literature that we now turn our attention.

Counselor Characteristics

The effectiveness of attempts to change others' attitudes and behavior depends in large part on how the source of the persuasive communication is perceived by the target or recipient of the message. In discussing the effects of "source characteristics" on attitude change, Hovland et al. (1953) focused primarily on the impact of communicator "credibility." Two aspects of credibility were examined in their work: *expertness* (the degree to which a communicator is perceived as being a source of valid information) and *trustworthiness* (the degree to which a communicator is perceived as having honest intentions). Not surprisingly, laboratory research in social psychology has shown that, in a variety of domains, communicators who are viewed as expert and trustworthy are more influential than those who are not (e.g., Aronson, Turner, & Carlsmith, 1963; Eagly & Himmelfarb, 1978; Hovland et al., 1953; Mills & Harvey, 1972; see, however, Powell, 1965). Although this relationship between credibility and influence is often regarded as a given among social psychologists, research that has explored the effects of counselor credibility has yielded mixed results.

Expertness

Studies of counselor expertness have usually introduced a therapist to a client in a manner that portrays the therapist as either highly trained and experienced or poorly trained and inexperienced. For example, counselors may be introduced to clients as Ph.D. psychologists with national reputations or as practicum students or undergraduates with little or no experience. Therapeutic outcomes are then assessed at the end of one or more counseling sessions.

At the risk of oversimplifying the results of this body of research, we can conclude that counselors can influence client change regardless of their presumed expertise, experience, or status. That is, some studies have found that even counselors described as inexperienced nonexperts produce client change relative to nontreatment control groups (Greenberg, 1969; Sprafkin, 1970). Thus, perceived counselor expertness is not necessary for therapy to be effective.

This finding has been a source of consternation for many well-trained therapists, but four points can be made about it. First, it is possible that the counselor role per se may carry considerable influence regardless of the characteristics of the individual who occupies it (Corrigan et al., 1980; Strong, 1968). That is, merely adopting counselor and client roles may create a situation in which the person in the client role makes an effort to attend to and comply with the counselor's recommendations, regardless of the counselor's expertise or experience. Second, casual observation in everyday life shows that people are often influenced and helped by others who are not in any way viewed as expert helpers. Even untrained individuals may be quite helpful to distressed persons if their relationship is characterized by understanding, empathy, trust, warmth, and support (Emrick, Lassen & Edwards, 1977; Truax & Carkhauff, 1967). Third, the initial effects of a counselor's presumed expertness (or lack of it) are likely to weaken once the counselor and client begin to interact. Even untrained counselors may be perceived as competent helpers, whereas some supposedly expert counselors are not (see Heppner & Dixon, 1978; Strong & Schmidt, 1970a). Most research dealing with the effects of expertness on influence, within both social psychology and counseling, has been based on a single interaction between communicator and target (or counselor and client). Perceived expertise may become less important with extended contact.

Most importantly, the fact that inexpert helpers have been shown to be effective in analogue counseling settings does not imply that perceived expertise has no effect at all. On the contrary, although ostensibly inexperienced counselors are sometimes as effective as those who are supposedly well trained and experienced (Sprafkin, 1970), most studies show that counselors who are believed to be expert do have a greater effect on clients, at least under certain conditions (e.g., Beutler, Jobe, & Elkins, 1974; Binderman, Fretz, Scott, & Abrams, 1972; Greenberg, 1969; Heppner & Dixon, 1978; McKee & Smouse, 1983; Strong & Schmidt, 1970a). Thus, although perceived expertise may not be absolutely necessary, a counselor's effectiveness is usually enhanced if the client perceives the counselor to be well trained and/or experienced.

But what of actual, rather than merely perceived, expertise? *Are* experienced therapists more effective than inexperienced ones? Exhaustive reviews of the literature by Auerbach and Johnson (1977) and Parloff, Waskow, and Wolfe (1978) concluded that the results relevant to this question are quite mixed. Although there is evidence that experienced therapists establish better relationships with their clients than less experienced ones, the relationship between therapist experience and therapeutic outcome is surprisingly weak (Auerbach & Johnson, 1977).

In any case, because perceived expertise often facilitates treatment effectiveness, several studies have explored factors that lead clients to infer that a therapist is expert. These studies show that perceived expertness is heightened by factors such as the possession of advanced degrees, the extent of the therapist's experience, the presence of diplomas in the therapist's office, the use of professional jargon, professional (as opposed to casual) clothing, and socially skilled nonverbal behavior (Atkinson & Carskaddon, 1975; Carkhuff, 1969; Greenberg, 1969; Kerr & Dell, 1976; Scheid, 1976; Schmidt & Strong, 1970; Sprafkin, 1970; Strong & Schmidt, 1970a). Such findings raise the issue of whether counselors and psychotherapists should purposefully manage their impressions in ways that portray them as expert, intentionally using diplomas, clothing, nonverbal cues, and so on to suggest expertise (cf. Korda, 1976; Waxer, 1978). Many therapists find the thought repugnant, whereas others argue that if such simple strategies heighten their effectiveness with clients, they should be considered.

Trustworthiness

Trust in a communicator is a primary determinant of attitude change in any encounter (e.g., McGuire, 1969), and it is particularly important in counseling settings. As Tyler (1965, p. 16) put it, "the client's confidence in the counselor, the assumption that he can *believe* what this person tells him, is the essential foundation for the whole counseling process." Not only are clients unlikely to heed the advice of counselors they distrust, but they are less likely to risk openly disclosing and confronting their difficulties when they do not trust the therapist. Unfortunately, despite the central role of trust in therapeutic relationships, little research has been conducted either on the factors that lead clients to trust their therapists or on the effects of trust on psychological change within therapy.

Strong (1968) suggested that whether a client perceives a counselor as trustworthy depends upon four factors: the counselor's reputation for honesty, the trustworthiness implied by the counselor's social role (being a minister or a physician, for example), the sincerity and openness of the counselor's interactions with the client, and the perceived lack of motivation for the counselor's personal gain. The few studies in the area have not specifically examined these determinants of trustworthiness, but have combined several within a single study. Studies show that interviewers who are inconsistent, inaccurate, unethical (violating confidentiality), or even overweight appear less trustworthy to clients (e.g., McGee & Smouse, 1983; Rothmeier & Dixon, 1980). In general, perceptions of trustworthiness appear to be affected more by the therapist's general manner than what he or she says (Kaul & Schmidt, 1971; Roll, Schmidt, & Kaul, 1972).

If social psychological research can be generalized to the counseling setting, we would predict that trustworthiness is a necessary (though not sufficient) precondition for successful counseling, perhaps more important than expertness (Kelman & Hovland, 1953; Walster, Aronson, & Abrahams, 1966; see also Corrigan et al., 1978). Although a few counseling outcome studies have obtained effects of trustworthiness (e.g., Rothmeier & Dixon, 1980), others have not (Strong & Schmidt, 1970b), and much more work on the topic is needed.

Attractiveness

Attractiveness refers to the degree to which a client likes the therapist. Research both in social psychology and in analogue therapy settings reveals that interpersonal attraction mediates social influence under some circumstances. However, considerably more research has been conducted on the factors that lead clients to like their therapists than on the effects of liking on therapy outcome.

As social psychological studies would predict (e.g., Berscheid & Walster, 1974), physically attractive counselors are generally rated more positively than unattractive ones. For example, Lewis and Walsh (1978) found that attractive counselors were judged to be more professional, interesting, and competent than unattractive counselors (see also Cash, Begley, McGown, & Weise, 1975; Cash & Kehr, 1978). The nature of the relationship between physical attractiveness and liking for a counselor is interesting; there is evidence that being unattractive reduces a client's liking for the counselor, but that being attractive does not necessarily increase liking (Corrigan et al., 1980).

Not surprisingly, warm and attentive counselors are liked better than cold and aloof ones (Patton, 1969; Schmidt & Strong, 1971). Similarly, nonverbal behaviors indicating attentiveness and interest (such as eye contact, nodding, smiling, forward lean) create greater liking for counselors (Claiborn, 1979; Kleinke, Staneski, & Berger, 1975; LaCrosse, 1975; Strong, Taylor, Bratten, & Loper, 1971).

Social psychological research also demonstrates that similarity enhances attraction (Byrne, 1971), and, again, counseling research supports this pattern. When clients are told that they and their counselor are similar or that they share certain attitudes, their liking for the counselor increases (Goldstein, 1971; Hogan, Hall, & Blank, 1972). However, initial information about similarity may be offset by new information gleaned during future therapy sessions. The effects of attitudinal similarity on attraction weaken beyond the initial counseling session (Goldstein, 1971).

Thus, counselor attractiveness is affected by various cues regarding appearance, nonverbal behavior, warmth, and similarity, but the question arises whether attraction toward a therapist enhances the outcome of therapy. Although research in experimental social psychology suggests that better liked communicators are more influential (Berscheid, 1966; Byrne, 1971;

McGuire, 1969), the findings in counseling studies are mixed. Some studies show positive effects of counselor attractiveness on treatment effectiveness (Patton, 1969; Strong & Dixon, 1971), whereas others do not (Dell, 1973; Schmidt & Strong, 1971; Sell, 1974; see Abramowitz, Berger, and Weary, 1982, Corrigan et al., 1980, and Dorn, 1984, for reviews).

In part, this complex pattern of results may reflect the fact that attractiveness may heighten counselors' influence only under certain conditions. For example, if a therapist is already perceived as competent and trustworthy, whether the client likes the therapist may be irrelevant because the client may participate fully in therapy anyway. However, if the therapist is viewed as less competent, clients may be less committed to the therapeutic relationship unless they are attracted to the therapist as an individual. As Goldstein (1971) pointed out, attraction may affect therapeutic outcomes by increasing the likelihood that the client will return for future sessions and participate actively and willingly in them. The authors know a woman who remains in therapy despite the fact that she doesn't view her therapist as particularly effective simply because she *likes* her therapist. Indeed, Strong and Dixon (1971) found that attractiveness increased counselors' influence only when they were viewed as inexpert rather than expert.

Critique of Research on Counselor Characteristics

It seems, then, that counselors who are perceived as experts are usually more effective than nonexperts even though nonexperts are often effective; that trustworthiness may contribute to therapeutic effects, though more work is needed; and that attractiveness may help inexpert counselors but is of limited value to expert counselors. Thus, these interpersonal variables affect counseling outcomes, but the results are not as straightforward as either social psychological research or clinical wisdom would lead one to expect. There are several possible reasons for this.

First, the experiments designed to test the impact of counselor characteristics upon the counselor's effectiveness usually employ analogue counseling situations involving a single contact between the counselor and client. As such, they tell us only about the impact of counselor characteristics during the first 60 minutes (or less) of an initial counseling session. The effects of some counselor variables may strengthen over time, whereas others may attenuate. For example, liking may become a more important determinant of therapeutic outcome as therapy progresses over time and the client persists in therapy, despite urges to quit, because he or she likes the counselor. On the other hand, reputed experience may be important only initially, until the client forms his or her own impressions of the counselor. Although existing research highlights potential contributors to the outcome of treatment, more work is needed in ongoing, long-term relationships between counselors and clients.

Second, many source characteristics may have their effects by increasing the receiver's attention to the message (Hovland et al., 1953). For example, people may pay more attention to credible and attractive sources than to less credible communicators. Although this attentional difference may have a strong effect on counselor effectiveness in real counseling encounters, it may be less important in research settings where "clients" usually know they are subjects in an experiment. Being subjects, they may attend closely to all the details of the session, regardless of the characteristics of the counselor, thereby making inexpert counselors appear more effective than they would normally be.

Third, the kinds of changes targeted in counseling are usually more involving and complex than those of interest in basic social psychological research. It may be that the psychological changes of interest in counseling and psychotherapy typically require stronger manipulations of credibility and attractiveness over a longer period of time.

In sum, although expertness, trustworthiness, and attractiveness do affect treatment outcomes, the complexity of the results should prompt additional research, preferably in clinical field studies, with increased attention to improved theory and methodology.

Message Characteristics

In comparison to the extensive research on counselor characteristics, message and client characteristics have received short shrift in counseling research. Message characteristics that social psychologists have studied include one-sided versus two-sided messages, messages that elicit fear, the degree of discrepancy between the message and the target's initial opinion, whether the communicator draws explicit conclusions, repetition of the message, and message style (the degree to which the presentation of the message is dynamic versus subdued, for example). Within counseling and psychotherapy, most attention has been devoted to message discrepancy, fear appeals, and stylistic factors.

Message Discrepancy

For every person who seeks counseling or psychotherapy, there is a gap between how the individual perceives his or her circumstances and how the individual would like things to be. Part of the role of the counselor is to help the client minimize this discrepancy by various cognitive and behavioral means (Strong & Claiborn, 1982), including direct suggestions regarding how the client might develop more functional ways of thinking and acting. Given that a therapist wishes to induce a cognitive or behavioral change in a client, how discrepant from the client's initial position should the therapist's recommendation be?

In general, social psychological research has demonstrated a positive, linear relationship between the magnitude of the discrepancy and the amount of resultant change (see McGuire, 1969). That is, the greater the discrepancy between the position advocated by a communicator and that initially held by a target, the greater the eventual change in the target's position. There is an upper limit to this effect, however, a point beyond which increasingly discrepant messages are dismissed outright and are less influential.

Overall, experimental and correlational investigations in counseling settings support this pattern—the greater the initial difference between the client's position and that advocated by the therapist, the greater the change that is likely to ultimately occur (Beutler, 1971; Beutler, Jobe, & Elkins, 1974; Beutler, Johnson, Neville, & Workman, 1972; Binderman et al., 1972; Patton, 1969). However, consistent with basic researach (e.g., Aronson, Turner, & Carlsmith, 1963; Bergin, 1962), there is an upper limit to how discrepant a counselor's communication may be and still produce change (Strong and Dixon, 1971).

The Effects of Fear-Laden Messages

Throughout history, a common means of changing others' attitudes and behavior has been to instill in them the fear of dire consequences that will result if one's advice or commands are not followed. For example, physicians describe the adverse effects of failure to comply with medical regimens, evangelists detail the horrors of hell to potential converts, and parents stress to their children the painful consequences of their misdeeds.

Several studies have examined the impact of fear-laden messages during attempts to persuade subjects to change dysfunctional behaviors such as smoking, improper dental care, and failing to use seat belts (see Higbee, 1969; Leventhal, 1970; McGuire, 1969; for reviews). This research shows that messages that induce fear can facilitate attitude and behavior change, as long as the fear produced by the message is relatively strong, the target believes that the fearful event has a high probability of occurring, and the target thinks that the fearful events will be avoided by changing his or her attitudes or behavior (Mewborn & Rogers, 1979; Rogers, 1975). Although therapists may be reluctant to use fear therapeutically, there are instances (such as those in which a client's behavior is dangerous to himself or herself or to others) in which other modes of persuasion may be buttressed by the use of fear to the client's benefit.

Communicator Style

A few studies have examined the effects of communicator style on social influence, seeking to determine whether active, dynamic communicators are more effective than less active, subdued ones. Their findings are mixed, the results seeming to depend on the attributions the target makes about the communicator on the basis of message delivery.

For example, an early study found that "dynamic" presentations were less effective in producing attitude change and were more likely to be viewed by subjects as propaganda, suggesting that subjects inferred that dynamic communicators were trying to manipulate them (Dietrich, 1946). On the other hand, communicators who talk quickly are sometimes more effective than slow talkers, possibly because fast speech connotes knowledgeability and honesty, whereas slower paced talking seems overly cautious and suspicious (Apple, Streeter, & Krauss, 1979; Maclachlan, 1979; Miller, Maruyama, Beaber, & Valone, 1976).

Within the context of therapy, such stylistic factors have been found to be related to therapist-client interactions, but rarely to the outcome of therapy (see Pope, 1977, for a review). For example, Pope concluded that, although a high activity level eases the strain of the interaction between therapists and clients, there is no evidence that a high activity level is more therapeutic.

However, the degree to which a therapist is directive (offering explicit interpretations and advice, structuring and guiding the client's train of thought) versus nondirective does appear to have an impact on therapeutic outcomes. Specifically, clients who have an internal locus of control, who are defensive at the outset of therapy, or who are more highly educated prefer and benefit most from a nondirective therapist, whereas externally oriented, nondefensive, less educated clients do better with directive approaches (see Berzins, 1977; Goldstein, 1971; Pope, 1977). Thus, contrary to the schools of therapy that recommend either a directive or a nondirective therapeutic style (such as rational-emotive versus client-centered approaches), the scanty research available suggests that each approach may be optimal for certain client groups.

Nonverbal Behavior

A therapist's effectiveness is also affected by his or her nonverbal behaviors (Waxer, 1978). Researchers have identified a set of nonverbal behaviors that enhance clients' ratings of the counselor and therapeutic effectiveness: a high degree of eye contact, a forward body lean, an attentive and concerned facial expression, maintaining a close interpersonal distance to the client (within three feet or so), smiling at the appropriate times, spontaneous (rather than "mindless") head nodding, and a relaxed, open body position (Lee, Hallberg, Kocsis, & Haase, 1980; Lee, Zingle, Patterson, Ivey, & Haase, 1976; Smith-Hanen, 1977).

The impact of these sorts of behaviors upon therapeutic outcome appears to be mediated by the inferences clients draw from them. Counselors who use attentive, socially skilled nonverbal behaviors are perceived as more expert, trustworthy, attractive, and persuasive and, thus, stimulate clients to be more open and to adopt the counselor's suggestions (Waxer, 1978). Indeed, in one study counselors who used "inattentive" nonverbal behaviors were rated only half as positively as "attentive" counselors (Krumboltz, Varenhorst, & Thoresen, 1967).

Critique of Research on Message Characteristics

Clearly, more research is required before solid conclusions regarding the impact of message characteristics in counseling can be drawn and applied with confidence to therapeutic settings. Future research dealing with therapeutic style should pay close attention to the inferences clients draw from therapist behaviors, because the impact of therapist style is probably mediated by such inferences. Further, because there are great cross-cultural differences in how various stylistic and nonverbal behaviors are interpreted, researchers and practitioners should be cognizant of the limitations of this line of research (see Yuen & Tinsley, 1981).

Client Characteristics

A good deal of social psychological research has examined how characteristics of the recipients of a persuasive communication mediate the degree to which they are influenced by it, but this topic has not been explored seriously in counseling and psychotherapy research. Instead, most research has studied how similarities between clients and therapists affect the counseling session.

YAVIS Factors

The strongest data relating client characteristics to the therapeutic process are provided by Goldstein's (1971) study of "YAVIS" clients (young, attractive, verbal, intelligent, and successful), who are generally more similar to their therapists in background, values, and life-style than are non-YAVIS clients. This similarity may affect not only the client's perceptions of the therapist but also the therapist's reactions to the client. Studies have shown, for example, that lower-class individuals are less likely to be accepted for counseling and psychotherapy, less likely to receive intensive therapy, and more likely to terminate treatment prematurely (Lorion, 1974; Parloff, Waskow, & Wolfe, 1978). Further, the socioeconomic status of a therapist's family of origin is related to his or her willingness to see lower-class patients (Kandel, 1966).

When therapists see non-YAVIS clients, their attitudes may be conveyed to the client in subtle ways that have an indirect effect on the outcome of therapy. For example, counselors tend to rate more positively clients who are physically attractive, are verbally fluent, and participate more fully in their therapy (Lewis, Davis, Walker, & Jennings, 1981); this attitude thus favors YAVIS clients. Not surprisingly, YAVIS and non-YAVIS clients react differently to counselors with varying characteristics (Goldstein, 1971).

Personality Variables

The effects of clients' personalities and, specifically, the degree of similarity between clients' and therapists' personality profiles have received a modicum of attention. A variety of personality measures have been used, including the MMPI, the Myers-Briggs Type Indicator, the Fundamental Interpersonal Relations Orientation Scale (FIRO-B), the Personality Research Form, and a number of specific trait scales (see Abramowitz et al., 1982; Berzins, 1977; Parloff et al., 1978, for reviews).

The most consistent results have been obtained using the FIRO-B. The FIRO-B assesses the compatibility of two people in terms of their needs to originate and receive behaviors along three dimensions: inclusion, control, and affection. Without going into specific details, studies using the FIRO-B show that increased compatibility on some dimensions is related to treatment outcome. In the Goldstein (1971) study mentioned above, for example, non-YAVIS clients were more attracted to their therapists over a 12-week period when they were highly compatible on the FIRO-B. Apparently, compatible therapist-client dyads find it easier to communicate than do incompatible dyads, thereby facilitating the therapeutic relationship and the outcome of therapy.

Finally, a few studies have examined the relationship between client personality and responsiveness to particular kinds of treatment under the assumption that people may be predisposed to prefer certain therapeutic approaches over others. We have already noted that internally controlled and well-educated clients prefer nondirective therapies, whereas externally controlled and less well educated persons prefer therapists who provide more structure and direction (Berzins, 1977; Goldstein, 1971). Further, subjects classified as "thinking" types on the Myers-Briggs Type Indicator rate rational-emotive therapy (which is highly cognitive) more highly than do "feeling" types, and indicate that they would be more likely to choose a rational-emotive therapist in the future (Stoltenberg, Maddux, & Pace, 1986).

Summary

The sparse research on client characteristics suggests that they interact with counselor characteristics and types of therapy to affect the therapeutic relationship and, in some instances, the outcome of therapy. The available data do not identify which client variables are most important, but the existing studies should sensitize researchers and practitioners to the fact that not all therapeutic approaches are equally effective on all types of clients (Leary, in press-b). This point was discussed by Kiesler (1966), who argued that researchers and therapists implicitly operate under a "myth of uniformity" that assumes that clients constitute a relatively homogeneous group. Future research is needed to identify important client characteristics that are related to therapist influence and client change as a function of specific difficulties and treatments.

Critique of the Social Influence Model of Counseling

As we reviewed the research based upon the social influence model of counseling and psychotherapy, we purposefully refrained from critiquing specific studies or the model upon which they are based. Our review completed, it is now important to discuss three general issues regarding the social influence model of counseling and psychotherapy.

Inconsistency of the Results

Although many of the findings of counseling research are consistent with those in experimental social psychology, some inconsistencies have emerged both between the counseling and the social psychological studies and among several of the counseling studies themselves. For example, the effects of counselor attractiveness on clients' acceptance of therapeutic "messages" is not as strong or as straightforward as experimental social psychological research would suggest. Similarly, within counseling research, some studies have found effects of counselor trustworthiness, but many others have not.

Although social psychological and counseling researchers purport to study many of the same variables (credibility, fear-inducing communications, and so on), the studies themselves differ so markedly that it is nearly impossible to compare them directly. As a result, it is difficult to know whether failures to conceptually replicate basic social psychological findings using counseling paradigms are due to the validity of the hypotheses being tested, the generalizability of the effects from one domain to another, or differences in methods and subjects used. Although many of the findings of basic attitude change research do generalize to real and analogue counseling settings, the inconsistencies are troublesome and suggest that tighter lines should be drawn between the conceptualizations and research strategies used in basic and applied research.

Generalizability to Real Therapy Settings

Researchers and practitioners in counseling and psychotherapy are understandably interested in whether the findings of research studies generalize to real therapy settings. Three considerations relevant to this issue emerge from the social influence literature.

First, although most counseling studies contain essential ingredients of real therapy settings (at minimum, a "counselor" and a "client"), they differ from real-world therapy in important ways that affect the generalizability of their results. As noted earlier, most counseling studies involve a single contact between a counselor and client, and client change is often assessed as early as 20 minutes after the start of the session. Thus, though acceptably designed and well controlled, these studies are most relevant to the initial stages of therapy. (This is not to say that they are not relevant to later stages of therapy, only that their relevance is unclear.) Future research should investigate factors that affect counseling processes later in the thera- peutic relationship, possibly drawing on models of relationship development in social psychology (e.g., Levinger, 1980).

Second, most social influence research, whether in social or counseling psychology, deals with psychological changes that are less complex than most of the issues for which people seek professional help. Although at- tempts have been made to address behaviors relevant to real counseling settings, it is difficult to study the remediation of problems as complex and intense as those seen regularly by practicing psychologists. This is not to berate the work that has been done, but to highlight its limitations and the need for studies of more serious client difficulties.

Third, most social influence research assumes, as a convenient fiction, that influence in therapy is unidirectional and static. In part, this is so be- cause the social influence model was developed in the context of studies of mass communication in which the assumption of unidirectional influence from a speaker to an audience is tenable. However, when dealing with dyadic interactions, such as those found in therapy, this approach portrays only one aspect of the interpersonal process. Although dynamic, "systems" models of behavior that incorporate interdependence and mutual influence between the individuals are complex and typically difficult to test, such approaches may be needed to capture more faithfully the interpersonal dy- namics of therapy (see Strong & Claiborn, 1982). We will return to this point momentarily.

Having discussed issues dealing with the generalizability of the social influence studies, we should make two other points. First, contrary to what is commonly assumed, the external validity of a study does not depend upon the degree to which the experimental setting mirrors the situation to which one would like the results to generalize (i.e., mundane realism). Regardless of the experimental setting or the subjects used, the external validity of a study is always an empirical question that requires conceptual replications in other settings using other subjects. Thus, a clinical field study using real therapists and a clinical sample is not inherently more generalizable than a laboratory experiment on social influence using artificial tasks and college sophomores (see Mook, 1983).

To take the point a step further, a strong case can be made that the results of specific studies should *never* be generalized to the real world, no matter where the study was conducted, what methods were used, or what kinds of subjects were employed. Generally speaking, research studies such as those reviewed in this chapter are conducted to evaluate hypotheses derived from theory. Only after repeated tests of theoretical propositions confirm a the- ory's merit should the theory be applied toward understanding, predicting, and controlling events in the real world. Viewed in this manner, *any* empiri- cal finding is too suspect to be generalized outside of the immediate study in which it was obtained. The problem, however, is that little of the research discussed in this chapter was designed to test theoretical notions about social influence and psychological change.

Lack of Theory

The greatest weakness of the social influence literature, both within social psychology and counseling, is its generally atheoretical nature. By and large, research findings in the area represent a loosely organized collection of empirical generalizations, unconnected by an overriding theoretical framework. To some degree, this problem can be traced to the original work by Hovland et al. (1953), which was only loosely based on a formal theoretical model. Studies of social influence have been revealing and useful, but as a whole they have done little to contribute to a deeper understanding of the *processes* involved in psychological change. Thus, we devote the last section of this chapter to a brief examination of three integrative theoretical models of social influence.

Theoretical Considerations

A complete examination of theories of attitude change and social influence relevant to counseling and psychotherapy would go far beyond the objectives of this book, but a brief overview of three important models may help explicate the interpersonal processes discussed in this chapter.

The Yale Research Program and Learning Theory

Although the original studies reviewed by Hovland et al. (1953) were not designed to construct or test a systematic theory of persuasion, they were based loosely on learning theory. In this framework, attitude change is regarded as a learning process, and change itself depends upon factors that facilitate the learning of the persuasive message. According to this view, whether an attitude is learned depends upon the degree to which the message is *attended to, comprehended, and accepted.* Thus, the various source, message, and recipient factors that faciliate attitude change may lead people to attend to, understand, and/or accept persuasive messages.

For example, people may pay greater attention to credible than noncredible sources and evaluate their arguments less critically, increasing the probability of acceptance. Similarly, fear-inducing messages heighten both attention and acceptance. The usefulness of this framework within counseling settings has not been fully evaluated, but it is at least plausible and simplistic enough to serve as a rough rule of thumb. When in doubt, counselors and psychotherapists may wish to proceed in a manner that promotes attention, comprehension, and acceptance of their communications to the client.

The Dynamic-Interdependence Approach

As noted earlier, traditional approaches to psychological change view social influence as unidirectional. Arguing that linear models of influence do not capture the richness of actual therapy relationships, Johnson and Matross (1977) have presented a "dynamic" approach to psychotherapy. In this model, counselor and client are said to have an interdependent relationship in which they negotiate the definition and achievement of mutual goals. The relationship between counselor and client involves mutual influence, with each affecting the other's beliefs, emotions, and behavior. Further, Johnson and Matross apply research on mixed-motive situations to analyze the process through which influence occurs.

According to this model, influence occurs because both the counselor and the client have resources upon which the other is dependent. Consistent with social psychological models of influence, Johnson and Matross maintain that influence requires that one party be dependent upon the other for valued resources (Thibaut & Kelley, 1959). To state their thesis in a single proposition:

> A therapist influences a client to the extent that the therapist furnishes resources needed by the client for the accomplishment of highly valued goals and to the extent that the client cannot obtain these resources at a lower cost from other relationships. (Johnson & Matross, 1977, p. 405).

From this perspective, the factors that mediate social influence are those that cause the client to believe that the therapist possesses the resources needed for accomplishment of the client's goals.

An important feature of this model is that it acknowledges the dynamic nature of therapeutic relationships, focusing on the relationship over time and taking into account the many variables involved, the bidirectional nature of influence, and the possibility of feedback loops. Although the dynamic approach has not been widely studied or used, it highlights factors not included in other models of influence.

The Elaboration Likelihood Model

The newest theory to be applied to psychotherapeutic change is the elaboration likelihood model (ELM; Petty & Cacioppo, 1981). According to this approach, there are two distinct routes by which attitudes change as a result of persuasive communication. The *central route* involves attitude change that occurs as the result of conscious consideration of the merits of a communication. For central-route processing to occur, however, the individual must be both motivated and able to assess the merits of the received message. If these two conditions are met, whether the message will be influential depends primarily upon the individual's analysis of its merit.

However, if the individual lacks either the motivation or the ability to think about the message, attitudes may be affected by extraneous factors, such as characteristics of the source or message, or by prexisting biases to accept or reject the message. Such factors may affect attitude change via the *peripheral route* without the individual having to do any extensive cognitive manipulation of the incoming message. According to Petty and Cacioppo (1981), attitude change that occurs via the peripheral route is less enduring than change that occurs centrally.

Although the ELM has been tested in only a handful of studies, it has the potential for making sense out of the complex patterns of results described in this chapter. Effects of counselor, message, and client factors may be inconsistent because other relevant factors (such as the client's motivation and ability to think about the message) were not taken into account. For example, according to the ELM, an important determinant of whether a communication is processed in a central or peripheral manner is the involvement of the target in the issue under consideration. Highly involved targets are more likely to process a message centrally, whereas less involved targets should use peripheral cues. Thus, the theory identifies an important factor not included in other models.

Both laboratory experiments (e.g., Petty, Cacioppo, & Goldman, 1981) and analogue counseling studies (Stoltenberg, Cacioppo, Petty, & Davis, 1985; Stoltenberg, & McNeill, 1984) provide empirical support for ELM, although the full extent of its usefulness has not yet been assessed.

Conclusions

That counseling and psychotherapy involve interpersonal influence processes is beyond question. What is not clear, however, is how this process should best be conceptualized. Although a huge body of research has identified factors that contribute to counselor influence, there is a pressing need for a theoretical model that can account for the available results. In our view, this model must deal both with the intricacies of the relationship between counselor and client and with the processes within the client that mediate cognitive, emotional, and behavioral change.

Chapter 10

Behavioral Compliance and Psychological Change

Underlying the social influence model discussed in the previous chapter is the assumption that, if people can be persuaded to change their beliefs or attitudes, changes in dysfunctional behavior should occur. Thus, the focus of the influence model is on factors that make the client more receptive to the counselor's interpretations, suggestions, and teachings.

Although cognitive change can result in behavioral change, the opposite process also occurs: Inducing someone to change his or her behavior can, if certain conditions are met, result in cognitive change. As Madsen and Madsen (1972, p. 31) put it, "It is much easier to act your way into a new way of thinking than to think your way into a new way of acting." This simple fact suggests a useful mechanism for promoting psychological change. Simply stated, inducing a client to engage in new, more functional ways of acting can result in new, more functional ways of thinking and feeling. This process constitutes our focus in this chapter.

Attitude-Discrepant Behavior and Psychological Change

Within experimental social psychology, the impact of behavior on cognitive change has often been studied within what is known as the "forced compliance paradigm." In hundreds of studies, subjects have been induced to say or do things that are inconsistent with their existing beliefs, and their resultant beliefs or attitudes have been assessed. Typically, people who engage in these counterattitudinal or attitude-discrepant actions subsequently change their attitudes so that they are more consistent with their prior behavior. (The "boring task" study, in which subjects were induced to lie to another subject [Festinger & Carlsmith, 1959], is probably familiar to most readers).

Hundreds of studies over the past 25 years have demonstrated the forced compliance effect as researchers have attempted to identify the conditions under which the performance of attitude-discrepant behavior does and does not result in cognitive change. Although the phenomenon has proven to be quite complex, a few necessary conditions have been isolated. In particular, there is general agreement that in order for counterattitudinal behavior to result in attitude change the individual must feel responsible for his or her actions and their consequences. In other words, the person must have some degree of choice in performing the action and must have foreseen the consequences of the behavior (Wicklund & Brehm, 1976). As we will see, this caveat is important in applying counterattitudinal procedures to clinical practice.

Lest the reader fail to see the relationship between the forced compliance research paradigm and the processes of counseling and psychotherapy, we should point out that many therapeutic techniques require clients to behave in ways in which they prefer not to behave. Clients may be urged to discuss distressing topics, engage in actions that produce anxiety or are inconsistent with their prevailing values, role-play positions with which they do not agree, abandon enjoyable vices, or otherwise engage in unpleasant, effortful, or attitude-discrepant tasks. For example, in marital therapy, feuding spouses may be told to convincingly argue one another's positions. In other cases, therapists may urge their clients to engage in atypical, counterattitudinal behavior by being assertive, more independent, or less authoritarian. Many clients seek professional help in order to relinquish dysfunctional but enjoyable habits such as smoking, gambling, or overeating. In each of these examples, clients are in a type of forced compliance situation—they are induced to behave in an attitude-discrepant fashion—and it is of considerable importance for clinicians and counselors to understand what is involved when they induce clients to do things they prefer not to do.

Theoretical Explanations of the Effect

Before discussing the clinical implications of forced compliance research, let us briefly examine three theories that provide explanations of it. A full discussion of each of these approaches would go far beyond the confines of this chapter, so we will refer the interested reader to useful sources as we proceed.

Cognitive dissonance theory. The earliest studies that examined the effects of counterattitudinal behavior on cognitive change were conducted as tests of cognitive dissonance theory (see Brehm & Cohen, 1962). According to this approach (Festinger, 1957), a state of dissonance is created when an individual has two cognitions (thoughts about oneself or the world) that imply the obverse of one another. For example, believing oneself to be highly intelligent is dissonant with scoring in the lowest quartile on an IQ test. Similarly, abhorring the Ku Klux Klan is dissonant with being best friends with the Grand Master of the local KKK. According to Festinger, the state of dissonance is aversive, thereby motivating the individual to avoid dissonance when possible and to reduce dissonance once it has been aroused.

People may reduce dissonance by modifying their cognitions in ways that restore a state of consonance. For example, they can add new consonant elements or eliminate dissonant cognitions regarding the issue, such as when the friend of the KKK Grand Master justifies his friendship by concluding that what his friends do in their spare time is none of his business. Dissonance may also be reduced by changing dissonant cognitions into consonant ones. According to the theory, this is what happened in Festinger and Carlsmith's (1959) "boring task" study. To relieve dissonance, subjects who had told someone that the boring task was interesting changed their attitude so that their attitudes and behavior were no longer discrepant.

According to the theory, people will not experience dissonance if they have no choice but to perform the behavior or are unable to foresee its consequences. From the perspective of the theory, it is simply not dissonance-arousing to do counterattitudinal things with the proverbial gun to one's head. For this reason, research has obtained less attitude change following counterattitudinal behavior the greater the pressures on the individual to perform the action. For example, subjects who are offered a large sum of money to behave in a counterattitudinal fashion typically experience less dissonance, and less subsequent cognitive change, than subjects who are paid less. With little justification for their actions, people experience greater dissonance and are more likely to change their cognitions to bring them in line with their behavior. The clinical implications of this fact will become clearer below.

Self-perception theory. An alternative explanation of the effects of counterattitudinal behavior has been offered by Bem (1972). According to his self-perception theory, people sometimes come to know their personal attitudes and other internal states by examining their behavior and the conditions under which it occurs. When people do not have well-formed attitudes or beliefs in a particular domain, they infer their attitudes from their behavior, much in the same way that they infer other people's attitudes.

According to self-perception theory, subjects in forced compliance studies seem to change their attitudes following counterattitudinal behavior not because they experience dissonance, but because they have inferred their attitudes from their behavior. Having told the waiting individual that the boring task was interesting, subjects in the Festinger and Carlsmith (1959) study inferred that they thought the task *was* interesting, for example.

Like dissonance theory, self-perception theory emphasizes the importance of perceived responsibility. If people do not feel personally responsible for their behavior, they are unlikely to infer that they wanted to behave as they did or believed what they said. Thus, providing a large inducement to perform an action may lead to behavioral compliance but will not lead individuals to infer that they agree with their behavior.

Self-presentation theory. In the quest for attitude-discrepant behavior, the typical forced compliance study induces subjects to cheat, lie, harm others, or otherwise appear immoral, unattractive, irrational, or incompetent to others in the experimental setting. In light of this, it is possible that the attitude change observed following counterattitudinal behavior reflects a self-presentational strategy designed to control how others view the subject (Tedeschi & Rosenfeld, 1981; Tedeschi, Schlenker, & Bonoma, 1971; chapter 5, this volume).

When people think they are viewed in a socially undesirable fashion, they offer accounts in an attempt to lead others to interpret their behavior in more acceptable terms (Goffman, 1955; Schlenker, 1980). Imagine a subject who has lied in return for money, as in the Festinger and Carlsmith study. When subsequently asked his evaluation of the boring task, the subject has two options: He can either admit that the task was excrutiatingly boring, in which case he clearly has lied to an unwitting person for profit, or he can maintain that the task was really not so boring after all, which portrays his actions in a more acceptable light. By espousing attitudes that are consistent with the behavior they have just performed, people may be viewed as consistent and honest rather than as inconsistent and deceitful. Thus, the self-presentation approach argues that what appears to be attitude change is really an interpersonal face-saving strategy.

As with dissonance and self-perception theories, personal responsibility is central to the self-presentation formulation. People will perceive a need to save face in others' eyes only if they are seen as responsible for their undesirable behavior and its consequences. If one is forced to lie under penalty of death, there is no need to account for one's action by insisting that one believed the lie.

Critique of the Three Approaches

Space does not permit a discussion of the enormous literatures that have been built around these three approaches, but a brief statement of their relative merits may be helpful. Although research exists that supports all three theories, support for the self-perception theory seems to be the weakest. The biggest problem with self-perception theory is that it applies only when the individual does not hold salient or important attitudes. As Taylor (1975, p. 131) observed, self-perception theory holds only under "conditions where one is asked one's attitude about an inconsequential issue."

When attitudes or beliefs are strongly held, data tend to support predictions derived from dissonance theory (Fazio, Zanna, & Cooper, 1977; Green, 1974; Ross & Shulman, 1973; Woodward, 1972). However, this theory, too, has been criticized extensively and has undergone extensive revisions that have shifted its focus from cognitive inconsistency per se to a focus on behaviors that threaten one's self-concept. Nevertheless, dissonance theory has strong empirical support and provides a broad framework in which a great deal of behavior can be explained.

Because the self-presentation approach is rather new, the verdict on its utility is still out. However, initial experimental results have been supportive. In a series of three studies, Schlenker, Forsyth, Leary, and Miller (1980) provided strong evidence that attitude change following counterattitudinal behavior serves self-presentational functions. For example, "dissonance-like" effects were obtained only when subjects expressed their attitudes to others who had observed their counterattitudinal, socially undesirable actions. When subjects expressed their attitudes to those who had not observed their actions, no effects were obtained, strongly suggesting that subjects strategically modified their attitude statements in order to "save face" (see Tedeschi & Rosenfeld, 1981).

Clinical Applications

We commend the reader's patience during this whirlwind tour of the social psychological literature dealing with the effects of counterattitudinal behavior. Armed with these theoretical perspectives, we can now turn our attention to the implications of this phenomenon for clinical and counseling practice.

Role-Playing

Many counseling and clinical psychologists use role-playing techniques to promote change in their clients. These techniques are commonly used in cases in which the client is in conflict with another individual (such as marriage counseling or organizational conflict resolution) and the therapist wants the client to understand better the perspective of the "opponent." Alternatively, the client may be asked to role play himself or herself in situations that are distressing or threatening, such as those requiring assertiveness. A considerable body of research has demonstrated the effectiveness of role playing in these contexts (Janis & Gilmore, 1965; Johnson, 1971; Muney & Deutsch, 1968). For example, in dyadic problem-solving and negotiation settings, people who role-play their opponent's position change their attitudes more than people who negotiate without role reversal or who only listen to their partner engage in role reversal (Johnson, 1967, 1971). Although it is clear that role playing promotes cognitive change, researchers and practitioners disagree regarding the best explanation of role-playing effects.

Early role-playing studies showed that improvising speeches in support of positions with which one disagrees produces more attitude change than either listening to a persuasive speech or reading a prepared speech (Greenwald & Albert, 1968; Janis & Gilmore, 1965; Janis & King, 1954; King

& Janis, 1956). The original explanation offered for these findings posited that attitude change occurs during active role playing because, in the process of improvising their speeches, people are brought into greater "cognitive contact" with opposing positions. The role-playing individual thinks up and uses those arguments that he or she finds most convincing, and thus generates persuasive arguments that are tailored to himself or herself. In essence, role playing helps convince the individual of the correctness of the other's position (Elms & Janis, 1965; Janis & Gilmore, 1965).

One corollary of this explanation is that the greater the incentive offered to the individual to role-play, the better the arguments he or she should generate (à la reinforcement theory) and the more attitude change should occur. However, as we have seen, greater inducements to perform attitude-discrepant actions typically result in less rather than more attitude change (see, however, Janis & Gilmore, 1965). According to cognitive dissonance theory, this is because the effects of role playing depend upon the generation of dissonance, which is minimized by external inducements that decrease personal responsibility. Within marriage therapy, for example, dissonance theory would advise that clients should perceive that they are role playing by choice and should be urged to improvise their own roles rather than rely on prompts from the therapist or spouse. The greater the perceived responsibility for one's behavior in a role-playing session, the greater the dissonance that is aroused; the realization that "I am freely arguing for positions with which I don't agree" produces maximum dissonance. And greater dissonance results in greater cognitive change toward the counterattitudinal position one has just argued.

Self-perception and self-presentation theories make precisely the same recommendation, although for different reasons. To the degree that people infer their attitudes from their behavior only when their actions are not controlled by situational factors (Bem, 1972), self-perception theory suggests that the woman who role-plays her husband's position during marriage counseling will infer she endorses his position only to the extent that she argues it freely. Of course, in most cases in which role reversal is used in therapy, Bem's precondition that existing attitudes be weak or ambiguous seldom is met. Spouses who seek counseling, for example, usually enter treatment with strong, polarized positions. In such situations, self-perception theory has limited or no utility.

According to the self-presentation approach, role reversal results in attitude change because the individual finds himself or herself in a self-presentational dilemma. Having convincingly argued his wife's side in a marital dispute, a husband will later have great difficulty trying to maintain that he does not understand her position or that it has absolutely no merit. Role playing may put people in the position of having to concede to others' views or risk appearing inconsistent and ridiculous.

In brief, although these three theoretical approaches explain the effectiveness of role playing in different ways, they agree that external pressure on the individual to role-play effectively should be *just sufficient* to get him or her to participate in the exercise. Stronger pressure will, according to all three theories, lead to less cognitive change.

Effort Expenditure by the Client

All successful therapy requires clients to exert effort. Not only must the client go to the trouble to contact a psychologist, travel to his or her office, and give up time from other activities, but therapy itself exacts certain costs in terms of effort, distress, and, usually, money. In light of this fact (and, often, to keep the client from terminating treatment), therapists sometimes try to minimize the effort involved. They may rearrange schedules to suit the client, minimize the discomfort produced by the therapy session itself, maintain flexible payment systems, and so on. Interestingly, each of the theories discussed above argues against this approach, suggesting instead that effort expenditure by the client is therapeutically beneficial and that the amount of effort exerted by the client is positively related to psychological change.

For the cognitive dissonance theorist, dissonance is created when people freely expend considerable effort on a task that they recognize may not be worth the cost. People may come to evaluate the task more positively as a way of justifying the effort and energy they have devoted to it, thereby reducing dissonance. As Festinger (1961, p. 11) noted, people "come to love things for which they have suffered." In an early demonstration of this *effort justification effect,* Aronson and Mills (1959) showed that female subjects who underwent a severe "initiation" in order to participate in a boring group discussion rated the discussion and its participants more favorably than subjects who underwent a mild "initiation" or none at all (see Gerard & Mathewson, 1966; Zimbardo, 1965). Having freely exerted considerable effort to join the group, subjects would have experienced dissonance had they admitted to themselves that the experience was not worth the effort.

Self-perception theory also predicts that increased effort enhances one's liking for an activity. According to this approach, people will be likely to infer that they like and are committed to activities for which they expend a great deal of effort.

Self-presentation theory maintains that people become more attracted to effortful activities because they want to justify their effort to others, rather than to themselves. Having publicly expended a great deal of effort, energy, time, or money in a particular endeavor, people may be compelled to justify their actions to others, and may do so by enhancing their endorsement of the activity (Alexander & Sagatun, 1973; Schlenker, 1975b).

Whatever the best theoretical explanation of the effect (and there is evidence that all three processes may operate), effort justification plays an important role in psychological change. In fact, Cooper and Axsom (1982) suggested that effort is a necessary, if not a primary ingredient of successful psychotherapy. In the course of exerting effort, the goals of therapy become

more attractive, and the client becomes increasingly committed to the therapeutic objectives and involved in therapy itself. Cooper and Axsom reviewed earlier studies suggesting that, in some cases, the exertion of effort
per se is sufficient to promote positive change, regardless of the specific
activity on which effort is exerted. For example, subjects in control groups
who engage in effortful but nontherapeutic tasks often improve as much as
subjects who undergo standard psychotherapeutic techniques (e.g., Marcia,
Rubin, & Efran, 1969; Sloane et al., 1975).

Taking the effort justification idea a step further, Cooper and Axsom
(1982) suggested that *any* activity may have therapeutic benefits if it requires
sufficient effort. In a study designed to test this notion, Cooper (1980) exposed snake-phobic subjects to a 40-minute session involving either implosive therapy or a bogus "effort therapy." The latter required subjects to
engage in 40 minutes of physical exercises, including jumping rope, running
in place, and winding a stick that had a 5-pound weight attached. (Subjects
were told that this activity reduced fear by increasing emotional sensitivity.)
In addition, subjects either were or were not given the option of withdrawing
from the study after learning that the procedures could be "effortful and
anxiety-provoking."

Results showed that, when decision freedom was high and subjects had
the choice of whether or not to continue, both implosive therapy and "effort
therapy" worked, but when decision freedom was low neither approach
produced effects. To the degree that both treatments were effortful, change
occurred only when subjects felt responsible for their participation, as the
theories predict.

In a conceptual replication, Cooper (1980) gave subjects either a common
assertive behavior rehearsal treatment or a meaningless "effort therapy"
similar to that described above. In addition, subjects were again given low or
high choice regarding their participation. Using a clever dependent variable
in which subjects were deliberately underpaid by a receptionist, Cooper
showed that subjects who were given a choice regarding participation were
more assertive in demanding the correct payment than those who had no
choice, regardless of the treatment they had received. We consider this
finding quite remarkable: A treatment designed to teach assertiveness was
no more effective than a nonsensical "effort therapy," as long as subjects
exerted effort and perceived they had high choice.

The importance of clients' perceptions that they have choice in their treatment was further highlighted by Mendonca and Brehm's (1983) study of
weight reduction. In this study, some overweight children were given a
choice regarding which weight-control program they would follow, whereas
others were given no choice. In reality, children in both experimental groups
were assigned to the same program, an effortful weight-loss regimen that
required restriction of caloric intake, regular exercise, and detailed records
of food consumption. The effects of the program clearly demonstrated the
importance of perceived choice: Children who had the perception that they

had chosen their program lost significantly more weight than those who had no choice, and this difference was maintained at a 4-week follow-up.

In perhaps the most striking demonstration of the effort justification effect in counseling, Axsom and Cooper (1985) recruited overweight women for a weight-loss program. All of the women participated in four sessions of "therapy." In these sessions, the women engaged in perceptual and cognitive tasks that they were told would enhance their emotional sensitivity in a way that helps lead to weight reduction. In reality, these tasks had nothing to do with weight loss, involving activities such as matching the length of lines on a tachistoscope.

The women were assigned to one of two groups that differed in the amount of cognitive effort required by these tasks; for half of the women, the tasks were relatively easy, whereas for the others they required sustained mental effort over a longer period of time. After only four sessions of these nonsensical activities, the women in the high-effort group had lost signficantly more weight than those in either the low-effort group or a no-treatment control group (neither of which had lost any weight at all). A 6-month follow-up showed that the high-effort group continued to lose weight, weighing an average of 8 pounds less than they had at the start of the study, whereas the women in the low-effort and control groups lost no weight at all. These group differences were maintained up to a year after "treatment."

Thus, using different target behaviors (phobias, assertiveness, weight control) and different procedures (physical versus cognitive "effort therapies"), these studies demonstrate that effort expenditure per se can have therapeutic effects in the absence of any intervention that could reasonably be expected to produce change. However, effortful therapies were only effective when subjects felt a sense of choice and responsibility regarding their participation in them, a finding that is consistent with all three theoretical explanations of the effect.

Although Cooper (1980) interpreted the effort justification effects within a cognitive dissonance framework, they are as easily handled by the alternative approaches. According to self-perception theory, subjects who exert high effort under high-choice conditions are more likely to infer that they really wanted to change than those who engaged in low effort therapy or had no choice in the matter. According to self-presentation theory, subjects who engaged in an effortful "therapy" under high-choice conditions experienced pressure to show that the treatment was effective, either to publicly justify their involvement (so as not to look foolish for wasting their time in a worthless project) or to please the experimenter. Future research should test alternative explanations of effort justification effects using clinically relevant procedures, such as those employed by Cooper (1980) and Axsom and Cooper (1985).

One further therapeutic implication of the effort justification phenomenon is worthy of mention. Harari (1983) noted that clients are often required to complete extensive batteries of tests before undergoing treatment. Although many practitioners regard these "intake" procedures as detrimental to therapy, Harari showed just the opposite. He randomly assigned some clients in a mental health center to undergo an *increased* number of preliminary procedures. As laboratory research on effort justification predicts, clients who completed extensive intake procedures were more satisfied with therapy and their therapists, were less likely to miss their therapy sessions, and were less likely to terminate therapy prematurely.

In brief, research suggests that effort expenditure facilitates psychological change, at least under certain circumstances. Of course, if the effort required of clients is too great, they are likely to withhold full effort or to terminate therapy. But until that point is reached, greater effort is associated with greater change.

Paradoxical Therapy

In paradoxical therapy, the therapist attempts to eliminate the client's dysfunctional behavior by instructing the client to engage willfully in the undesired behavior (Haley, 1963). The behaviors targeted for paradoxical injunctions usually involve those such as insomnia, smoking, procrastination, and overeating, that are resistant to traditional "talk therapies." For example, a student who is a habitual procrastinator might be directed to sit in front of her books but put off studying for some prespecified time each day (e.g., Lopez & Wambach, 1982; Wright & Strong, 1982). Or an insomniac who normally takes 4 hours to go to sleep each night might be instructed to lie awake for at least 6 hours. An adolescent who is in constant conflict with his parents might be instructed to purposefully argue with his parents at prespecified times each day.

In a variation of this theme known as "reframing," the therapist interprets the client's difficulties in a positive fashion and encourages their continuance. For example, Palazzoli, Boscolo, Cecchin, and Prata (1978) found that interpreting pathological family interactions in a positive fashion (as demonstrating sensitivity and self-sacrifice, for example) reduced the dysfunctional interaction patterns among family members. Similarly, Beck and Strong (1981) demonstrated that reinterpreting clients' depressive symptoms in a positive fashion resulted in greater long-term reduction of symptoms than did a more traditional therapy.

Paradoxically, then, paradoxical directives and reframing are often effective in reducing or eliminating undesired behavior (Jackson & Haley, 1968; Rohrbaugh, Tennen, Press, & White, 1981; Strong, 1982; Watzlawick, Beavin, & Jackson, 1967; Weeks & L'Abate, 1979). However, the psychological processes mediating these effects are not at all clear. Several explanations have been offered to explain the effectiveness of paradoxical therapy, but only some of them concern us here.

Reactance theory. Perhaps the most widely accepted explanation of paradoxical effects is based on reactance theory, which deals with people's reactions to events that threaten their behavioral freedom (Brehm, 1966; chapter 3, this volume). Under certain circumstances, events that threaten individuals' behavioral freedom motivate them to restore their freedom, resulting in behavior contrary to the social pressure. In the case of paradoxical therapy, the therapist's insistence that the client perform the problem behaviors in particular ways at prespecified times may threaten the client's sense of freedom and autonomy and result in an oppositional attempt by the client to prevent the symptoms from occurring.

Cognitive dissonance theory. Alternatively, explanations based on dissonance theory emphasize the fact that, in most instances, clients assume that their "symptoms" are beyond their voluntary control. However, clients who follow a therapist's instructions to purposefully engage in the behavior soon learn that their behavior can, to some degree, be turned off and on at will. To the degree that this realization is inconsistent with the belief that one's behavior is out of one's control, the clients may experience dissonance, which can be resolved by concluding that their symptoms are controllable after all. Once this point is reached, the clients are able to exert conscious control over the problem behavior.

Self-perception and attributional explanations. Attributional explanations offer two other insights regarding paradoxical therapy. First, it has long been recognized that intrinsic interest in an activity is diminished when external rewards are offered for engaging in the activity (Deci, 1975; Lepper, Greene, & Nisbett, 1973). In one classic study, children who were rewarded for engaging in activities they previously enjoyed showed a subsequent decrease in interest in those activities (Lepper et al., 1973). According to self-perception theory, when people do something for no obvious external reason, they infer that they are doing so for internal reasons, and may conclude that they enjoy the activity (Bem, 1972). However, when external inducements are offered, people infer that they are performing the behavior to gain those external rewards, and their intrinsic motivation declines. In the same way, clients tend to make internal attributions for dysfunctional behaviors that occur for no obvious external reason (such as chronic insomnia or procrastination). Once the therapist orders that the behavior be performed, the internal reasons for doing so diminish in importance, and the dysfunction seems less dispositional.

Further, clients who attribute their problems to themselves may conclude that their behavior is uncontrollable and experience learned helplessness in that regard (see chapter 3). However, when the behavior appears to occur voluntarily in compliance with the demands of the therapist, clients may conclude that the behavior is, in fact, controllable, either by the therapist or by themselves. Thus, paradoxical therapy may be effective because it leads clients to conclude that the problem behavior is controllable.

In chapter 2, we discussed problems such as insomnia that are exacerbated when people make internal attributions for them (Storms & McCaul, 1976). Paradoxical therapy may have the additional effect of leading clients to attribute their difficulties externally (away from themselves), thereby reducing their distress over the problem and breaking the exacerbation cycle. For example, the insomniac who attempts to force himself or herself to stay awake has a plausible explanation for his or her sleeplessness, an explanation that reduces the degree to which he or she worries about going to sleep on any particular night. With this source of anxiety gone, the individual may fall asleep more quickly (e.g., Ascher & Efran, 1978).

Self-presentation. A self-presentation approach to paradoxical therapy suggests two routes to behavior change. First, the "reactance" effects discussed above may reflect impression management strategies rather than intrapsychic attempts to restore behavioral freedom (Wright & Brehm, 1982). That is, clients may disobey the therapist's directives so as to be viewed as autonomous and self-directed. Clients may purposefully control their symptomatic behavior in order to show the therapist that they are not under his or her control.

Additionally, as noted earlier, most clients maintain that their dysfunctional behavior is beyond their voluntary control. Once it is demonstrated that a certain degree of control is possible (e.g., I can fight with my parents "on demand"), the client faces a self-presentational dilemma. If the client continues to engage in maladaptive behavior even in the face of public evidence that he or she has some control over it, negative evaluations and reactions from others will result. Thus, the client may begin to control the dysfunctional behavior as much as possible.

Interactional approaches. Many writers have pointed out that dysfunctional behavior may serve interpersonal functions (Artiss, 1959; Carson, 1969). People sometimes engage in dysfunctional reactions as a way of controlling or punishing others. As noted in chapter 5, intimidating and supplicating strategies are quite effective in inducing others to respond in desired ways by instilling fear, guilt, pity, or some other reaction. The effectiveness of these strategies is due in part to their undesirability as people respond to the "disturbed" individual in a manner that will eliminate the undesirable behavior.

Thus, reinterpreting problem behaviors in a positive fashion may deprive the client of the use of these sorts of strategies. Just as a child who throws a tantrum on the kitchen floor will stop once his parents calmly thank him for dusting the linoleum, clients may forgo their "symptoms" when they no longer offend, intimidate, or control others (see Beck & Strong, 1981; Omer, 1981; Palazzoli et al., 1978; Weeks & L'Abate, 1982).

Summary and conclusions. We have mentioned how reactance, dissonance, attribution, self-presentation, and interactional approaches can explain the effectiveness of paradoxical therapy in order to make two points. First, although paradoxical treatments are clearly effective in many instances, we have little empirical evidence that elucidates the processes involved. At this juncture, each of these explanations of the effect is plausible. This seems to be a very important topic for future research, for advances in the use of these techniques will depend on a more complete understanding of the factors underlying them.

Second, as this chapter has amply demonstrated, more than one social psychological theory may be applied to many behavioral phenomena. Although this state of affairs is often regarded as frustrating and discouraging by professionals and students alike, this is not necessarily a bad state of affairs. On the one hand, there is no reason to assume a priori that any one of these theories can explain *all* instances in which paradoxical therapy or any other treatment is effective. To the degree that behavioral and emotional problems are multiply determined and various treatments have multiple effects on the client, it is possible that each of these theories, or at least some subset of them, are needed to understand every instance in which paradoxical treatment is effective. For example, paradoxical injunctions may serve an attributional function for an insomniac if she attributes her sleeplessness to her willful attempts to remain awake, rather than to her personal problems, and consequently stops worrying about it. For a schizophrenogenic mother, paradoxical techniques may serve to reframe her manipulative symptoms in more positive terms, thereby diminishing their effectiveness. The point is that paradoxical therapy may work for different disorders and for different people for different reasons. Only future research will uncover the relevant variables.

Beyond that, having several theories that explain a single phenomenon encourages strong empirical tests of the various positions by the competing camps, thereby stimulating a great deal of creative and enlightening research (Elms, 1975). Feyerabend, a noted philosopher of science, argues that science is best served not by monotheoretical "normal science" (Kuhn, 1962) but by the presence of competing theories. Feyerabend noted that, "this plurality of theories must not be regarded as a preliminary stage of knowledge which will at some time in the future be replaced by the One True Theory" (Feyerabend, 1970, p. 321). Having just one accepted theory neither ensures nor indicates that the theory is the best one.

Conclusions

This chapter has examined three therapeutic strategies that share an emphasis on inducing clients to engage in behaviors that they would prefer not to perform. In role playing, clients act in ways that are atypical of their behavior or are counterattitudinal; in effort justication paradigms, clients engage in effortful treatment regimens; and in paradoxical therapy, clients are told to consciously create their dysfunctional behaviors in prescribed ways. Each of these procedures can, under appropriate conditions, create therapeutic change, but the mechanisms responsible for these changes are imperfectly understood, and they can be explained equally well by different theories. The picture is complicated further by the possibility that more than one process is involved in these effects. Improved use of these procedures in counseling settings awaits additional research, both basic and applied, that elucidates the processes involved.

Chapter 11
Expectancies and Behavior Change

Envision an unattractive, wary, poorly educated client encountering a pessimistic, burned-out counselor who dreads coming to work each morning. Then contrast that scenario with that of an attractive, trusting, well-educated client meeting an enthusiastic, confident counselor who is glad to be of help. Both intuition and research results (Garfield, 1978) predict that therapeutic change is more likely in the latter case than in the former, but why exactly is that so? A number of explanations are possible, but this chapter focuses on the possibility that change is more likely in the second scenario because both counselor and client *expect* it to occur. Their expectations may influence the outcome of therapy by leading to behavior that produces desirable changes that, in the absence of those expectations, would not have occurred. In short, the belief that change will occur may be a powerful component in psychological therapy.

The expectations with which both client and counselor enter the therapeutic relationship have long been of interest to clinical researchers (e.g., Goldstein, 1962). There are many variables to forecast—whether the participants will like each other, how long therapy will last, what it will be like, whether it will be successful—and clients' global expectations determine whether they enter therapy to begin with (Tinsley, Brown, de St. Aubin, & Lucek, 1984). Furthermore, once therapy begins, clients' expectations of what it involves may determine whether they continue treatment or drop out (see Garfield, 1978, for a review). Clients who expect direct advice and rapid cures, for instance, are often disappointed, and it is valuable to prepare clients for therapy by showing them in advance exactly what it entails (e.g., Wilson, 1985). In addition, it is desirable that therapist and client share the same expectations regarding the nature of treatment (Garfield, 1978), and there is even evidence that certain therapies are better suited than others to clients with particular expectancies (Abramowitz, Abramowitz, Roback, & Jackson, 1974; Kilmann, Albert, & Sotile, 1975).

We focus in this chapter on one role of expectations in counseling and psychotherapy, drawing on social psychological studies that show how our beliefs can become behavioral realities. We examine the possibility that expectations of psychological change on the part of both therapists and clients can facilitate or even create such change. For their part, therapists may occasionally construct self-fulfilling prophecies, obtaining certain therapeutic outcomes largely because they expect to. Clients, too, make predictions regarding the outcome of treatment, and they may master their problems mainly because they believe they can. Indeed, we examine the argument that psychological therapies succeed by enhancing clients' estimates of their personal abilities, or judgments of self-efficacy. Finally, we address the possibility that the expectation of change underlies most successful therapies.

Therapist Expectancies

For decades, clinical researchers have grappled with the methodological difficulties of demonstrating that psychological treatments have effects above and beyond the "nonspecific" or "placebo" effects of coming under a therapist's care (for thoughtful discussion of this issue see Critelli & Neumann, 1984; Frank, 1973; Lick & Bootzin, 1975; Rosenthal & Frank, 1956; and Shapiro & Morris, 1978). It is widely recognized that simply meeting an attentive, supportive therapist can have desirable effects regardless of the techniques the therapist employs. One influential component of these placebo effects is the therapist's expectation that he or she can help and that treatment will be successful. Even reviewers who prefer to make little of therapist expectancy effects grudgingly admit that therapy is dramatically affected by the therapist's beliefs about the likelihood of change (Wilkins, 1977).

Importantly, a therapist's expectation of improvement is not merely a predictor of beneficial change; such expectations can create change that would not otherwise occur. Berman and Wenzlaff (1983) randomly manipulated the expectations of 17 therapists at a university counseling center by informing them that pretests had indicated that one of their new clients would rapidly improve; for a second (control) client, the therapists were told that no firm prediction could be made. When each therapist and both of his or her clients were monitored through six counseling sessions, a clear effect of positive expectations was obtained. The therapists believed that clients whom they had expected to improve had improved more than the controls, and the clients shared those views. The positive-expectancy clients actually reported substantially greater reductions in anxiety and depression (though the groups did not differ in interpersonal problems and somatic complaints). It seems undeniably true, as Goldstein (1962) suggested years ago, that all else being equal, prospective clients should be assigned to the therapists who hold the most favorable prognostic expectations for them.

Why do therapists' expectations have these positive effects? As we saw in chapter 8, one possibility is that the improvement is more apparent than real; an expectation of change may lead both counselor and client to overestimate how much change has actually occurred (Conway & Ross, 1984). The benefits of therapy are often far from illusory, however. How might positive expectations become behavioral realities?

Self-Fulfilling Prophecies

By acting in accord with their favorable expectations, therapists may set into motion self-fulfilling prophecies. They may treat clients more warmly, encourage them more, praise small successes more highly, and in general behave very differently than they would have had their expectations been less positive. Such generous, attentive treatment may then elicit from clients more desirable change than would have been obtained had the therapists not been so supportive. In short, the therapists' (potentially false) expectations of success may become true largely because the therapists' beliefs lead them to behave in ways that make them come true.

A wide variety of social psychological studies demonstrate that such processes occur. Perhaps the best known example is Rosenthal and Jacobson's (1968) study of teacher expectations and student achievement. These researchers led elementary school teachers to believe that randomly selected students, whatever their prior achievements, would improve substantially during the school year. Indeed, at the end of the year, those students had improved more than their classmates. Further study showed that such remarkable effects do not always occur (Rosenthal & Rubin, 1978), but when they do they are often sizeable. In turn, students' expectations regarding the quality of the teaching they will receive can affect their teachers' behavior as well (Feldman & Prohaska, 1979; Feldman & Theiss, 1982).

The teacher expectation studies demonstrate that self-fulfilling prophecies can have happy endings, but, unfortunately, negative expectations can also come true. We saw in chapter 8, for example, that men who believed their female partners were unattractive elicited drab behavior from them (Snyder et al., 1977). Similarly, when men know they are interacting with women they often elicit more feminine, sex-typed behavior from them than they do when they falsely believe their female partners are other men (Skrypnek & Snyder, 1982).

In fact, it is possible for negative expectations to become regrettably persistent realities. Snyder and Swann (1978b) showed that behavior elicited from a person in response to a self-fulfilling prophecy can mold that person's responses in later situations as well. In their study, pairs of male subjects competed on a reaction-time task, and on alternating trials each man had an aversive "noise weapon" at his disposal. One of the subjects, the "perceiver," was told that his opponent, the "target," was either sensitive, kind, and cooperative (in short, nonhostile) or aggressive, competitive, and cruel.

Both subjects were also informed that extensive use of the noise weapon was usually either a dispositional characteristic, depending on the type of person one was, or a situational strategy, depending on the play of one's opponent. In any case, the "perceivers" who believed they were playing a hostile, cruel opponent began the game by delivering higher levels of noise than did those who thought their partners were nonhostile, and in line with a self-fulfilling prophecy, the "hostile" targets responded with more noise of their own. In brief, perceivers who expected hostility got it.

The most provocative results of this study, however, came when the perceivers were replaced with new naïve subjects and the "hostile" targets again played the game. If they had been led to believe that their frequent use of the noise weapon was a dispositional characteristic, they continued to act in a hostile manner, delivering more noise than did those who believed their earlier aggression had been largely situational. Under some circumstances, then, the targets of prejudicial personal evaluations not only come to act in a manner that confirms those judgments, but continue to act that way even when no one expects them to (cf. Fazio et al., 1981). One can imagine how it could be hard for a "mental patient" who is widely feared or rejected to act in a manner that is neither threatening nor withdrawn. People often elicit from others the behavior they expect, whether or not it is desirable.

Darley and Fazio (1980) have delineated the specific steps by which self-fulfilling prophecies may occur (Figure 11-1). Their analysis focuses on the preconceptions and expectations of one member of a dyad, examining how that person's judgments can ultimately affect the other's behavior. (They do recognize, however, that both members of a dyad may have preconceptions that come to influence the behavior of their partners.)

First, the person, or *perceiver, forms an expectancy* about the other person, or target, that predicts how the target will behave. Various information about the target, such as age, race, sex, physical attractiveness, and social class, may affect the perceiver's judgments in ways of which the perceiver is unaware, and if the perceiver is able to observe the target's behavior, the personalistic bias makes dispositional attributions likely (see chapter 8).

In an important second step, the *perceiver acts,* usually in accord with his or her expectancy. The perceiver's judgments are not always reflected in his or her behavior; if subjects expect hostility from another person, for instance, they may begin interaction by being especially pleasant, hoping to divert the other's wrath (Ickes, Patterson, Rajecki, & Tanford, 1982). However, it is usually hard for people to keep from subtly communicating what they really think about others (DePaulo et al., 1985). For example, when Word, Zanna, and Cooper (1974) asked white subjects to interview both white and black job applicants (all of whom were highly trained confederates), they found that the black applicants received shorter interviews and heard more speech errors from the interviewers, who sat further away. The whites' relative uneasiness during the interviews with the black applicants was manifest, whether they knew it or not. Indeed, comprehensive meta-

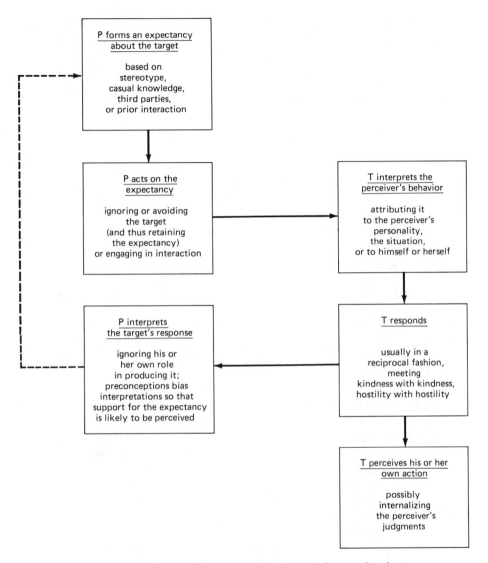

Figure 11-1. The confirmation of expectancies through interaction between a perceiver (P) and his or her target (T). From "Expectancy Confirmation Processes Arising in the Social Interaction Sequence" by J. M. Darley and R. H. Fazio, 1980, *American Psychologist, 35,* pp. 867–881. Copyright © 1980 by the American Psychological Association. Adapted by permission of the authors.

analyses of 136 expectancy studies by Harris and Rosenthal (1985) have shown that perceivers' expectancies influence a wide range of their nonverbal behavior toward their targets. Perceivers with favorable expectations, for instance, interact longer and more often with their targets, sharing more eye contact, sitting closer, smiling more, asking more questions, and encouraging more responses than do perceivers with less positive expectancies. Our earlier supposition that therapists with favorable expectations are likely to be more encouraging, enthusiastic, and supportive may be close to the mark; perceivers with positive expectations create altogether warmer interpersonal climates for their targets.

The third step of Darley and Fazio's (1980) model involves the *target's interpretation* of the perceiver's behavior. If the perceiver's behavior is seen as being caused by the perceiver's personality, the self-fulfilling prophecy created in this interaction can generalize to entirely new interactions with the perceiver later on. Alternatively, the target may believe that he or she is the cause of the perceiver's action; in this instance, if the target feels the perceiver has misread him or her, the target may try to change the perceiver's judgments, blocking the self-fulfilling prophecy (as we will shortly see). In any case, the target draws some conclusion from the perceiver's behavior. In a second interview study, Word et al. (1974) trained two confederates to portray the same relaxed or uneasy interviewing styles that white interviewers had displayed with white and black applicants, respectively. Real subjects were then interviewed by the confederates, and whether they were black or white, the applicants judged the "uneasy" interviewer to be unfriendly. The subjects were clearly aware of how the interviewer was acting, and, like most observers, they attributed his behavior to his dispositions.

In the fourth step, the *target responds* to the perceiver. Unless the target is actively trying to dispel the perceiver's expectancy, this response is usually similar to the perceiver's action. Enthusiasm is usually met with interest (Snyder et al., 1977), hostility with counteraggression (Snyder & Swann, 1978b). In the study by Word et al. (1974), subjects who interacted with "uneasy" interviewers sat further away, spoke more haltingly, appeared more nervous, and came off less positively than those speaking with interviewers who were relaxed (cf. Harris & Rosenthal, 1985).

Such is the nature of a self-fulfilling prophecy that, as the *perceiver interprets* the target's response in the fifth step of the model, the perceiver is unlikely to recognize the role he or she played in producing it. Perhaps without a word being said, the perceiver may find in the target the behavior he or she expected; what better evidence is there that the expectancy was accurate?

Consider a real-life analogue of the Word et al. (1974) study. A white vocational counselor with a stereotypical conception of blacks is uneasy at the thought of interviewing them, and, without meaning to, acts that way. Black job-seekers faced with a distant, apparently unfriendly interviewer become uneasy themselves and appear inept. The interviewer finds, once again, that his or her expectations have been confirmed and becomes even more certain that, "It's too bad, but they just can't cut it." What is more, it is possible, in a final step of Darley and Fazio's (1980) model, for a target to interpret his or her actions in the same way as the perceiver does, internalizing them and continuing to behave that way on other occasions (Fazio et al., 1981; Snyder & Swann, 1978b).

Thus, a perceiver's expectations can substantially influence a target's behavior as both parties base their actions on their judgments of the other and on their prior interaction. As well as describing the perpetuation of social stereotypes, self-fulfilling prophecies help explain the effects of therapists' expectations. It is likely that the positive expectations of the therapists in Berman and Wenzlaff's (1983) study created positive outcomes for their clients by directly influencing the "nonspecific" therapy the clients received. When counselors held favorable expectations, clients probably received more positive regard, were encouraged to attempt more by a more enthusiastic and attentive counselor, and were urged to internalize their successes to a greater degree. They might even have spent more time with their counselors overall (Fehrenbach & O'Leary, 1982).

Given the potential benefits of positive expectations and the corresponding harmful potential of negative expectations, a therapist's optimism is a desirable component of any strategy of behavior change. Of course, positive expectations do not always produce results, and interpersonal prophecies do not always fulfill themselves, as any clinician knows.

When Prophecies Fail

Although others' expectations for us have powerful effects, it may be quite difficult to convince us that we are something we firmly feel we are not. While our self-concepts are open to change, they are not so malleable that any stranger with a new opinion of us can substantially alter our self-views. Indeed, we tend to refute and reject information about ourselves that is inconsistent with our self-concepts, preferring instead to hear things that verify and support what we already think about ourselves (Swann, 1985). For instance, when Swann and Hill (1982) provided social feedback that was discrepant with subjects' self-evaluations of dominance or submissiveness— telling a submissive person, for instance, that she really appeared to be forceful and dominant—the subjects went out of their way to be even more dominant or submissive than usual, proving they were not what the evaluator believed.

If people reject straightforward feedback about themselves with which they do not agree, what happens when a perceiver's more subtle expectancy about a target contradicts that target's self-concept? Can the perceiver elicit from the target behavior that just does not fit the target's self-view? Swann and Ely (1984) examined this issue, asking female subjects to evaluate the introversion or extraversion of people who viewed themselves as either extraverted or introverted. Each subject was equipped with either a strong or a weak expectancy that contradicted the self-description of the target she would meet, and was asked to test that expectancy using the hypothesis-testing procedure of Snyder and Swann (1978a; see chapter 8). Judges' ratings of three separate trials revealed that the perceivers' expectancies became self-fulfilling prophecies only when strong expectations in the perceivers were pitted against rather uncertain self-conceptions in the targets. If both perceivers and targets held uncertain judgments, or if the targets were sure of themselves, the perceivers failed to elicit the behavior they expected; the targets continued to describe themselves in ways that were consistent with their self-concepts, despite the implicit demands from their partners to describe themselves as something else.

Swann and Ely's (1984) study was not a strong test of self-fulfilling prophecies because it only involved verbal communication between perceivers and targets who could not see one another. Nevertheless, it indicates that even strong expectations may fail to influence behavior that is central to a person's self-concept. Whether or not it is dysfunctional, behavior that helps affirm a person's self-image may be unlikely to change in response to others' expectations, leaving the opposing prophecies of others uniformly unfulfilled.

In many therapeutic situations, of course, the therapist has no wish to contradict the client's self-conceptions completely. Therapy often involves an effort to provide willing clients with new interpretations of their feelings and abilities, not wholesale revisions of their self-views. Even if a therapist has such revisionist aspirations, his or her credibility, prestige, and attractiveness might make therapeutic expectancies much more influential than Swann and Ely's (1984) study would suggest (see Aronson et al., 1963, and chapter 9). Still, it is likely that therapists' expectations have the greatest impact on relatively interested, motivated clients who care what their therapists think and who are receptive to their advice. In the absence of those facilitating conditions, even the most favorable expectations may be unlikely to influence resistant clients. And even if desirable change is achieved in the controlled therapeutic environment, it may attenuate when clients have the chance to reaffirm their self-images on their own (cf. Swann and Hill, 1982). For all the value and potential benefit of therapists' positive expectations, clients' expectations of success are probably more vital still. If clients do not believe in themselves, lasting change may be difficult to achieve.

Backfiring Expectations

High expectations can have hidden costs. People sometimes "choke" under pressure, performing poorly when the importance of their actions is magnified. In an intriguing series of studies, Baumeister (1984) and his colleagues showed that high expectations from an audience can backfire, causing people to do less well than they otherwise would. For example, an archival analysis of championship games in major league baseball and basketball demonstrated that it may actually be disadvantageous to play the final game of a championship series before an adoring home crowd (Baumeister & Steinhilber, 1984). Home teams win over 60% of the first two games of the

World Series, but they lose over 60% of the decisive seventh games. Similar results occur in basketball, and analysis of team performances reveals that the home teams "choke"—committing errors, missing free throws—to a greater extent than the visiting teams excel. Curiously, the performance decrement is associated not with the fear of failure, but with the chance to achieve success; when facing elimination in a sixth game of a World Series, home teams win 73% of the time, but when they have the chance to win the championship instead, they do so only 38% of the time.

The key to these remarkable results may be the extent to which the performers share the audience's lofty expectations. Baumeister, Hamilton, and Tice (1985) found that an audience's expectations of success increase the pressure on a performer and are likely to harm performance unless they are so credible, persuasive, and compelling that the performer privately expects success as well. In the Baumeister et al. studies, a person's private expectation of success invariably facilitated that person's skillful performance. By contrast, if a person was privately sure he or she would fail, high expectations from an audience made matters worse, debilitating the person further. If the person came to share a credible audience's positive expectations, however, performance improved. Thus, high expectations from others (e.g., therapists) can have either a beneficial or a detrimental impact, depending upon the individual's own beliefs. It is very likely that most therapists are credible enough that their confident projections of success have a desirable influence on their uncertain clients. However, if the clients are unwilling participants in therapy or are convinced of their own incompetence, high therapist expectations may backfire, impeding progress. Once again, clients' expectations are of fundamental importance to the therapeutic enterprise.

Client Expectations

Clients' expectations that their therapy will be successful probably do much more than just make them willing, compliant participants in their treatments. Reviewers of "nonspecific" therapies and placebo effects have noted several ways that clients' positive expectations facilitate change. First, hopeful expectations contribute to positive moods and higher motivation, which may help clients learn new skills or understand new frames of reference (Bootzin, 1985; Lick & Bootzin, 1975). In a similar fashion, expectations of improvement may reduce clients' anxiety about their problems, calming the worrying that may exacerbate them (Ross & Olson, 1982; see chapter 2).

Second, a hopeful outlook may lead clients to "accentuate the positive," noticing and attaching importance to small successes they would otherwise overlook (Ross & Olson, 1982). They may even test their expectations of improvement in a biased, confirmatory manner so that their hopes are supported, encouraging them to continue treatment (Lick & Bootzin, 1975). If they fail to find any factual evidence of success, they may resolve the resulting cognitive dissonance by convincing themselves they are feeling better anyway (Shapiro & Morris, 1978).

Third, to the extent a client has enjoyed prior success with therapy, the therapeutic situation itself may be a conditioned stimulus that promotes improvement, alleviating anxiety and decreasing depression (Ross & Olson, 1982; Shapiro & Morris, 1978). Finally, Ross and Olson speculated that positive expectations might produce physiological changes that have palliative effects (stimulating the production of morphine-like endorphins in the brain, for instance).

In addition to these potential benefits, the expectation that one's behavior will change may actually make one's behavior more likely to change. Merely predicting how we will act increases the likelihood that we will do what we predicted (a personal self-fulfilling prophecy). Sherman (1980) found that when people were asked to volunteer to collect money for the American Cancer Society, only 4% complied. However, if people instead were asked to predict whether or not they would volunteer, 48% believed they would, and when that entire prediction group was later asked to volunteer, 31% complied. The different rates of compliance reflect the channeling effects of behavioral predictions, and expecting that one will stop smoking, begin dating, be more assertive, or control one's temper may make those behaviors more likely to occur. Thus, having clients make public predictions about the desirable changes they hope to achieve during therapy may be beneficial.

Of course, one's beliefs about what one *can* do will substantially influence one's beliefs about what one will do, and that brings us to consideration of the most important client expectancies of all.

Self-Efficacy

In a provocative and heuristic analysis of behavior change, Bandura (1977, 1978, 1982, 1984) has suggested that clients' estimates of their specific competencies largely determine how they cope with their problems. For Bandura, a person's "efficacy expectancies" describe that person's beliefs about his or her particular skills and capabilities, and they determine how the person reacts behaviorally, cognitively, and emotionally to problematic events. Perceptions of self-efficacy determine what activities people attempt, how hard they try, and how long they persist in the face of failure. Burdened with low efficacy expectations, clients are likely to avoid their problems, expend little effort, give up prematurely, dwell on their inadequacies, and suffer considerable anxiety and stress. By contrast, those with high efficacy expectations are likely to set challenging goals, persevere in the face of frustration, approach therapy tasks without anxiety, and, in short, attain more (Bandura, 1984).

Bandura (e.g., 1982, 1984) makes an important distinction between an efficacy expectancy, which is the subjective probability that one can successfully execute a certain behavior, and an outcome expectancy, which is the subjective probability that a particular behavior will lead to particular outcomes. Your conviction that you can run an entire marathon would be an efficacy expectancy, for example, whereas your anticipation of the accompanying praise and respect from your spouse and friends would be an outcome expectancy. Although they are not always easy to discriminate, the distinction between the two types of expectancy is important because either may be a source of dysfunctional behavior (see chapter 6). A shy person may consciously shy away from rewarding interaction either because she believes she lacks the skills to engage in small talk or because she believes that her partner will reject her no matter how well she does (Leary & Atherton, 1986). Thus we may fear failure either because of perceived personal inadequacy or because of an unresponsive, punitive environment that we believe will leave our best efforts unrewarded.

In fact, Bandura (1982) posited four sets of interactive effects of the combination of independent efficacy and outcome expectancies. If both types of expectancy are high, people are sure of themselves and believe the environment is facilitative, and assured, confident behavior should result. If both expectancies are low, dispirited apathy and helplessness result (Devins et al., 1982). When self-efficacy is high but the environment is thought to be unresponsive, frustration, protest, and active efforts to change the environment are likely. Perhaps the worst case of all, however, is the combination of personal inefficacy and positive outcome expectancies; success seems available if only one were competent enough to attain it, in which case depression, despondency, and diminished self-esteem are all likely.

The obvious scope of Bandura's analysis and his argument that perceptions of self-efficacy play a central, causal role in mediating behavior change have drawn critics from far and wide. We will examine the most common criticisms of self-efficacy theory as a means of introducing the volumes of studies that bear on the theory.

Is self-efficacy a redundant construct? Bandura's early studies of self-efficacy (e.g., Bandura, Adams, & Beyer, 1977) showed that as subjects with snake phobias progressed through therapy, the changes in their self-efficacy expectancies closely tracked their actual behavioral accomplishments. Self-efficacy was a very good predictor of performance, but Borkovec (1978), Eysenck (1978), and Wolpe (1978) argued that one need not resort to a construct of self-efficacy to explain such results. Changes in conditioned anxiety and arousal could also be responsible, they reasoned, and would provide a more parsimonious explanation. Bandura and Adams (1977) were able to show, however, that once phobic subjects were completely desensitized, entirely eliminating their anxiety, their efficacy expectancies still closely predicted the (widely variable) behaviors they were able to perform. (This ability to predict the differential response of individuals receiving the same type of treatment, and the levels of change attained by different treatments [Bandura et al., 1977; Bandura, Adams, Hardy, & Howells, 1980], is a key advantage of a self-efficacy perspective.) Williams and his colleagues (Williams, Turner, & Peer, 1985; Williams & Watson, 1985) have since shown that anxiety and perceived danger are much poorer predictors of phobics' behavior than is self-efficacy.

Does self-efficacy have causal impact? The alert reader may have already anticipated a criticism like that raised by Eysenck (1978), Kazdin (1978), and Wolpe (1978): Given the close correlation between self-efficacy and behavior, do perceptions of self-efficacy *causally* affect behavior, or do they simply follow from witnessing one's actions? Bandura (1982) admitted that, as an estimation of one's competencies, self-efficacy is influenced by one's performance. Efficacy expectations are based on one's *interpretation* of one's performances, however, and because of the inferential ambiguities involved (with external aid, task difficulty, one's effort, etc., all affecting the conclusions one draws) judgments of self-efficacy are not simple reflections of behavioral accomplishments (Bandura, 1984). More importantly, efficacy expectancies do, in turn, direct behavior. Self-efficacy is a better predictor of future performance than is past performance, accurately predicting performance on tasks people have never attempted before (Bandura, Reese, & Adams, 1982). Manipulations of self-efficacy not only determine subjects' coping behavior but affect their heart rates, blood pressures, and levels of plasma epinephrine and norepinephrine as well (Bandura, et al., 1982; Bandura, Taylor, Williams, Mefford, & Barchas, 1985). Introducing low efficacy expectancies creates a depressive mood, but introducing a depressive mood does not create low efficacy expectancies (Stanley & Maddux, 1985). It seems, overall, that the causal link between self-efficacy and behavior is reciprocal, with each partially determining the other.

Are outcome or efficacy expectations more important? In two different ways self-efficacy theory has been criticized for neglecting the importance of outcome expectancies in directing behavior. The stronger form of this argument is again that self-efficacy is an unnecessary construct; Borkovec (1978) and Teasdale (1978) suggested that quantification of the outcomes and incentives that follow operant behavior is sufficient to explain behavior change, and that we need not propose cognitive mediators such as self-efficacy. However, a wide range of studies have demonstrated that efficacy expectancies are much more closely related to one's actual behavior than are outcome expectancies. For instance, Barling and Abel (1983) examined 12 components of subjects' tennis performance (such as their anticipation, concentration, footwork, competitiveness, and power and spin) and found that the subjects' perceptions of self-efficacy were closely linked to their performances whereas their outcome expectancies were not. Similar findings have been obtained in studies of subjects' assertiveness (Lee, 1984a), ability to handle snakes (Lee, 1984b), and persistence after failure (Jacobs, Prentice-Dunn, & Rogers, 1984).

Thus, behavior can be predicted from people's perceptions of what they can do as well as from their perceptions of the rewards and punishments available to them. If people feel, rightly or wrongly, that they cannot perform a certain action well, they are unlikely to do well whatever the rewards available to them. Self-efficacy provides predictive power that outcome expectancies do not provide, a fact that seems particularly important when clinically relevant behaviors are considered. Efficacy expectancies significantly predict clients' ability to stop smoking, identifying those who are likely to remain nonsmokers and accurately predicting situations in which relapses are likely to occur (Coelho, 1984; Condiotte & Lichtenstein, 1981; DiClemente, Prochaska, & Gibertini, 1985). Similarly, they predict who will drop out of weight-loss programs (Mitchell & Stuart, 1984) and how much weight the remaining clients will have lost after 6 weeks and 6 months (Bernier & Poser, 1984). Efficacy expectancies even predict university faculty research productivity (Taylor, Locke, Lee, & Gist, 1984). Thus, self-efficacy is far from redundant with outcome expectancies; efficacy expectancies can tell us much about people's behaviors that rewards and costs do not.

A weaker form of the efficacy-versus-outcome criticism suggests that self-efficacy does have effects, but that Bandura's theory overlooks just how influential outcome expectancies really are (Eastman & Marzillier, 1984; Kirsch, 1985; Marzillier & Eastman, 1984). Even though, as we have just seen, efficacy expectations are much more closely linked to the parameters of actual performance than are outcome expectations (e.g., Barling & Abel, 1983; Jacobs et al., 1984), this criticism has some merit. Maddux and Barnes (1985) suggested that because self-efficacy reflects perceived skillfulness, clients' *intentions* to engage in certain behaviors, rather than their performance of those behaviors, are a better test of the relative contributions of efficacy and outcome expectations. Research shows that both types of expectations independently predict behavioral intentions, but when both are experimentally manipulated, only changes in outcome expectancies *cause* significant changes in subjects' intentions (Maddux, Norton, & Stoltenberg, in press; Maddux, Sherer, & Rogers, 1982). Efficacy expectations still add to our ability to *predict* intentions even when outcome expectancies are accounted for, however, and both appear to provide important, nonredundant information about people's plans of action (Maddux et al., in press). We may conclude, then, that both the competencies people perceive and the outcomes they expect influence what they believe they will do, whereas efficacy judgments alone are the primary determinants of how much they actually accomplish (Eccles, Adler, & Meece, 1984).

Maddux and his colleagues suggested the positive or negative *value* of potential outcomes as a third independent predictor of behavior, apart from the outcome expectancy that certain behaviors will obtain the outcomes (Maddux & Barnes, 1985; cf. Kirsch, 1985), but so far it has proven difficult to disentangle outcome value from outcome expectancy (Maddux et al., in press; Stanley & Maddux, 1985, 1986). For that matter, it is not always easy to differentiate efficacy expectations from outcome expectations (Maddux et al., 1982); for example, a potential marathoner with low efficacy expectations may expect very different outcomes (e.g., ripped muscles, lasting metabolic disorders) than another runner with higher self-efficacy (e.g., sore muscles, temporary fatigue) as a result of their different efficacies, not their perceptions of the rewards available.

What should we make, then, of the concept of self-efficacy? Some of its conceptual links to other determinants of behavior need clarification, and it needs to be considered as only one of several causes of a person's actions, as Bandura (e.g., 1984) has repeatedly emphasized. Still, efficacy expectancies are probably vitally important to the amelioration of dysfunctional behavior, since many troubled clients already possess the behavioral competencies needed to help their problems, but do not implement them because they do not believe they can. Arnkoff and Glass (1982) recalled the story of Dumbo, the flying elephant who could remain aloft as long as he was holding what he thought was a magic feather. This was a workable arrangement until Dumbo dropped the feather; he then started to plummet to the ground, and not until he was (hurriedly) convinced that he could fly did he again start using the skills he had possessed all along. Human clients may face similar dilemmas, and the successes of insight, client-centered, and rational-emotive therapies, for example, may depend largely on the extent to which they are able to influence clients' conceptions of the life skills they already have. When specific new skills are taught to clients in participant modeling or relaxation training, for instance, clients must still develop the confidence and certainty in their newfound talents that enable them to employ those skills when needed. Clients' expectations for their own successes appear to be of fundamental importance, and influencing clients' efficacy expectancies may be an indispensable part of any therapeutic endeavor.

Enhancing self-efficacy expectations. Indeed, Bandura (1977, 1982) suggested that, whatever their specific procedures, all effective strategies of behavior change have beneficial effects in part by influencing clients' perceptions of self-efficacy. He posed four broad ways a person's self-efficacy can be changed.

The most influential source of efficacy expectations is a client's own behavioral accomplishments. By actually demonstrating their mastery of a new skill or an old fear, clients gain straightforward evidence that they are capable, at least under some circumstances, of successfully enacting important behaviors. For example, Williams et al. (1985) showed that guided mastery of specific tasks in an eight-story parking garage was of greater and more lasting benefit to subjects with acrophobia than was a desensitization treatment in which the subjects merely faced the feared eight-story drop. The extent to which efficacy expectations are affected by performance accomplishments, of course, depends on the person's attributions for his or her success; attributions to internal, stable, global, and, especially, controllable factors are likely to lead to the greatest change in self-efficacy (see chapter 2).

Vicarious experience through the observation of others is a second source of efficacy information. Although not as influential as enactive mastery (Bandura et al., 1977), modeling treatments can have reliable effects on self-efficacy depending on the similarity of the models to the client, the number of models employed, and other situational variables (Bandura, 1977). Witnessing the successes of others can influence one's expectancies of performing similar actions.

Third, verbal persuasion affects self-efficacy. Although persuasion is not presumed to be as great an influence as performance-based treatments (since a single behavioral failure may undo all that is accomplished through persuasion), it can have desirable impact, particularly when it leads a client to attempt or persist at activities in which success is later obtained. Persuaders may also be able to remind clients of past successes and to point out internal causes for success that clients have overlooked (Goldfried & Robins, 1982, 1983). The credibility and attractiveness of the persuaders will likely determine how much persuasive influence they have (see chapter 9).

Finally, physiological states of arousal may affect perceptions of self-efficacy because people generally read signs of arousal in problematic situations as evidence of their vulnerability (cf. Leary & Atherton, 1986; Leary, Atherton, Hill, & Hur, in press). When they are cool and calm in the face of calamity, clients may be more confident of their abilities to cope with their predicaments. Biofeedback and symbolic desensitization may thus be useful treatments, removing arousal as a cue of low self-efficacy.

As Goldfried and Robins (1983) suggested, many therapies probably provide more than one source of efficacy information. A relaxation procedure not only reduces arousal, but also teaches a new behavioral skill that clients gradually master. Cognitive restructuring persuades a client of a new point of view but also reduces worried arousal. With these multiple effects in mind, we prefer, instead of contrasting therapies, to note their many commonalities as a means of summarizing this chapter. Bandura's analysis suggests that diverse treatments all share a common means of facilitating behavior change by influencing perceptions of self-efficacy.

Common Features of Strategies of Behavior Change

Observers of psychotherapies generally agree that there are several features shared by even disparate treatments (Brady et al., 1980; Critelli & Neumann, 1984; Frank, 1973; Goldfried, 1980; Strong & Claiborn, 1982). Examination of that list underscores the reliance of therapies upon the expectations of both therapist and client in influencing behavior.

First, psychotherapies involve a *therapist* who usually seems competent, caring, and confident. Second, there exists a *relationship* between therapist and client and a therapeutic setting that is a crucible for change. Third, the therapy provides a credible *rationale* for change that allows an expectancy of improvement. Finally, the therapy involves *new experiences* in the form of effortful procedures that both enhance the client's self-confidence and implicitly demand improvement. Together, these characteristics provide social support, successful experiences, and hope for improvement that, rather than mere nuisance variables to be controlled in effectiveness studies, may be a fundamental basis for the effectiveness of psychological treatment (Critelli & Neumann, 1984; Frank, 1973).

Along with whatever specific procedures are used to provide new experiences to clients, these common features are all likely to influence clients' beliefs that change is possible and that they will get better. Nearly all therapies involve a persuasive therapist who believes that change will occur, an interactive relationship that allows the therapist to communicate those expectancies, and an acceptable explanation for why change is attainable. Given the fact that many therapies have yet to demonstrate that they are any more effective than these positive expectancy-inducing features alone (Critelli & Neumann, 1984; Prioleau, Murdock, & Brody, 1983), the vital contribution of clients' positive expectations of change and the facilitating role of therapists' favorable expectations cannot be taken lightly. Whether or not it is explained in terms of self-efficacy, intentional or unintentional impact on clients' beliefs that favorable change is possible seems to be a universal factor in strategies of behavior change.

Conclusions

A therapist's confident expectations of success are a boon to any strategy of behavior change, frequently setting in motion self-fulfilling prophecies that increase the likelihood of psychotherapeutic change. The therapist's expectations probably have these beneficial effects in part by influencing the client's private expectations of what he or she can achieve. The client's expectations are of foremost importance, as they have direct influence on the client's behavioral capacities. Thus, enhancing clients' expectations of mastery, or self-efficacy, may be a vital part of any therapeutic enterprise. Happily, whatever their specific procedures, most psychological therapies share common elements that are likely to enhance a client's self-efficacy expectations.

Chapter 12

Areas and Issues

The preceding 11 chapters have provided an extensive overview of areas in which social psychological perspectives may be useful in understanding, diagnosing, and treating emotional and behavioral problems. Although we have examined what we feel are central topics in social-dysgenic, social-diagnostic, and social-therapeutic psychology, other topics have not even been mentioned. In this brief concluding chapter, we draw the reader's attention to those relevant topics that have not been discussed. We conclude with a discussion of professional issues that have emerged from recent interest in the area, adding a few remarks about the future of the interface.

Other Topics of Interest

To examine comprehensively all the potential integrations of social and clinical-counseling psychology this book would have to be at least twice its present size. Following are brief overviews of other topics in abnormal, clinical, and counseling psychology that involve interpersonal processes.

Group Therapy

Although counseling and psychotherapy evolved as a dyadic interaction between a therapist and a client, much counseling and psychotherapy today occurs within group settings involving a therapist and a number of clients (usually between four and eight). The use of therapy groups introduces several factors into the therapeutic setting that do not occur in dyadic therapy sessions, and the extensive social psychological literature dealing with group dynamics is relevant to understanding and managing what occurs when several individuals come together for treatment.

Topics within social psychology relevant to group therapy include conformity, leadership emergence, the development of group norms, coalition formation, conflict and conflict reduction, ingroup/outgroup biases, social facilitation, group polarization, deindividuation, proxemics, social loafing, and scapegoating, to name some of the more obvious. Space does not permit an examination of the relevance of each of these phenomena for group therapy, but details can be found in Forsyth (1983), Shaw (1981), and Sheras and Worchel (1979).

Family Relationships and Systems

Both the healthy and the unhealthy members of a closely knit group such as a family may unwittingly collaborate to maintain or exacerbate the psychological difficulties of a group member (Helmersen, 1983; Jacob, 1975). Studies of such interpersonal systems generally focus on either the structural aspects of family life (power relationships, coalitions, roles, etc.) or on the processes of family interaction, particularly communication (Hoffman, 1981). Thus, social psychological understanding of group process is relevant to understanding dysfunctional relationships within families, although social psychologists are just beginning to turn their attention to family systems (e.g., Gottsegen, 1985).

Cultural and Socioeconomic Factors

Various psychological disorders are not distributed evenly across all groups within society. Rather, behavioral and emotional problems vary markedly as a function of variables such as social class, race, sex, geographical area of residence (such as urban versus rural), religious affiliation, and country of birth (Freeman & Giovannoni, 1969). For example, in the classic project by Hollingshead and Redlich (1958), the prevalence of schizophrenia was found to be eight times greater among persons in low rather than high social strata. On the other hand, a greater proportion of upper-class persons were under treatment for neurotic disturbances and manic-depressive psychoses.

What remains unclear 25 years after this groundbreaking research is whether these patterns result from different stresses and coping mechanisms among people in different classes, from different manifestations of similar psychological problems as a function of class, or from therapists' tendency to diagnose problems differently depending on the social status of the client. In any case, the processes at work are social psychological in nature. Unfortunately, social psychologists are far less interested in the impact of sociocultural variables upon behavior than they were 20 years ago, and current work in the area is being conducted in other disciplines, such as sociology.

Aggression

Many individuals who seek psychological help have problems with hostility and aggression, such as juvenile offenders, child and spouse abusers, and highly combative personalities. The extensive social psychological literature on aggression is quite relevant to understanding and treating these individuals (Baron, 1983; Tavris, 1982). For example, people who have poor social skills and, thus, have difficulty influencing others in socially appropriate ways are more likely to be aggressive than are socially skilled individuals. Teaching aggressive people through modeling, role playing, and instruction to interact more adroitly may reduce their propensity to resort to aggression.

Also, the occurrence of aggression depends in part on the aggressor's attributions regarding others' actions. There is evidence that chronically aggressive individuals tend to attribute hostile intentions to others, interpreting their accidental transgressions as deliberate attacks (Nasby, Hayden, & DePaulo, 1980). To the degree that negatively biased attributions underlie aggressiveness, attributional training may reduce aggression in some cases.

Social Support

Not all help for psychological problems comes from trained professionals. Indeed, it is much more common for people to obtain advice, support, and consolation from friends and family. In light of this fact, researchers have recently become interested in informal helping relationships and their role in reducing behavioral and emotional difficulties (Kessler, Price, & Wortman, 1985). Simply being the member of a social network of individuals who can be counted on in times of need reduces anxiety, aggression, and depression, and improves the individual's ability to cope with stressful events (e.g., Turner, 1981). Further, having a supportive social network is associated with having fewer physical complaints, such as headaches, dizziness, and fatigue (Miller, Ingham, & Davidson, 1976). Among the elderly, the presence of an intimate friend or "confidant" seems to provide a buffer against the dysfunctional psychological consequences of stressful events, such as retirement and the death of one's spouse (Lowenthal & Haven, 1968).

However, at present it is unclear precisely why social support has these effects, why some people have good support systems and others do not, or how people may be helped to develop better social support networks. Within the growing literature on relationships, social support deserves a great deal more attention from social psychologists (e.g., Brehm, 1984).

Reactions to Receiving Help

Although people often seek help from both psychologists and friends, research suggests that they sometimes react negatively to the help they receive. Receiving help from others often implies weakness, engenders dependency, and creates an inequitable situation when one can not "repay" the helper for his or her assistance. Indeed, people may refuse to seek needed help or refuse help when it is offered if the proferred assistance damages their self-esteem or creates a debt (e.g., Fisher & Nadler, 1976). In light of this, practicing psychologists should understand how best to package their services so that people take full advantage of them. In addition, work is needed that examines ways of decreasing people's reluctance to seek help when needed (DePaulo, 1982).

Health Psychology

Health psychology involves the application of psychology to the prevention and treatment of illness, the maintenance of health-related behaviors, the identification of illness (both by medical personnel and the patient), and the delivery of health care (Matarazzo, 1982). Although the psychological aspects of health care have been long ignored, recent years have seen an influx of psychologists of all specialties into health-related settings (S. Hendrick, 1983; Hendrick & Hendrick, 1984). Even more have become involved in basic research on topics with implications for health and illness.

Within social psychology, this interest is manifested in studies dealing with factors that affect patients' compliance with physicians' orders, the effects of social support on adjustment following catastrophic accidents (Schulz & Decker, 1982), hypochondriasis (Snyder & Smith, 1982), antecedents and correlates of coronary-prone behavior (Glass, 1977), factors that minimize the effects of stressful events on the individual (such as "hardiness"; Kobasa, Maddi, & Kahn, 1982), physician-patient interactions (Stiles, Putman, & Jacob, 1982), the reduction of stress among patients facing aversive medical procedures (Langer, Janis, & Wolfer, 1975), and the prevention of unhealthy behavior such as smoking (Rogers, 1983), to name just a few. By all accounts, the social psychology of health and illness stands as an important, but relatively untapped area for investigation and practice.

Organizational Factors

The organizations in which people work contribute to both their well-being and their distress. In recent years, psychologists have become increasingly interested in how characteristics of organizations—work roles, on-the-job relationships, physical surroundings, job duties, organizational structure, and so on—contribute to stress and other dysfunctional reactions (see, for example, Osipow & Spokane, 1984; Parker & DeCotiis, 1983; Schuler, 1984). Not only does job stress interfere with performance and satisfaction on the job, but it can influence an employee's family life as well (Jackson & Maslach, 1982).

The effects of job stress are of dual interest to psychologists and other helping professionals. Not only do many of their clients have occupational concerns of various types, but mental health professionals themselves are particularly susceptible to certain forms of job stress or burnout (Maslach, 1982).

Environmental Factors

Finally, social psychologists have for many years been interested in the deleterious effects of the physical environments in which people live and work. Environmental conditions such as crowding, noise, and pollution can have serious psychological and physical effects. For example, airport noise is associated with increased admissions to mental hospitals (Meecham & Smith, 1977), birth defects (Timnick, 1978), and deaths from strokes (Dellinger, 1979). Similarly, although crowding does not produce all of the problems once attributed to it, it can have deleterious effects on both mood and behavior (see Altman, 1975; Freedman, 1975).

Conclusions

Few human problems do not include an interpersonal component. As demonstrated above and throughout the book, interpersonal processes underlie a variety of difficulties. And even when problems are created by impersonal forces, such as birth trauma, genetic factors, disease, or a natural disaster, the remediation of those problems invariably involves interpersonal events. Thus, the potential applicability of social psychology is quite broad, but the entrance of social psychologists into areas of applied psychology raises new questions regarding the professional identity of social psychologists vis-á-vis their clinical and counseling colleagues. In particular, what part should social psychologists play in the study and treatment of dysfunctional behavior?

Social Psychologists as Therapists?

With social psychologists' foray into the study of clinically relevant phenomena, some observers have asked whether social psychologists should engage in direct clinical practice. C. Hendrick (1983) asserted that they should, arguing that, given the content of their field, social psychologists have a birthright to practice interpersonal therapies. He based this assertion on two observations that echo themes carried throughout this book: Many, if not most, behavioral and emotional disturbances are "disturbances in interpersonal behavior" (p. 68), and psychotherapy is, at its base, a mode of social interaction. Thus, of all specialists within psychology, said Hendrick, social psychologists have the strongest background in theory and research that is relevant to understanding and treating dysfunctional behavior. He proposed that a new specialty of "clinical social psychology" be developed that would train social psychologists to be practitioners.

Although we are in basic agreement with C. Hendrick's point that social psychological theory and research is quite relevant to psychological practice, we also agree with S. Hendrick's (1983) argument that, in order for social psychologists to undertake seriously the prospect of doing clinical or counseling practice, doctoral training in social psychology would require additional work dealing with unhealthy, maladaptive behavior. Although theory and research in traditional social psychology *are* relevant to clinical and counseling practice, most of it deals with "normal" phenomena, and clinical social psychologists would need extensive work in the study of dysfunctional behavior.

Further, it seems to us that the sorts of activities for which social psychologists are best prepared involve work with minor clinical problems—those that involve the remediation of adjustment and interpersonal difficulties such as loneliness, troubled relationships, shyness, nonassertiveness, interpersonal conflict, stress, and so on (cf. S. Hendrick, 1983). Not only have these topics received extensive attention from social psychologists, but the treatments involved (e.g., social-skills training, self-management, assertiveness training, role playing) are systemized extensions of everyday interpersonal processes. This is *not* to say that social psychology is not relevant to more serious disorders, such as schizophrenia or severe depression, but less attention has been devoted to these phenomena by social psychologists.

The vast majority of social psychologists, even those who are interested in dysfunctional phenomena, do not wish to become engaged in providing direct services. However, as this volume demonstrates, increasing numbers are becoming interested in investigating the development, diagnosis, and treatment of dysfunctional behavior from social psychological perspectives. Most of these individuals were trained as basic social psychologists, with little, if any, advanced work in abnormal, clinical, or counseling psychology; their expertise in the social psychology of dysfunctional behavior developed through their own efforts after graduate school. Graduate programs are needed that train social psychologists in clinical problems, methods, and issues which "would result in a researcher who is well prepared to tackle some of the pressing practical problems of clinical and counseling psychology." (Maddux & Stoltenberg, 1983a, p. 296; see Leary, in press-a, for a full discussion of this issue).

In short, it seems shortsighted to believe that the knowledge and skills needed to treat dysfunctional behavior can be obtained only through traditional clinical and counseling training programs. However, social psychologists who wish to provide direct services need additional training to complement their basic knowledge and skills in social psychology. As more social psychologists become interested in topics traditionally of interest to counseling and clinical psychologists, changes will be required in how certain social psychologists are trained.

To the Future

To speculate too grandly about the future of the interface between social and professional psychology at this juncture is hazardous. Like the parents of young children who try to imagine their offspring as adolescents or adults, we find that the field is still far too new and undeveloped to predict the directions it will take, the issues it will raise, or even whether the recent burst of interest in social-dysgenic, social-diagnostic, and social-therapeutic topics represents the emergence of a genuine subspecialty in psychology or just a flash in the pan. All indications suggest that social psychology offers many useful perspectives on dysfunctional behavior, both with theories to guide research and with models upon which to base psychological interventions. Whether these perspectives will, in the long run, advance our understanding and treatment of psychological difficulties must be left to all of us, researchers and practitioners alike, to determine.

References

Abbey, A. (1982). Sex differences in attributions for friendly behavior: Do males misperceive females' friendliness? *Journal of Personality and Social Psychology, 42*, 830–838.

Abramowitz, C. V., Abramowitz, S. I., Roback, H. B., & Jackson, C. (1974). Differential effectiveness of directive and nondirective group therapies as a function of client internal-external control. *Journal of Consulting and Clinical Psychology, 42*, 849–853.

Abramowitz, C. V., & Dokecki, P. R. (1977). The politics of clinical judgment: Early empirical returns. *Psychological Bulletin, 84*, 460–476.

Abramowitz, S. I., Berger, A., & Weary, G. (1982). Similarity between clinician and client: Its influence on the helping relationship. In T. A. Wills (Ed.), *Basic processes in helping relationships* (pp. 357–380). New York: Academic Press.

Abramson, L. Y., & Sackheim, H. A. (1977). A paradox in depression: Uncontrollability and self-blame. *Psychological Bulletin, 84*, 835–851.

Abramson, L. Y., Seligman, M. E. P., & Teasdale, J. D. (1978). Learned helplessness in humans: Critique and reformulation. *Journal of Abnormal Psychology, 87*, 49–74.

Adler, A. (1930). Individual psychology. In C. Murchinson (Ed.), *Psychologies of 1930* (pp. 395–405). Worcester, MA: Clark University Press.

Alexander, C. N., Jr., & Sagatun, I. (1973). An attributional analysis of experimental norms. *Sociometry, 36*, 127–142.

Allen, C. M., & Straus, M. A. (1980). Resources, power, and husband-wife violence. In M. Straus and G. Hotaling (Eds.), *The social causes of husband-wife violence* (pp. 188–208). Minneapolis: University of Minnesota Press.

Alloy, L. B. (1982). The role of perceptions and attributions for response-outcome noncontingency in learned helplessness: A commentary and discussion. *Journal of Personality, 50*, 443–479.

Alloy, L. B., & Abramson, L. Y. (1979). Judgment of contingency in depressed and nondepressed students: Sadder but wiser? *Journal of Experimental Psychology: General, 108*, 441–485.

Alloy, L. B., & Abramson, L. Y. (1982). Learned helplessness, depression, and the illusion of control. *Journal of Personality and Social Psychology, 42*, 1114–1126.

Alloy, L. B., Abramson, L. Y., & Viscusi, D. (1981). Induced mood and the illusion of control. *Journal of Personality and Social Psychology, 41*, 1129–1140.

Alloy, L. B., & Tabachnik, N. (1984). Assessment of covariation by humans and animals: The joint influence of prior expectations and current situational information. *Psychological Review, 91,* 112–149.

Allport, G. (1955). *Becoming.* New Haven, CT: Yale University Press.

Allyon, T., Haughton, E., & Hughes, H. B. (1965). Interpretation of symptoms: Fact or fiction? *Behavior Research and Therapy, 3,* 1–7.

Altmaier, E. M., Leary, M. R., Forsyth, D. R., & Ansel, J. C. (1979). Attribution therapy: Effects of locus of control and timing of treatment. *Journal of Counseling Psychology, 26,* 481–486.

Altman, I. (1975). *The environment and social behavior.* Monterey, CA: Brooks/ Cole.

Andersen, S. M., & Bem, S. L. (1981). Sex typing and androgyny in dyadic interaction: Individual differences in responsiveness to physical attractiveness. *Journal of Personality and Social Psychology, 41,* 74–86.

Anderson, C. A. (1982). Inoculation and counterexplanation: Debiasing techniques in the perseverance of social theories. *Social Cognition, 1,* 126–139.

Anderson, C. A. (1983a). Motivational and performance deficits in interpersonal settings: The effect of attributional style. *Journal of Personality and Social Psychology, 45,* 1136–1147.

Anderson, C. A. (1983b). Abstract and concrete data in the perseverance of social theories: When weak data lead to unshakeable beliefs. *Journal of Experimental Social Psychology, 19,* 93–108.

Anderson, C. A., & Arnoult, L. H. (1985). Attributional style and everyday problems in living: Depression, loneliness, and shyness. *Social Cognition, 3,* 16–35.

Anderson, C. A., Horowitz, L. M., & French, R. (1983). Attributional style of lonely and depressed people. *Journal of Personality and Social Psychology, 45,* 127–136.

Anderson, C. A., Lepper, M. R., & Ross, L. (1980). Perseverance of social theories: The role of explanation in the persistence of discredited information. *Journal of Personality and Social Psychology, 39,* 1037–1049.

Anderson, C. A., New, B. L., & Speer, J. R. (1985). Argument availability as a mediator of social theory perseverence. *Social Cognition, 3,* 235–249.

Andrews, G. R., & Debus, R. L. (1978). Persistence and causal perception of failure: Modifying cognitive attributions. *Journal of Educational Psychology, 70,* 154–166.

Antaki, C. (1982). A brief introduction to attribution and attributional theories. In C. Antaki & C. Brewin (Eds.), *Attributions and psychological change: Applications of attributional theories to clinical and educational practice* (pp. 3–21). New York: Academic Press.

Antill, J. K. (1983). Sex role complementarity versus similarity in married couples. *Journal of Personality and Social Psychology, 45,* 145–155.

Apple, W., Streeter, L. A., & Krauss, R. B. (1979). Effects of pitch and speech rate on personal attributions. *Journal of Personality and Social Psychology, 37,* 715–727.

Ard, B. N., Jr. (1977). Avoiding destructive jealousy. In G. Clanton & L. G. Smith (Eds.), *Jealousy* (pp. 166–179). Englewood Cliffs, NJ: Prentice-Hall.

Argyle, M. (1975). *Bodily communication.* London: Methuen.

Argyle, M. (1981). Social competence and mental health. In M. Argyle (Ed.), *Social skills and health* (pp. 159–187). London: Methuen.

Arieti, S. (1959). *American handbook of psychiatry.* New York: Basic Books.

Arkes, H. R. (1981). Impediments to accurate clinical judgment and variable ways to minimize their impact. *Journal of Consulting and Clinical Psychology, 49,* 323–330.

Arkes, H. R., & Harkness, A. R. (1980). Effect of making a diagnosis on subsequent recognition of symptoms. *Journal of Experimental Psychology: Human Learning and Memory, 6,* 568–575.

Arkin, R. M. Self-presentation styles. (1981). In J. T. Tedeschi (Ed.), *Impression management theory and social psychological research* (pp. 311–333). New York: Academic Press.

Arkin, R. M., Lake, E. A., & Baumgardner, A. H. (1985). Shyness and self-presentation. In W. H. Jones, J. M. Cheek, & S. R. Briggs (Eds.), *Shyness: Perspectives on research and treatment* (pp. 189–203). New York: Plenum Press.

Arkowitz, H., Hinton, R., Perl, J., & Himadi, W. (1978). Treatment strategies for dating anxiety in college men based on real-life practice. *The Counseling Psychologist, 7*, 41–46.

Arkowitz, H., Lichtenstein, E., McGovern, K., & Hines, P. (1975). The behavioral assessment of social competence in males. *Behavioral Therapy, 6*, 3–13.

Arnkoff, D. B., & Glass, C. R. (1982). Clinical cognitive constructs: Examination, evaluation, and elaboration. In P. C. Kendall (Ed.), *Advances in cognitive-behavioral research* (Vol. 1, pp. 1–32). New York: Academic Press.

Aronson, E. (1968). Dissonance Theory: Progress and problems. In R. Abelson et al. (Eds.), *Theories of cognitive consistency: A sourcebook* Chicago: Rand McNally.

Aronson, E., & Mills, J. (1959). The effect of severity of initiation on liking for a group. *Journal of Abnormal and Social Psychology, 59*, 177–181.

Aronson, E., Turner, J., & Carlsmith, J. (1963). Communication credibility and communication discrepancy as determinants of opinion change. *Journal of Abnormal and Social Psychology, 67*, 31–36.

Artiss, K. L. (Ed.) (1959). *The symptom as communication in schizophrenia.* New York: Grune & Stratton.

Asch, S. E. (1946). Forming impressions of personality. *Journal of Abnormal and Social Psychology, 41*, 258–290.

Ascher, L. M., & Efran, J. S. (1978). Use of paradoxical intention in a behavioral program for sleep onset insomnia. *Journal of Consulting and Clinical Psychology, 46*, 547–550.

Atkinson, D. R., & Carskaddon, G. (1975). A prestigious introduction, psychological jargon, and perceived counselor credibility. *Journal of Counseling Psychology, 22*, 180–186.

Atkinson, J., & Huston, T. L. (1984). Sex role orientation and division of labor early in marriage. *Journal of Personality and Social Psychology, 46*, 330–345.

Auerbach, A. H., & Johnson, M. (1977). Research on the therapist's level of experience. In A. S. Gurman & A. M. Razin (Eds.), *Effective psychotherapy* (pp. 84–102). New York: Pergamon Press.

Axsom, D., & Cooper, J. (1985). Cognitive dissonance and psychotherapy: The role of effort justification in inducing weight loss. *Journal of Experimental Social Psychology, 21*, 149–160.

Bander, K. W., Steinke, G. V., Allen, G. J., & Mosher, D. L. (1975). Evaluation of three dating-specific treatment approaches for heterosexual dating anxiety. *Journal of Consulting and Clinical Psychology, 43*, 259–265.

Bandura, A. (1969). *Principles of behavior modification.* New York: Holt, Rinehart and Winston.

Bandura, A. (1973). *Aggression: A social learning analysis.* Englewood Cliffs, NJ: Prentice-Hall.

Bandura, A. (1977). Self-efficacy. Towards a unifying theory of behavioral change. *Psychological Review, 84*, 191–215.

Bandura, A. (1978). Reflections on self-efficacy. *Advances in Behaviour Research and Therapy, 1*, 237–269.

Bandura, A. (1982). Self-efficacy mechanism in personal agency. *American Psychologist, 37*, 122–147.

Bandura, A. (1984). Recycling misconceptions of perceived self-efficacy. *Cognitive Therapy and Research, 8*, 231–255.

Bandura, A., & Adams, N. E. (1977). Analysis of self-efficacy theory of behavioral change. *Cognitive Therapy and Research, 1,* 287–310.

Bandura, A., Adams, N. E., & Beyer, J. (1977). Cognitive processes mediating behavioral change. *Journal of Personality and Social Psychology, 35,* 125–139.

Bandura, A., Adams, N. E., Hardy, A. B., & Howells, G. N. (1980). Tests of the generality of self-efficacy. *Cognitive Therapy and Research, 4,* 39–66.

Bandura, A., Reese, L., & Adams, N. E. (1982). Microanalysis of action and fear arousal as a function of differential levels of perceived self-efficacy. *Journal of Personality and Social Psychology, 43,* 5–21.

Bandura, A., Taylor, C. B., Williams, S. L., Mefford, I. N., & Barchas, J. D. (1985). Catecholamine secretion as a function of perceived coping self-efficacy. *Journal of Consulting and Clinical Psychology, 53,* 406–414.

Barefoot, J. C., & Girodo, M. (1972). The misattribution of smoking cessation symptoms. *Canadian Journal of Behavioral Science, 4,* 358–363.

Barling, J., & Abel, M. (1983). Self-efficacy beliefs and tennis performance. *Cognitive Therapy and Research, 7,* 265–272.

Baron, R. A. (1983). The control of human aggression: An optimistic perspective. *Journal of Social and Clinical Psychology, 1,* 97–119.

Batson, C. D. (1975). Attribution as a mediator of bias in helping. *Journal of Personality and Social Psychology, 32,* 455–466.

Batson, C. D., Jones, C. H., & Cochran, P. J. (1979). Attributional bias in counselors' diagnoses: The effect of resources. *Journal of Applied Social Psychology, 9,* 377–393.

Batson, C. D., & Marz, B. (1979). Dispositional bias in trained therapists' diagnoses: Does it exist? *Journal of Applied Social Psychology, 9,* 476–489.

Batson, C. D., O'Quin, K., & Pych, V. (1982). An attribution theory analysis of trained helpers' inferences about clients' needs. In T. A. Wills (Ed.), *Basic processes in helping relationships* (pp. 59–80). New York: Academic Press.

Baucom, D. H. (1983). Sex role identity and the decision to regain control among women: A learned helplessness investigation. *Journal of Personality and Social Psychology, 44,* 334–343.

Baumeister, R. F. (1982). A self-presentational view of social phenomena. *Psychological Bulletin, 91,* 3–26.

Baumeister, R. F. (1984). Choking under pressure: Self-consciousness and paradoxical effects of incentives on skillful performance. *Journal of Personality and Social Psychology, 46,* 610–620.

Baumeister, R. F., Hamilton, J. C., & Tice, D. M. (1985). Public versus private expectancy of success: Confidence booster or performance pressure? *Journal of Personality and Social Psychology, 48,* 1447–1457.

Baumeister, R. F., & Jones, E. E. (1978). When self-presentation is constrained by the target's knowledge: Consistency and compensation. *Journal of Personality and Social Psychology, 36,* 608–618.

Baumeister, R. F., & Steinhilber, A. (1984). Paradoxical effects of supportive audiences on performance under pressure: The home field disadvantage in sports championships. *Journal of Personality and Social Psychology, 47,* 85–93.

Baumgardner, A. H., & Arkin, R. M. (1985, August). *Playing it safe? Social anxiety and protective self-presentation.* Paper presented at the meeting of The American Psychological Association, Los Angeles.

Beach, S. R. H., Abramson, L. Y., & Levine, F. M. (1981). Attributional reformulation of learned helplessness and depression: Therapeutic implications. In J. F. Clarkin & H. I. Glazer (Eds.), *Depression: Behavioral and directive intervention strategies* (pp. 131–145). New York: Garland STPM Press.

Beck, A. T., Rush, A. J., Shaw, B. F., & Emery, G. (1979). *Cognitive therapy of depression.* New York: Guilford Press.

Beck, J. T., & Strong, S. R. (1981). *Positive connotation: Stimulating therapeutic change with paradoxical interpretations.* Unpublished manuscript, Virginia Commonwealth University, Richmond.

Bellack, A. S., & Hersen, M. (Eds.) (1979). *Research and practice in social skills training.* New York: Plenum Press.

Bem, D. J. (1972). Self perception theory. In L. Berkowitz (Ed.), *Advances in experimental social psychology* (Vol. 6, pp. 1–62). New York: Academic Press.

Bem, S. L., & Lenney, E. (1976). Sex typing and the avoidance of cross-sex behavior. *Journal of Personality and Social Psychology, 33,* 48–54.

Berg, J. H., Blaylock, T., Camarillo, J., & Steck, L. (1985, April). *Taking another's outcomes into consideration.* Paper presented at the annual meeting of the Southeastern Psychological Association, Atlanta.

Bergin, A. E. (1962). The effect of dissonant persuasive communications upon changes in a self-referring attitude. *Journal of Personality, 30,* 423–438.

Berglas, S., & Jones, E. E. (1978). Drug choice as a self-handicapping strategy in response to a noncontingent success. *Journal of Personality and Social Psychology, 36,* 405–417.

Berkowitz admits inventing demons. Associated Press. *Gainesville (FL) Sun,* Feb 23, 1979, p. 4B.

Berley, R. A., & Jacobson, N. S. (1984). Causal attributions in intimate relationships: Toward a model of cognitive-behavioral marital therapy. In P. C. Kendall (Ed.), *Advances in cognitive-behavioral research and therapy* (Vol. 3, pp. 1–60). Orlando, FL: Academic Press.

Berman, J. S., & Bennett, J. B. (1982, August). *Love and power: Testing Waller's principle of least interest.* Paper presented at the annual meeting of the American Psychological Association, Washington, DC.

Berman, J. S., & Wenzlaff, R. M. (1983, August). *The impact of therapist expectancies on the outcome of psychotherapy.* Paper presented at the annual meeting of the American Psychological Association, Anaheim, CA.

Bernier, M., & Poser, E. G. (1984). The relationship between self-efficacy, attributions, and weight loss in a weight rehabilitation program. *Rehabilitation Psychology, 29,* 95–105.

Berscheid, E. (1966). Opinion change and communicator-communicatee similarity and dissimilarity. *Journal of Personality and Social Psychology, 4,* 670–680.

Berscheid, E., & Fei, J. (1977). Romantic love and sexual jealousy. In G. Clanton & L. G. Smith (Eds.), *Jealousy* (pp. 101–109). Englewood Cliffs, NJ: Prentice-Hall.

Berscheid, E., & Walster, E. (1974). Physical attractiveness. In L. Berkowitz (Ed.), *Advances in experimental social psychology* (Vol. 7, pp. 157–215). New York: Academic Press.

Berzins, J. I. (1977). Therapist-patient matching. In A. S. Gurman & A. M. Razin (Eds.), *Effective psychotherapy: A handbook of research.* New York: Pergamon Press.

Beutler, L. E. (1971). Predicting outcomes of psychotherapy: A comparison of predictions from two attitude theories. *Journal of Consulting and Clinical Psychology, 37,* 411–416.

Beutler, L. E., Jobe, A. M., & Elkins, D. (1974). Outcomes in group psychotherapy: Using persuasion theory to increase treatment efficiency. *Journal of Consulting and Clinical Psychology, 42,* 547–553.

Beutler, L. E., Johnson, D. T., Neville, C. W., Jr., & Workman, S. N. (1972). Effort expended as a determiner of treatment evaluation and outcome: The honor of a prophet in his own country. *Journal of Consulting and Clinical Psychology, 39,* 495–500.

Binderman, R. M., Fretz, B. C., Scott, N. A., & Abrams, M. H. (1972). Effects of interpreter credibility and discrepancy level of results on responses to test results. *Journal of Counseling Psychology, 19,* 399–403.

Birchler, G. R., Weiss, R. L., & Vincent, J. P. (1975). Multimethod analysis of social reinforcement exchange between maritally distressed and non-distressed spouse and stranger dyads. *Journal of Personality and Social Psychology, 31,* 349–362.

Bishop, J. B., & Richards, T. F. (1984). Counselor theoretical orientation as related to intake judgments. *Journal of Counseling Psychology, 31,* 398–401.

Bloom, B. L., Asher, S. J., & White, S. W. (1978). Marital disruption as a stressor: A review and analysis. *Psychological Bulletin, 85,* 867–894.

Bohime, W. (1960). Depression as a practice: Dynamics and psychotherapeutic considerations. *Comprehensive Psychiatry, 1,* 194–201.

Bond, C. F. (1985). The next-in-line effect: Encoding or retrieval deficit? *Journal of Personality and Social Psychology, 48,* 853–862.

Bootzin, R. R. (1985). The role of expectancy in behavior change. In L. White, G. Schwartz, & B. Tursky (Eds.), *Placebo: Clinical phenomena and new insights* (pp. 196–210). New York: Guilford press.

Bootzin, R. R., Herman, C. P., & Nicassio, P. (1976). The power of suggestion: Another examination of misattribution and insomnia. *Journal of Personality and Social Psychology, 34,* 673–679.

Borkovec, T. D. (1978). Self-efficacy: Cause or reflection of behavioral change? *Advances in Behavior Research and Therapy, 1,* 163–170.

Borkovec, T. D., & Glasgow, R. E. (1973). Boundary conditions of fake heart-rate feedback effects on avoidance behavior: A resolution of discrepant results. *Behavior Research and Therapy, 11,* 171–177.

Borkovec, T. D., Stone, N. M., O'Brien, G. T., & Kaloupek, D. G. (1974). Evaluation of a clinically relevant target behavior for analog outcome research. *Behavior Therapy, 5,* 503–513.

Borkovec, T. D., Wall, R. L., & Stone, N. M. (1974). False physiological feedback and the maintenance of speech anxiety. *Journal of Abnormal Psychology, 83,* 164–168.

Borys, S., & Perlman, D. (1985). Gender differences in loneliness. *Personality and Social Psychology Bulletin, 11,* 63–74.

Bowers, K. (1968). Pain, anxiety, and perceived control. *Journal of Consulting and Clinical Psychology, 32,* 596–602.

Bowers, K. S. (1975). The psychology of subtle control: An attributional analysis of behavioral persistence. *Canadian Journal of Behavioral Science, 7,* 78–95.

Brady, J. P., Davison, G. C., Dewald, P. A., Egan, G., Fadiman, J., Frank, J. D., Gill, M. M., Hoffman, I., Kempler, W., Lazarus, A. A., Raimy, V., Rotter, J. B., & Strupp, H. H. (1980). Some views on effective principles of psychotherapy. *Cognitive Therapy and Research, 4,* 269–306.

Braginsky, B., & Braginsky, D. (1967). Schizophrenic patients in the psychiatric interview: An experimental study of their effectiveness at manipulation. *Journal of Consulting Psychology, 30,* 295–300.

Braginsky, B. M., Braginsky, D. D., & Ring, K. (1982). *Methods of madness: The mental hospital as a last resort.* Lanham, MD: University Press of America.

Braginsky, B. M., Grosse, M., & Ring, K. (1966). Controlling outcomes through impression management: An experimental study of the manipulative tactics of mental patients. *Journal of Consulting Psychology, 30,* 295–300.

Bramel, D. A. (1963). Selection of a target for defensive projection. *Journal of Abnormal and Social Psychology, 66,* 318–324.

Brehm, J. W. (1966). *A theory of psychological reactance.* New York: Academic Press.

Brehm, J. W. (1972). *Responses to loss of freedom: A theory of psychological reactance.* Morristown, NJ: General Learning Press.

Brehm, J. W., & Cohen, A. R. (1962). *Explorations in cognitive dissonance*. New York: Wiley.

Brehm, S. S. (1976). *The application of social psychology to clinical practice*. Washington, DC: Hemisphere.

Brehm, S. S. (1984). Social support processes. In J. C. Masters & K. Yarkin-Levin (Eds.), *Boundary areas in social and developmental psychology* (pp. 107–129). Orlando, FL: Academic Press.

Brehm, S. S. (1985). *Intimate relationships*. New York: Random House.

Brenner, M. (1973). The next-in-line effect. *Journal of Verbal Learning and Verbal Behavior, 12,* 320–323.

Brewin, C. R. (1984). Attributions for industrial accidents: Their relationship to rehabilitation outcome. *Journal of Social and Clinical Psychology, 2,* 156–164.

Brewin, C., & Antaki, C. (1982). The role of attributions in psychological treatment. In C. Antaki & C. Brewin (Eds.), *Attributions and psychological change: Applications of attributional theories to clinical and educational practice* (pp. 23–44). New York: Academic Press.

Brewin, C. R., & Shapiro, D. A. (1985). Selective impact of reattribution of failure instructions on task performance. *British Journal of Social Psychology, 24,* 37–46.

Brodt, S. E., & Zimbardo, P. G. (1981). Modifying shyness-related social behavior through symptom misattribution. *Journal of Personality and Social Psychology, 41,* 437–449.

Brown, B. R. (1968). The effects of need to maintain face on interpersonal bargaining. *Journal of Experimental Social Psychology, 4,* 107–122.

Brown, R. D. (1970). Experienced and inexperienced counselors' first impressions of clients and case outcomes: Are first impressions lasting? *Journal of Counseling Psychology, 17,* 550–558.

Bruner, J., & Tagiuri, R. (1954). The perception of people. In G. Lindzey (Ed.), *Handbook of social psychology* (Vol. 2, pp. 634–654). Cambridge, MA: Addison-Wesley.

Bruskin Associates. (1973, July). What are Americans afraid of? *The Bruskin Report: A Market Research Newsletter,* No. 53.

Bryant, B., & Trower, P. E. (1974). Social difficulty in a student sample. *British Journal of Educational Psychology, 44,* 13–21.

Burdg, N. B., & Graham, S. (1984). Effects of sex and label on performance ratings, children's test scores, and examiners' verbal behavior. *American Journal of Mental Deficiency, 88,* 422–427.

Burger, J. M. (1985). Desire for control and achievement-related behaviors. *Journal of Personality and Social Psychology, 48,* 1520–1533.

Burger, J. M., & Arkin, R. M. (1980). Prediction, control, and learned helplessness. *Journal of Personality and Social Psychology, 38,* 482–491.

Burger, J. M., Brown, R., & Allen, C. K. (1983). Negative reactions to personal control. *Journal of Social and Clinical Psychology, 1,* 322–342.

Burger, J. M., & Cooper, H. M. (1979). The desirability of control. *Motivation and Emotion, 3,* 381–393.

Buss, A. H. (1980). *Self-consciousness and social anxiety*. San Francisco: Freeman.

Buunk, B. (1982). Anticipated sexual jealousy: Its relationship to self-esteem, dependency, and reciprocity. *Personality and Social Psychology Bulletin, 8,* 310–316.

Buunk, B. (1984). Jealousy as related to attributions for the partner's behavior. *Social Psychology Quarterly, 47,* 107–112.

Byrne, D. (1971). *The attraction paradigm*. New York: Academic Press.

Cacioppo, J. T., Glass, C. R., & Merluzzi, T. V. (1979). Self-statements and self-evaluations: A cognitive response analysis of heterosocial anxiety. *Cognitive Therapy and Research, 3,* 249–262.

Cain, A. C. (1964). On the meaning of "playing crazy" in borderline children. *Psychiatry, 27,* 278–289.

Cantor, N. (1982). "Everyday" versus normative models of clinical and social judgment. In G. Weary and H. L. Mirels (Eds.), *Integrations of clinical and social psychology* (pp. 27–47). New York: Oxford University Press.

Caplan, N., & Nelson, S. D. (1973). On being useful: The nature and consequences of psychological research on social problems. *American Psychologist, 28,* 199–211.

Carkhuff, R. R. (1969). *Helping and human relations* (Vol. 2). New York: Holt, Rinehart & Winston.

Carretta, T. R., & Moreland, R. L. (1982). Nixon and Watergate: A field demonstration of belief perseverance. *Personality and Social Psychology Bulletin, 8,* 446–453.

Carson, R. C. (1969). *Interaction concepts of personality.* Chicago: Aldine.

Carver, C. S. (1979). A cybernetic model of self-attention processes. *Journal of Personality and Social Psychology, 31,* 1251–1281.

Cash, T. F., Begley, P. J., McGown, D. A., & Weise, B. C. (1975). When counselors are heard but not seen: Initial impact of physical attractiveness. *Journal of Counseling Psychology, 22,* 273–279.

Cash, T. F., & Kehr, J. (1978). Influence of nonprofessional counselors' physical attractiveness and sex on perceptions of counselor behavior. *Journal of Counseling Psychology, 25,* 336–342.

Chambliss, C., & Murray, E. J. (1979). Cognitive procedures for smoking reduction: Symptom attribution versus efficacy attribution. *Cognitive Therapy and Research, 3,* 91–95.

Chapin, M., & Dyck, D. G. (1976). Persistence in children's reading behavior as a function of N length and attribution retraining. *Journal of Abnormal Psychology, 85,* 511–515.

Chapman, L. J., & Chapman, J. P. (1967). Genesis of popular but erroneous psychodiagnostic observations. *Journal of Abnormal Psychology, 72,* 193–204.

Chapman, L. J., & Chapman, J. P. (1969). Illusory correlation as an obstacle to the use of valid psychodiagnostic signs. *Journal of Abnormal Psychology, 74,* 271–280.

Check, J. V. P., & Malamuth, N. M. (1983). Sex role stereotyping and reactions to depictions of stranger versus acquaintance rape. *Journal of Personality and Social Psychology, 45,* 344–356.

Cheek, J. M., & Buss, A. H. Shyness and sociability. (1981). *Journal of Personality and Social Psychology, 41,* 330–339.

Cheek, J. M., & Melchior, L. A. (1985, August). *Are shy people narcissistic?* Paper presented at the meeting of the American Psychological Association, Los Angeles.

Claiborn, C. D. (1979). Counselor verbal intervention, nonverbal behavior, and social power. *Journal of Counseling Psychology, 26,* 378–383.

Clanton, G., & Smith, L. G. (Eds.) (1977). *Jealousy.* Englewood Cliffs, NJ: Prentice-Hall.

Clark, J. V., & Arkowitz, H. (1975). Social anxiety and self-evaluation of interpersonal performance. *Psychological Reports, 36,* 211–221.

Clark, L. F., & Taylor, S. E. (1983, August). *Hypothesis-testing under different interaction conditions: The questions people ask.* Paper presented at the annual meeting of the American Psychological Association, Anaheim, CA.

Clark, M. S. (1985). Implications of relationship type for understanding compatibility. In W. Ickes (Ed.), *Compatible and incompatible relationships* (pp. 119–140). New York: Springer-Verlag.

Coelho, R. J. (1984). Self-efficacy and cessation of smoking. *Psychological Reports, 54,* 309–310.

Coleman, M., & Ganong, L. H. (1985). Love and sex role stereotypes: Do macho men and feminine women make better lovers? *Journal of Personality and Social Psychology, 49,* 170–176.

Coles, R. (1973). Shrinking history—Part one. *New York Review of Books, 20*(2), 15–21.

Colletti, G., & Kopel, S. A. (1979). Maintaining behavior change: An investigation of three maintenance strategies and the relationship of self-attribution to the long-term reduction of cigarette smoking. *Journal of Consulting and Clinical Psychology, 47,* 614–617.

Condiotte, M. M., & Lichtenstein, E. (1981). Self-efficacy and relapse in smoking cessation programs. *Journal of Consulting and Clinical Psychology, 49,* 648–658.

Conger, J. C., Conger, A. J., & Brehm, S. S. (1976). Fear level as a moderator of false feedback effects in snake phobias. *Journal of Consulting and Clinical Psychology, 44,* 135–141.

Constantine, L. L. (1977). Jealousy: Techniques for intervention. In G. Clanton & L. G. Smith (Eds.), *Jealousy* (pp. 190–198). Englewood Cliffs, NJ: Prentice-Hall.

Conway, M., & Ross, M. (1984). Getting what you want by revising what you had. *Journal of Personality and Social Psychology, 47,* 738–748.

Cooper, J. (1980). Reducing fears and increasing assertiveness: The role of dissonance reduction. *Journal of Experimental Social Psychology, 16,* 199–213.

Cooper, J., & Axsom, D. (1982). Effort justification in psychotherapy. In G. Weary & H. L. Mirels (Eds.), *Integrations of clinical and social psychology* (pp. 214–230). New York: Oxford University Press.

Corrigan, J. D., Dell, D. M., Lewis, K. N., & Schmidt, L. D. (1980). Counseling as a social influence process: A review. *Journal of Counseling Psychology, 27,* 395–441.

Coyne, J. C. (1976a). Depression and the response of others. *Journal of Abnormal Psychology, 85,* 186–193.

Coyne, J. C. (1976b). Toward an interactional description of depression. *Psychiatry, 39,* 28–40.

Coyne, J. C., & Gotlib, I. H. (1983). The role of cognition in depression: A critical appraisal. *Psychological Bulletin, 94,* 472–505.

Critelli, J. W., & Neumann, K. F. (1984). The placebo: Conceptual analysis of a construct in transition. *American Psychologist, 39,* 32–39.

Crocker, J. (1981). Judgment of covariation by social perceivers. *Psychological Bulletin, 90,* 272–292.

Crowne, D. P., & Marlowe, D. (1964). *The approval motive: Studies in evaluative dependence.* New York: Wiley.

Curran, J. P. (1975). An evaluation of a skills training program and a systematic desensitization program in reducing dating anxiety. *Behavior Research and Therapy, 13,* 65–68.

Curran, J. P. (1977). Skills training as an approach to the treatment of heterosexual-social anxiety. *Psychological Bulletin, 84,* 140–157.

Curran, J. P., & Gilbert, F. S. (1975). A test of the relative effectiveness of a systematic desensitization program and an interpersonal skills training program with date anxious subjects. *Behavior Therapy, 6,* 510–521.

Cutrona, C. E. (1982). Transition to college: Loneliness and the process of social adjustment. In L. A. Peplau & D. Perlman (Eds.), *Loneliness: A sourcebook of current theory, research and therapy* (pp. 291–309). New York: Wiley.

Cutrona, C. E., Russell, D., & Jones, R. D. (1984). Cross-situational consistency in causal attributions: Does attributional style exist? *Journal of Personality and Social Psychology, 47,* 1043–1058.

Dailey, C. A. (1952). The effects of premature conclusion upon the acquisition of understanding of a person. *Journal of Psychology, 33,* 133–152.

Dallas, M. E. W., & Baron, R. S. (1985). Do psychotherapists use a confirmatory strategy during interviewing? *Journal of Social and Clinical Psychology, 3,* 106–122.

Daly, J. A., & McCroskey, J. C. (1984). *Avoiding communication.* Beverly Hills, CA: Sage.

Danker-Brown, P., & Baucom, D. H. (1982). Cognitive influences on the development of learned helplessness. *Journal of Personality and Social Psychology, 43,* 793–801.

Darley, J. M., & Fazio, R. H. (1983). A hypothesis-confirming bias in labeling effects. *Journal of Personality and Social Psychology, 44,* 20–33.

Darley, J. M., & Gross, P. H. (1983). A hypothesis-confirming bias in labeling effects. *Journal of Personality and Social Psychology, 44,* 20–33.

Davidson, B. (1984). A test of equity theory for marital adjustment. *Social Psychology Quarterly, 47,* 36–42.

Davies, J. B. (1982). Alcoholism, social policy, and intervention. In J. R. Eiser (Ed.), *Social psychology and behavioral medicine* (pp. 235–260). London: Wiley.

Davis, D. A. (1979). What's in a name? A Bayesian rethinking of attributional biases in clinical judgment. *Journal of Consulting and Clinical Psychology, 47,* 1109–1114.

Davison, G. C., Tsujimoto, R. N., & Glaros, A. G. (1973). Attribution and the maintenance of behavior change in falling asleep. *Journal of Abnormal Psychology, 82,* 124–133.

Davison, G. C., & Valins, S. (1969). Maintenance of self-attributed and drug-attributed behavior change. *Journal of Personality and Social Psychology, 11,* 25–33.

Dawes, R. M. (1979). The robust beauty of improper linear models in decision making. *American Psychologist, 34,* 571–582.

Dawes, R. M. (1982). The value of being explicit when making clinical decisions. In T. A. Wills (Ed.), *Basic processes in helping relationships* (pp. 37–58). New York: Academic Press.

Dawes, R. M., & Corrigan, B. (1974). Linear models in decision making. *Psychological Bulletin, 81,* 95–106.

Dean, D., Braito, R., Powers, E., & Brant, B. (1975). Cultural contradiction and sex role revisited: A replication and reassessment. *The Sociological Quarterly, 16,* 207–215.

DeCharms, R. (1968). *Personal causation: The internal affective determinants of behavior.* New York: Academic Press.

Deci, E. L. (1975). *Intrinsic motivation.* New York: Plenum Press.

DeGree, C. E., & Snyder, C. R. (1985). Adler's psychology (of use) today: Personal history of traumatic life events as a self-handicapping strategy. *Journal of Personality and Social Psychology, 48,* 1512–1519.

Dell, D. M. (1973). Counselor power base, influence attempt, and behavior change in counseling. *Journal of Counseling Psychology, 20,* 399–405.

Dellinger, R. W. (1979). Jet roar: Health problems take off near airports. *Human Behavior, 8*(5), 50–51.

DePaulo, B. M. (1982). Social psychological processes in informal help-seeking. In T. Wills (Ed.), *Basic processes in helping relationships* (pp. 255–279). New York: Academic Press.

DePaulo, B. M., Stone, J. I., & Lassiter, G. D. (1985). Deceiving and detecting deceit. In B. R. Schlenker (Ed.), *The self and social life* (pp. 323–370). New York: McGraw-Hill.

Devins, G. M., Binik, Y. M., Gorman, P., Dattel, M., McCloskey, B., Oscar, G., & Briggs, J. (1982). Perceived self-efficacy, outcome expectancies, and negative mood states in end-stage renal disease. *Journal of Abnormal Psychology, 91,* 241–244.

DiClemente, C. C., Prochaska, J. O., & Gibertini, M. (1985). Self-efficacy and the stages of self-change of smoking. *Cognitive Therapy and Research, 9,* 181–200.

Diener, E. (1979). Deindividuation, self-awareness, and disinhibition. *Journal of Personality and Social Psychology, 37,* 1160–1171.

Dienstbier, R. A., & Munter, P. O. (1971). Cheating as a function of the labeling of natural arousal. *Journal of Personality and Social Psychology, 17,* 208–213.

Dietrich, J. E. (1946). The relative effectiveness of two modes of radio delivery in influencing attitudes. *Speech Monographs, 13,* 58–65.

Docherty, J. P., & Ellis, J. (1976). A new concept and findings in morbid jealousy. *American Journal of Psychiatry, 133,* 679–683.

Doherty, E. G. (1971). Social attraction and choice among psychiatric patients and staff: A review. *Journal of Health and Social Behavior, 12,* 279–290.

Dorn, F. J. C. (1984). *Counseling as applied social psychology.* Springfield, IL: Thomas.

Dryden, W. (1981). The relationships of depressed persons. In S. Duck & R. Gilmour (Eds.), *Personal relationships. 3: Personal relationships in disorder* (pp. 191–214). London: Academic Press.

Duck, S. (1980). The personal context: Intimate relationships. In P. Feldman & J. Orford (Eds.), *Psychological problems: The social context* (pp. 73–96). London: Wiley.

Duck, S. (Ed.) (1982). *Personal relationships. 4: Dissolving personal relationships.* London: Academic Press.

Duck, S. (Ed.) (1984). *Personal relationships. 5: Repairing personal relationshps.* London: Academic Press.

Duck, S., & Gilmour, R. (1981). *Personal relationships. 3: Personal relationships in disorder.* London: Academic Press.

Duncan, S., Jr. (1972). Some signals and rules for taking speaking turns in conversation. *Journal of Personality and Social Psychology, 23,* 283–292.

Dusek, J. B., Kermis, M. D., & Mergler, N. L. (1975). Information processing in low- and high-test-anxious children as a function of grade level and verbal labeling. *Developmental Psychology, 11,* 651–652.

Duval, S., & Wicklund, R. A. (1972). *A theory of objective self-awareness.* New York: Academic Press.

Dweck, C. S. (1975). The role of expectations and attributions in the alleviation of learned helplessness. *Journal of Personality and Social Psychology, 36,* 951–962.

Eagly, A. H., & Himmelfarb, S. (1978). Attitudes and opinions. *Annual Review of Psychology, 29,* 517–554.

Eastman, C., & Marzillier, J. S. (1984). Theoretical and methodological difficulties in Bandura's self-efficacy theory. *Cognitive Therapy and Research, 8,* 213–229.

Eccles (Parsons), J., Adler, T., & Meece, J. L. (1984). Sex differences in achievement: A test of alternate theories. *Journal of Personality and Social Psychology, 46,* 26–43.

Edinger, J. A., & Patterson, M. L. (1983). Nonverbal involvement and social control. *Psychological Bulletin, 93,* 30–56.

Edwards, J. N., & Saunders, J. M. (1981). Coming apart: A model of the marital dissolution decision. *Journal of Marriage and the Family, 41,* 379–389.

Efran, J. S., & Korn, P. R. (1969). Measurement of social caution: Self-appraisal, role playing, and discussion behavior. *Journal of Consulting and Clinical Psychology, 33,* 78–83.

Einhorn, H. J. (1972). Expert measurement and mechanical combination. *Organizational Behavior and Human Performance, 7,* 86–106.

Einhorn, H. J., & Hogarth, R. M. (1978). Confidence in judgment: Persistence of the illusion of validity. *Psychological Review, 85,* 395–416.

Ellis, A. (1962). *Reason and emotion in psychotherapy*. New York: Lyle Stuart.

Ellis, A. (1977a). The basic clinical theory of rational-emotive therapy. In A. Ellis & R. Grieger (Eds.), *Handbook of rational-emotive therapy* (pp. 3–34). New York: Springer.

Ellis, A. (1977b). Rational and irrational jealousy. In G. Clanton & L. G. Smith (Eds.), *Jealousy* (pp. 170–178). Englewood Cliffs, NJ: Prentice-Hall.

Elms, A. C. (1975). The crisis of confidence in social psychology. *American Psychologist, 30,* 967–976.

Elms, A. C., & Janis, I. L. (1965). Counter-norm attitudes induced by consonant versus dissonant conditions of role-playing. *Journal of Experimental Research in Personality, 1,* 50–60.

Emrick, C. D., Lassen, C. L., & Edwards, M. T. (1977). Nonprofessional peers as therapeutic agents. In A. S. Gurman & A. M. Razin (Eds.), *Effective psychotherapy: A handbook of research* (pp. 120–161). New York: Pergamon Press.

Eysenck, H. J. (1978). Expectations as causal elements in behavioural change. *Advances in Behaviour Research and Therapy, 1,* 171–175.

Farber, I. E. (1975). Sane and insane: Constructions and misconstructions. *Journal of Abnormal Psychology, 84,* 589–620.

Fazio, R. H., Effrein, E. A., & Falender, V. J. (1981). Self-perceptions following social interaction. *Journal of Personality and Social Psychology, 41,* 232–242.

Fazio, R. H., Zanna, M. P., & Cooper, J. (1977). Dissonance and self-perception: An integrative view of each theory's proper domain of application. *Journal of Experimental Social Psychology, 13,* 464–479.

Fehrenbach, P. A., & O'Leary, M. R. (1982). Interpersonal attraction and treatment decisions in inpatient and outpatient psychiatric settings. In T. A. Wills (Ed.), *Basic processes in helping relationships* (pp. 13–36). New York: Academic Press.

Feldman, R. S., & Prohaska, T. (1979). The student as Pygmalion: Effect of student expectation on the teacher. *Journal of Educational Psychology, 71,* 485–493.

Feldman, R. S., & Theiss, A. J. (1982). The teacher and student as Pygmalions: Joint effects of teacher and student expectations. *Journal of Educational Psychology, 74,* 217–223.

Felson, R. B. (1978). Aggression as impression management. *Social Psychology Quarterly, 41,* 205–213.

Fenigstein, A. (1979). Self-consciousness, self-attention, and social interaction. *Journal of Personality and Social Psychology, 37,* 75–86.

Feningstein, A., Scheier, M. F., & Buss, A. H. (1975). Public and private self-consciousness: Assessment and theory. *Journal of Consulting and Clinical Psychology, 43,* 522–527.

Festinger, L. (1954). A theory of social comparison processes. *Human Relations, 1,* 117–140.

Festinger, L. (1957). *A theory of cognitive dissonance*. Stanford, CA: Stanford University Press.

Festinger, L. (1961). The psychological effects of insufficient reward. *American Psychologist, 16,* 1–12.

Festinger, L., & Carlsmith, J. M. (1959). Cognitive consequences of forced compliance. *Journal of Abnormal and Social Psychology, 58,* 203–210.

Feyerabend, P. K. (1970). How to be a good empiricist: A plea for tolerance in matters epistemological. In B. Brody (Ed.), *Readings in the philosophy of science*. Englewood Cliffs, NJ: Prentice-Hall.

Fichten, C. S. (1984). See it from my point of view: Videotape and attributions in happy and distressed couples. *Journal of Social and Clinical Psychology, 2,* 125–142.

Fincham, F. D. (1983). Clinical applications of attribution theory: Problems and prospects. In M. Hewstone (Ed.), *Attribution theory: Social and functional extensions* (pp. 187–203). Oxford: Blackwells.

Fincham, F. D. (1985). Attribution processes in distressed and nondistressed couples: 2. Responsibility for marital problems. *Journal of Abnormal Psychology, 94*, 183–190.

Fincham, F., & O'Leary, K. D. (1983). Causal inferences for spouse behavior in maritally distressed and nondistressed couples. *Journal of Social and Clinical Psychology, 1*, 42–57.

Fischer, C. S., & Phillips, S. L. (1982). Who is alone? Characteristics of people with small networks. In L. A. Peplau & D. Perlman (Eds.), *Loneliness: A sourcebook of current theory, research and therapy* (pp. 21–39). New York: Wiley.

Fischer, J. L., & Narus, L. R., Jr. (1981). Sex roles and intimacy in same sex and other sex relationships. *Psychology of Women Quarterly, 5*, 444–455.

Fischetti, M., Curran, J. P., & Wessberg, H. W. (1977). A sense of timing: A skill deficit in heterosexual-socially anxious males. *Behavior Modification, 1*, 179–194.

Fischhoff, B. (1975). Hindsight ≠ foresight: The effect of outcome knowledge on judgment under uncertainty. *Journal of Experimental Psychology: Human Perception and Performance, 1*, 288–299.

Fischhoff, B. (1977). Perceived informativeness of facts. *Journal of Experimental Psychology: Human Perception and Performance, 3*, 349–358.

Fischhoff, B. (1982). Debiasing. In D. Kahneman, P. Slovic, & A. Tversky (Eds.), *Judgment under uncertainty: Heuristics and biases* (pp. 422–444). Cambridge, England: Cambridge University Press.

Fischhoff, B., & Beyth, R. (1975). "I knew it would happen"—Remembered probabilities of once-future things. *Organizational Behavior and Human Performance, 13*, 1–16.

Fischhoff, B., Slovic, P., & Lichtenstein, S. (1977). Knowing with certainty: The appropriateness of extreme confidence. *Journal of Experimental Psychology: Human Perception and Performance, 3*, 552–564.

Fisher, J. D., & Nadler, A. (1976). Effect of donor resources on recipient self-esteem and self-help. *Journal of Experimental Social Psychology, 12*, 139–150.

Fogel, L. S., & Nelson, R. O. (1983). The effects of special education labels on teachers' behavioral observations, checklist scores, and grading of academic work. *Journal of School Psychology, 21*, 241–251.

Follette, W. C., & Jacobson, N. S. (1985). Assessment and treatment of incompatible marital relationships. In W. Ickes (Ed.), *Compatible and incompatible relationships* (pp. 333–361). New York: Springer-Verlag.

Fontana, A. F., & Gessner, T. (1969). Patients' goals and the manifestation of psychopathology. *Journal of Consulting and Clinical Psychology, 33*, 247–253.

Fontana, A. F., & Klein, E. B. (1968). Self-presentation and the schizophrenic "deficit." *Journal of Consulting and Clinical Psychology, 32*, 250–256.

Fontana, A. F., Klein, E. B., Lewis, E., & Levine, L. (1968). Presentation of self in mental illness. *Journal of Consulting and Clinical Psychology, 32*, 110–119.

Försterling, F. (1985). Attributional retraining: A review. *Psychological Bulletin, 98*, 495–512.

Forsyth, D. R. (1980). The functions of attributions. *Social Psychology Quarterly, 43*, 184–189.

Forsyth, D. R. (1983). *An introduction to group dynamics.* Monterey, CA: Brooks/Cole.

Forsyth, N. L., & Forsyth, D. R. (1982). Internality, controllability, and the effectiveness of attributional interpretations in counseling. *Journal of Counseling Psychology, 29*, 140–150.

Forsyth, N. L., & Forsyth, D. R. (1983). The promise and peril of attributional counseling: A reply. *Journal of Counseling Psychology, 30*, 457–458.

Frank, J. D. (1961). *Persuasion and healing.* Baltimore: Johns Hopkins University Press.

Frank, J. D. (1973). *Persuasion and healing: A comparative study of psychotherapy* (rev. ed.). Baltimore: Johns Hopkins University Press.

Frankel, A., & Snyder, M. L. (1978). Poor performance following insolvable problems: Learned helplessness or egotism? *Journal of Personality and Social Psychology, 36,* 1415–1423.

Freedman, J. C. (1975). *Crowding and behavior.* San Francisco: Freeman.

Freedman, J. (1978). *Happy people: What happiness is, who has it, and why.* New York: Harcourt Brace Jovanovich.

Freeman, H. E., & Giovannoni, J. M. (1969). Social psychology of mental health. In G. Lindzey & E. Aronson (Eds.), *The handbook of social psychology* (2nd ed.) (Vol. 5, pp. 660–719). Reading, Mass.: Addison-Wesley.

Fremouw, W. J., & Zitter, R. E. (1978). A comparison of skills training and cognitive restructuring-relaxation for the treatment of speech anxiety. *Behavior Therapy, 9,* 248–259.

Friedlander, M. L., & Phillips, S. D. (1984). Preventing anchoring effects in clinical judgment. *Journal of Consulting and Clinical Psychology, 52,* 366–371.

Friedlander, M. L., & Stockman, S. J. (1983). Anchoring and publicity effects in clinical judgment. *Journal of Clinical Psychology, 39,* 637–643.

Gallup, G. G. (1977). Self-recognition in primates: A comparative approach to the bidirectional properties of consciousness. *American Psychologist, 32,* 329–338.

Garber, J., & Seligman, M. E. P. (Eds.) (1980). *Human helplessness.* New York: Academic Press.

Garfield, S. L. (1978). Research on client variables in psychotherapy. In S. L. Garfield & A. E. Bergin (Eds.), *Handbook of psychotherapy and behavior change* (2nd ed., pp. 191–232). New York: Wiley.

Gauron, E. G., & Dickinson, J. K. (1966). Diagnostic decision-making in psychiatry: 1. Information usage. *Archives of General Psychiatry, 14,* 225–232.

Geer, J. (1965). The development of a scale to measure fear. *Behaviour Research and Therapy, 3,* 45–53.

Geiss, S. K., & O'Leary, K. D. (1981). Therapist ratings of frequency and severity of marital problems: Implications for research. *Journal of Marital and Family Therapy, 7,* 515–520.

Gelles, R. J. (1976). Abused wives: Why do they stay? *Journal of Marriage and the Family, 38,* 659–668.

Gelles, R. J. (1980). Violence in the family: A review of research in the family. *Journal of Marriage and the Family, 42,* 873–885.

Gelles, R. J., & Straus, M. A. (1979). Determinants of violence in the family: Toward a theoretical integration. In W. Burr, R. Hill, F. I. Nye, & I. L. Weiss (Eds.), *Contemporary theories about the family: Research-based theories* (Vol. 1, pp. 549–581). New York: Free Press.

Gerard, H. B., & Mathewson, G. C. (1966). The effects of severity of initiation on liking for a group: A replication. *Journal of Experimental Social Psychology, 2,* 278–287.

Gergen, K. J. (1973). Social psychology as history. *Journal of Personality and Social Psychology, 26,* 309–320.

Gergen, K. J., & Gergen, N. N. (1984). *Historical social psychology.* Hillsdale, NJ: Erlbaum.

Gibbons, F. X., & Gaeddert, W. P. (1984). Focus of attention and placebo utility. *Journal of Experimental Social Psychology, 20,* 159–176.

Gilmour, R., & Duck, S. (Eds.) (1986). *The emerging field of personal relationships.* London: Academic Press.

Glasgow, R., & Arkowitz, H. (1975). The behavioral assessment of male and female social competence in dyadic heterosexual interactions. *Behavior Therapy, 6,* 488–498.

Glass, C. R., Gottman, J. M., & Shmurak, S. (1976). Response acquisition and cognitive self-statement modification approaches to dating-skills-training. *Journal of Counseling Psychology, 23,* 520–526.

Glass, D. C. (1977). *Behavior patterns, stress, and coronary disease.* Hillsdale, NJ: Erlbaum.

Glass, D. C., & Singer, J. E. (1972). *Urban stress.* New York: Academic Press.

Goetz, T. E., & Dweck, C. S. (1980). Learned helplessness in social situations. *Journal of Personality and Social Psychology, 39,* 246–255.

Goffman, E. (1955). On facework. *Psychiatry, 18,* 213–231.

Goffman, E. (1959). *The presentation of self in everyday life.* New York: Doubleday.

Goggin, W. C., & Range, L. M. (1985). The disadvantages of hindsight in the prevention of suicide. *Journal of Social and Clinical Psychology, 3,* 232–237.

Goldberg, L. R. (1970). Man versus model of man: A rationale, plus some evidence, for a method of improving on clinical inferences. *Psychological Bulletin, 73,* 422–432.

Goldfried, M. R. (1979). Anxiety reduction through cognitive-behavioral intervention. In P. C. Kendall & S. D. Hollon (Eds.), *Cognitive-behavioral interventions: Theory, research, and procedures.* New York: Academic Press.

Goldfried, M. R. (1980). Toward the delineation of therapeutic change principles. *American Psychologist, 35,* 991–999.

Goldfried, M. F., & Robins, C. (1982). On the facilitation of self-efficacy. *Cognitive Therapy and Research, 6,* 361–380.

Goldfried, M. R., & Robins, C. (1983). Self-schema, cognitive bias, and the processing of therapeutic experiences. In P. C. Kendall (Ed.), *Advances in cognitive-behavioral research and therapy* (Vol. 2, pp. 33–80). New York: Academic Press.

Goldfried, M. R., & Sobocinski, D. (1975). Effect of irrational beliefs on emotional arousal. *Journal of Consulting and Clinical Psychology, 43,* 504–510.

Golding, S. L., & Rorer, L. G. (1972). Illusory correlation and subjective judgment. *Journal of Abnormal Psychology, 80,* 249–260.

Goldstein, A. P. (1962). *Therapist-patient expectancies in psychotherapy.* New York: Macmillan.

Goldstein, A. P. (1966). Psychotherapy research by extrapolation from social psychology. *Journal of Counseling Psychology, 13,* 38–45.

Goldstein, A. P. (1971). *Psychotherapeutic attraction.* Elmsford, NY: Pergamon Press.

Goldstein, A. P., Heller, K., & Sechrest, L. B. (1966). *Psychotherapy and the psychology of behavior change.* New York: Wiley.

Golin, S., Terrell, F., & Johnson, B. (1977). Depression and the illusion of control. *Journal of Abnormal Psychology, 86,* 440–442.

Golin, S., Terrell, F., Weitz, J., & Drost, P. L. (1979). The illusion of control among depressed patients. *Journal of Abnormal Psychology, 88,* 454–457.

Goode, W. J. (1971). Force and violence in the family. *Journal of Marriage and the Family, 33,* 604–636.

Gordon, G. (1966). *Role theory and illness: A sociological perspective.* New Haven, CT: College and University Press.

Gottman, J. M. (1979). *Marital interaction: Experimental investigations.* New York: Academic Press.

Gottman, J. M., & Porterfield, A. L. (1981). Communicative competence in the nonverbal behaviour of married couples. *Journal of Marriage and the Family, 43,* 807–824.

Gottsegen, G. B. (Chair). (1985, August). *Integrating family and social psychology: New directions, new ideas.* Symposium conducted at the annual meeting of the American Psychological Association, Los Angeles.

Gove, W. R. (Ed.) (1975). *The labelling of deviance: Evaluating a perspective.* New York: Wiley.

Gove, W. R., Hughes, M., & Geerken, M. R. (1980). Playing dumb: A form of impression management with undesirable side-effects. *Social Psychology Quarterly, 43,* 89–102.

Green, D. (1974). Dissonance and self-perception analyses of "forced compliance:" When two theories make competing predictions. *Journal of Personality and Social Psychology, 29,* 819–828.

Greenberg, J., & Pysczynski, T. (1985). Proneness to romantic jealousy and responses to jealousy in others. *Journal of Personality, 53,* 468–479.

Greenberg, R. P. (1969). Effects of presession information on perception of the therapist in a psychotherapy analogue. *Journal of Consulting and Clinical Psychology, 33,* 425–429.

Greenwald, A. G. (1980). The totalitarian ego: Fabrication and revision of personal history. *American Psychologist, 35* 603–618.

Greenwald, A. G., & Albert, R. D. (1968). Acceptance and recall of improvised arguments. *Journal of Personality and Social Psychology, 8,* 31–35.

Grimm, L. G. (1980). The maintenance of self- and drug-attributed behavior change: A critique. *Journal of Abnormal Psychology, 89,* 282–285.

Grosz, H. J., & Grossman, K. G. (1964). The sources of observer variation and bias in clinical judgments: 1. The item of psychiatric history. *Journal of Nervous and Mental Disease, 138,* 105–113.

Haemmerlie, F. M. (1983). Heterosocial anxiety in college females: A biased interactions treatment. *Behavior Modification, 7,* 611–623.

Haemmerlie, F. M., & Montgomery, R. L. (1982). Self-perception theory and unobtrusively biased interactions: A treatment for heterosocial anxiety. *Journal of Counseling Psychology, 29,* 362–370.

Haemmerlie, F. M., & Montgomery, R. L. (1984). Purposefully biased interactions: Reducing heterosocial anxiety through self-perception theory. *Journal of Personality and Social Psychology, 47,* 900–908.

Haley, J. (1963). *Strategies of psychotherapy.* New York: Grune & Stratton.

Haley, W. (1985). Social skills deficits and self-evaluation among depressed and nondepressed psychiatric inpatients. *Journal of Clinical Psychology, 41,* 162–168.

Hall, J. A. (1984). *Nonverbal sex differences: Communication accuracy and expressive style.* Baltimore: Johns Hopkins University Press.

Hamilton, D. L. (1981). Illusory correlation as a basis for stereotyping. In D. Hamilton (Ed.), *Cognitive processes in stereotyping and intergroup behavior* (pp. 115–144). Hillsdale, NJ: Erlbaum.

Hammen, C., & Cochran, S. D. (1981). Cognitive correlates of life stress and depression in college students. *Journal of Abnormal Psychology, 92,* 173–184.

Hammen, C., & Mayo, R. (1982). Cognitive correlates of teacher stress and depressive symptoms: Implications for attributional models of depression. *Journal of Abnormal Psychology, 91,* 96–101.

Hansen, G. L. (1985). Perceived threats and marital jealousy. *Social Psychology Quarterly, 48,* 262–268.

Hansson, R. O., Jones, W. H., & Carpenter, B. N. (1984). Relational competence and social support. In P. Shaver (Ed.), *Review of personality and social psychology: 5* (pp. 265–284). Beverly Hills, CA: Sage.

Hanusa, B. H., & Schultz, R. (1977). Attributional mediators of learned helplessness. *Journal of Personality and Social Psychology, 35,* 602–611.

Harari, H. (1983). Social psychology *of* clinical practice and *in* clinical practice. *Journal of Social and Clinical Psychology, 1,* 173–192.

Harkness, A. R., DeBono, K. G., & Borgida, E. (1985). Personal involvement and strategies for making contingency judgments: A stake in the dating game makes a difference. *Journal of Personality and Social Psychology, 49,* 22–32.

Harris, M. J., & Rosenthal, R. (1985). Mediation of interpersonal expectancy effects: 31 meta-analyses. *Psychological Bulletin, 97,* 363–386.

Harvey, J. H. (1983). The founding of the *Journal of Social and Clinical Psychology. Journal of Social and Clinical Psychology, 1,* 1–13.

Harvey, J. H. (1985, April). *Attributions in relationships: Research and theoretical developments.* Paper presented to the California School of Professional Psychology Symposium on Attribution, Berkeley.

Harvey, J. H., & Weary, G. (1979). The integration of social and clinical psychology training programs. *Personality and Social Psychology Bulletin, 5,* 511–515.

Harvey, J. H., & Weary, G. (1982). *Perspectives on attributional processes.* Dubuque, IA: Brown.

Harvey, J. H., Town, J. P., & Yarkin, K. L. (1981). How fundamental is "the fundamental attribution error"? *Journal of Personality and Social Psychology, 40,* 346–349.

Harvey, J. H., Wells, G. L., & Alvarez, M. D. (1978). Attribution in the context of conflict and separation in close relationships. In J. H. Harvey, W. Ickes, & R. F. Kidd (Eds.), *New directions in attribution research* (Vol. 2, pp. 235–260). Hillsdale, NJ: Erlbaum.

Hatfield, E. (1984). The dangers of intimacy. In V. J. Derlega (Ed.), *Communication, intimacy, and close relationships* (pp. 205–220). Orlando, FL: Academic Press.

Hatfield, E., & Traupmann, J. (1980). Intimate relationships: A perspective from equity theory. In S. Duck & R. Gilmour (Eds.), *Personal relationships 1: Studying personal relationships* (pp. 165–178). London: Academic Press.

Hatfield, E., Traupmann, J., Sprecher, S., Utne, M., & Hay, J. (1985). Equity and intimate relations: Recent research. In W. Ickes (Ed.), *Compatible and incompatible relationships* (pp. 91–117). New York: Springer-Verlag.

Helmersen, P. (1983). *Family interaction and communication in psychopathology: An evaluation of recent perspectives.* New York: Academic Press.

Henderson, S. (1977). The social network, support, and neurosis: The function of attachment in adult life. *British Journal of Psychiatry, 131,* 185–191.

Hendrick, C. (1983). Clinical social psychology: A birthright reclaimed. *Journal of Social and Clinical Psychology, 1,* 66–87.

Hendrick, C., & Hendrick, S. (1984). Toward a clinical social psychology of health and disease. *Journal of Social and Clinical Psychology, 2,* 182–192.

Hendrick, S. (1983). Ecumenical (social and clinical and x, y, z . . .) psychology. *Journal of Social and Clinical Psychology, 1,* 79–87.

Heppner, P. P., & Dixon, D. N. (1978). Effects of client perceived need and counselor role on client's behaviors. *Journal of Counseling Psychology, 25,* 514–519.

Higbee, K. L. (1969). Fifteen years of fear arousal: Research on threat appeals, 1953–1968. *Psychological Bulletin, 72,* 426–444.

Hill, C. T., Rubin, Z., & Peplau, L. A. (1976). Breakups before marriage: The end of 103 affairs. *Journal of Social Issues, 32,* 147–168.

Hill, M. G., & Weary, G. (1983). Perspectives on the *Journal of Abnormal and Social Psychology:* How it began and how it was transformed. *Journal of Social and Clinical Psychology, 1,* 4–14.

Hirsch, P. A., & Stone, G. L. (1983). Cognitive strategies and the client conceptualization process. *Journal of Counseling Psychology, 30,* 566–572.

Hoffman, L. (1981). *Foundations of family life.* New York: Basic Books.

Hoffman, M. A., & Teglasi, H. (1982). The role of causal attributions in counseling shy subjects. *Journal of Counseling Psychology, 29,* 132–139.

Hogan, R., Hall, R., & Blank, E. (1972). An extension of the similarity-attraction hypothesis to the study of vocational behavior. *Journal of Counseling Psychology, 19,* 238–240.

Hogan, R., & Jones, W. H. (1983). A role theoretical model of criminal conduct. In

W. S. Laufer & J. M. Days (Eds.), *Personality theory, moral development, and criminal behavior*. Boston: Lexington.

Hogarth, R. M. (1981). Beyond discrete biases. Functional and dysfunctional aspects of judgmental heuristics. *Psychological Bulletin, 90,* 197–217.

Hollingshead, A. B., & Redlich, F. C. (1958). *Social class and mental illness*. New York: Wiley.

Holt, R. R. (1970). Yet another look at clinical and statistical prediction: Or is clinical psychology worthwhile? *American Psychologist, 25,* 337–349.

Holtzworth-Munroe, A., & Jacobson, N.S. (1985). Causal attributions of married couples: When do they search for causes? What do they conclude when they do? *Journal of Personality and Social Psychology, 48,* 1398–1412.

Hood, R. W., Jr. (1970). Effects of foreknowledge of death in the assessment from case history material of intent to die. *Journal of Consulting and Clinical Psychology, 34,* 129–133.

Horney, K. (1950). *Neurosis and human growth*. New York: Norton.

Horowitz, R., & Schwartz, G. (1974). Honor, normative ambiguity, and gang violence. *American Sociological Review, 39,* 238–251.

House, J. S., Robbins, C., & Metzner, H. L. (1982). The association of social relationships and activities with mortality: Perspective evidence from the Tecumseh Community Health study. *American Journal of Epidemiology, 116,* 123–140.

Houts, A. C., & Galante, M. (1985). The impact of evaluative disposition and subsequent information on clinical impressions. *Journal of Social and Clinical Psychology, 3,* 232–237.

Hovland, J., Janis, I. L., & Kelley, H. H. (1953). *Communication and persuasion: Psychological studies of opinion change*. New Haven, CT: Yale University Press.

Howes, M. J., Hokanson, J. E., & Loewenstein, D. A. (1985). Induction of depressive affect after prolonged exposure to a mildly depressed individual. *Journal of Personality and Social Psychology, 49,* 1110–1113.

Hull, J. G. (1981). A self-awareness model of the causes and effects of alcohol consumption. *Journal of Abnormal Psychology, 90,* 586–600.

Hull, J. G., Levenson, R. W., Young, R. D., & Sher, K. J. (1983). Self-awareness-reducing effects of alcohol consumption. *Journal of Personality and Social Psychology, 44,* 461–473.

Hull, J. G., & Levy, A. S. (1979). The organizational functions of the self: An alternative to the Duval and Wicklund model of self-awareness. *Journal of Personality and Social Psychology, 37,* 756–768.

Hull, J. G., & Young, R. D. (1983). The self-awareness reducing effects of alcohol consumption: Evidence and implications. In J. Suls & A. G. Greenwald (Eds.), *Psychological perspectives on the self* (Vol. 2, pp. 159–190). Hillsdale, NJ: Erlbaum.

Ickes, W. (Ed.). (1985a). *Compatible and incompatible relationships*. New York: Springer-Verlag.

Ickes, W. (1985b). Sex-role influences on compatibility in relationships. In W. Ickes (Ed.), *Compatible and incompatible relationships* (pp. 187–208). New York: Springer-Verlag.

Ickes, W., & Barnes, R. D. (1978). Boys and girls together—and alienated: On enacting stereotyped sex roles in mixed-sex dyads. *Journal of Personality and Social Psychology, 36,* 669–683.

Ickes, W., & Layden, M. A. (1978). Attributional styles. In J. H. Harvey, W. Ickes, & R. F. Kidd (Eds.), *New directions in attribution research* (Vol. 2, pp. 119–152). Hillsdale, NJ: Erlbaum.

Ickes, W., Patterson, M. L., Rajecki, D. W., & Tanford, S. (1982). Behavioral and cognitive consequences of reciprocal versus compensatory responses to preinteraction expectancies. *Social Cognition, 1,* 160–190.

Ickes, W., Schermer, B., & Steeno, J. (1979). Sex and sex-role influences in same-sex dyads. *Social Psychology Quarterly, 42,* 373–385.

Jackson, D. D., & Haley, J. (1968). Transference revisited. In D. Jackson (Ed.), *Therapy, communication, and change.* Palo Alto, CA: Science and Behavior Books.

Jackson, S. E., & Maslach, C. (1982). After-effects of job-related stress: Families as victims. *Journal of Occupational Behavior, 3,* 63–77.

Jacob, T. (1975). Family interaction in disturbed and normal families: A methodological and substantive review. *Psychological Bulletin, 82,* 33–65.

Jacobs, B., Prentice-Dunn, S., & Rogers, R. W. (1984). Understanding persistence: An interface of control theory and self-efficacy theory. *Basic and Applied Social Psychology, 5,* 333–347.

Jacobson, N. S., Follette, W. C., & Elwood, R. W. (1984). Outcome research on behavioral marital therapy: A methodological and conceptual reappraisal. In K. Hahlweg & N. Jacobson (Eds.), *Marital interaction: Analysis and modification* (pp. 113–129). New York: Guiford Press.

Jacobson, N. S., Follette, W. C., & McDonald, D. W. (1982). Reactivity to positive and negative behavior in distressed and nondistressed married couples. *Journal of Consulting and Clinical Psychology, 50,* 706–714.

Jacobson, N. S., & Margolin, G. (1979). *Marital therapy: Strategies based on social learning and behavior exchange principles.* New York: Brunner/Mazel.

Jacobson, N. S., McDonald, D. W., Follette, W. C., & Berley, R. A. (1985). Attributional processes in distressed and nondistressed married couples. *Cognitive Therapy and Research, 9,* 35–50.

Jacobson, N. S., Waldron, H., & Moore, D. (1980). Toward a behavioral profile of marital distress. *Journal of Consulting and Clinical Psychology, 48,* 696–703.

Janis, I. L., & Gilmore, J. B. (1965). The influence of incentive conditions on the success of role-playing modifying attitudes. *Journal of Personality and Social Psychology, 1,* 17–27.

Janis, I. L., & King, B. T. (1954). The influence of role-playing on opinion change. *Journal of Abnormal and Social Psychology, 49,* 211–218.

Janoff-Bulman, R. (1979). Characterological versus behavioral self-blame: Inquiries into depression and rape. *Journal of Personality and Social Psychology, 31,* 1798–1809.

Jeffrey, D. B. (1974). A comparison of the effects of external control and self-control on the modification and maintenance of weight. *Journal of Abnormal Psychology, 83,* 404–410.

Jelalian, E., & Miller, A. G. (1984). The perseverance of beliefs: Conceptual perspectives and research developments. *Journal of Social and Clinical Psychology, 2,* 25–56.

Jennings, D. L., Amabile, T. M., & Ross, L. (1982). Informal covariation assessment: Data-based versus theory-based judgments. In D. Kahneman, P. Slovic, & A. Tversky (Eds.), *Judgment under uncertainty: Heuristics and biases* (pp. 211–230). Cambridge, England: Cambridge University Press.

Jennings, D. L., Lepper, M. R., & Ross, L. (1981). Persistence of impressions of personal persuasiveness: Perseverance of erroneous self-assessments outside the debriefing paradigm. *Personality and Social Psychology Bulletin, 7,* 257–263.

Johnson, D. L., Rusbult, C. E., & Morrow, G. D. (1983, August). *Responses to dissatisfaction in longstanding relationships: Predictors and consequences.* Paper presented at the annual meeting of the American Psychological Association, Anaheim, CA.

Johnson, D. W. (1967). The use of role reversal in intergroup competition. *Journal of Personality and Social Psychology, 7,* 135–141.

Johnson, D. W. (1971). The effectiveness of role reversal: The actor or the listener. *Psychological Reports, 28,* 275–282.

Johnson, D. W., & Matross, R. P. (1977). Interpersonal influence in psychotherapy: A social psychological view. In A. S. Gurman & A. M. Razin (Eds.), *Effective psychotherapy* (pp. 395–432). New York: Pergamon Press.

Johnson, J. E., Petzel, T. P., & Sperduto, V. W. (1983). An evaluation of the Scale of Attributional Style using college students preselected on level of depression. *Journal of Social and Clinical Psychology, 1,* 140–145.

Johnson, W. G., Ross, J. M., & Mastria, M. A. (1977). Delusional behavior: An attributional analysis of development and modification. *Journal of Abnormal Psychology, 86,* 421–426.

Jones, E. E., & Berglas, S. (1978). Control of attributions about the self through self-handicapping strategies: The appeal of alcohol and the role of underachievement. *Personality and Social Psychology Bulletin, 4,* 200–206.

Jones, E. E., & Harris, V. A. (1967). The attribution of attitudes. *Journal of Experimental Social Psychology, 3,* 1–24.

Jones, E. E., & Nisbett, R. E. (1971). *The actor and the observer: Divergent perceptions of the causes of behavior.* Morristown, NJ: General Learning Press.

Jones, E. E., & Pittman, T. S. (1982). Toward a general theory of strategic self-presentation. In J. Suls (Ed.), *Psychological perspectives on the self.* Hillsdale, NJ: Erlbaum.

Jones, E. E., Rhodewalt, F., Berglas, S., & Skelton, J. A. (1981). Effects of strategic self-presentation on subsequent self-esteem. *Journal of Personality and Social Psychology, 41,* 409–421.

Jones, E. E., Rock, L., Shaver, K. G., Goethals, G. R., & Ward, L. M. (1968). Pattern of performance and ability attribution: An unexpected primacy effect. *Journal of Personality and Social Psychology, 10,* 317–340.

Jones, R. A. (1983). Academic insularity and the failure to integrate social and clinical psychology. *SASP Newsletter, 9*(6), 10–13.

Jones, S. C. (1973). Self- and interpersonal evaluations: Esteem theories versus consistency theories. *Psychological Bulletin, 79,* 185–199.

Jones, W. H. (1981). Loneliness and social contact. *Journal of Social Psychology, 113,* 295–296.

Jones, W. H. (1982, April). *The psychology of loneliness: Personality, behavioral and situational determinants of interpersonal disruption.* Paper presented at the Annual Meeting of the Southwestern Psychological Association, Dallas.

Jones, W. H., Cheek, J. M., & Briggs, S. R. (Eds.), (1986). *Shyness: Perspectives on research and treatment.* New York: Plenum Press.

Jones, W. H., Freemon, J. R., & Goswick, R. A. (1981). The persistence of loneliness: Self and other determinants. *Journal of Personality, 49,* 27–48.

Jones, W. H., Hobbs, S. A., & Hockenbury, D. (1982). Loneliness and social skill deficits. *Journal of Personality and Social Psychology, 42,* 682–689.

Jones, W. H., Sansone, C., & Helm, B. (1983). Loneliness and interpersonal judgments. *Personality and Social Psychology Bulletin, 9,* 437–442.

Kahn, A. (in press). The power war: Male response to power loss under equality. *Psychology of Women Quarterly.*

Kahn, M. (1970). Nonverbal communication and marital satisfaction. *Family Process, 9,* 449–456.

Kamhi, A. G., & McOsker, T. G. (1982). Attention and stuttering: Do stutterers think too much about speech? *Journal of Fluency Disorders, 7,* 309–321.

Kandel, D. B. (1966). Status homophily, social context, and participation in psychotherapy. *American Journal of Sociology, 71,* 640–650.

Kanfer, F. H., & Seidner, M. L. (1973). Self-control: Factors enhancing tolerance of noxious stimulation. *Journal of Personality and Social Psychology, 25,* 381–389.

Kanfer, R., & Zeiss, A. M. (1983). Depression, interpersonal standard settings, and judgments of self-efficacy. *Journal of Abnormal Psychology, 92,* 319–329.

Kanter, N. J., & Goldfried, M. R. (1979). Relative effectiveness of rational restructuring and self-control desensitization in the reduction of interpersonal anxiety. *Behavior Therapy, 10,* 472–490.

Katz, D. (1960). The functional approach to the study of attitudes. *Public Opinion Quarterly, 24,* 163–204.

Kaul, T., & Schmidt, L. (1971). Dimensions of interview trustworthiness. *Journal of Counseling Psychology, 18,* 542–548.

Kayne, N. T., & Alloy, L. B. (in press). Clinician and patient as aberrant actuaries: Expectation-based distortions in assessment of covariation. In L. Y. Abramson (Ed.), *Attribution processes and clinical psychology.* New York: Guilford Press.

Kazdin, A. E. (1978). Conceptual and assessment issues raised by self-efficacy theory. *Advances in Behavior Research and Therapy, 1,* 177–185.

Kazdin, A. E. (1979). Sociopsychological factors in psychopathology. In A. S. Bellack & M. Hersen (Eds.), *Research and practice in social skills training* (pp. 41–73). New York: Plenum Press.

Kelley, H. H. (1973). The processes of causal attribution. *American Psychologist, 28,* 107–128.

Kelley, H. H. (1979). *Personal relationships: Their structures and processes.* Hillsdale, NJ: Erlbaum.

Kelley, H. H. (1984). The theoretical description of interdependence by means of transition lists. *Journal of Personality and Social Psychology, 47,* 956–982.

Kelley, H. H., Berscheid, E., Christensen, A., Harvey, J. H., Huston, T. L., Levinger, G., McClintock, E., Peplau, L. A., & Peterson, D. R. (1983). *Close relationships.* New York: Freeman.

Kelley, H. H., & Michela, J. L. (1980). Attribution theory and research. *Annual Review of Psychology, 31,* 457–501.

Kellogg, R., & Baron, R. S. (1975). Attribution theory, insomnia, and the reverse placebo effect: A reversal of Storm's and Nisbett's findings. *Journal of Personality and Social Psychology, 32,* 231–236.

Kelly, F. S., Farina, A., & Mosher, D. L. (1971). Ability of schizophrenic women to create a favorable or unfavorable impression on an interviewer. *Journal of Consulting and Clinical Psychology, 36,* 404–409.

Kelman, H. C., & Hovland, C. I. (1953). "Reinstatement" of the communication in delayed measurement of opinion change. *Journal of Abnormal and Social Psychology, 48,* 327–335.

Kerr, B. A., & Dell, D. M. (1976). Perceived interviewer expertise and attractiveness: Effects of interviewer behavior and attitude and interview setting. *Journal of Counseling Psychology, 23,* 553–556.

Kessler, R. C., Price, R. H., & Wortman, C. B. (1985). Social factors in psychopathology: Stress, social support, and coping processes. *Annual Review of Psychology, 36,* 531–572.

Kiesler, D. J. (1966). Some myths of psychotherapy research and the search for a paradigm. *Psychological Bulletin, 65,* 110–136.

Kilman, P. R., Albert, N. M., & Sotile, V. M. (1975). Relationship between locus of control, structure of therapy and outcome. *Journal of Counseling and Clinical Psychology, 43,* 588.

King, B. T., & Janis, I. L. (1956). Comparison of the effectiveness of improvised versus nonimprovised role-playing in producing opinion changes. *Human Relations, 9,* 177–186.

King, D. A., & Heller, K. (1984). Depression and the response of others: A reevaluation. *Journal of Abnormal Psychology, 93,* 477–480.

Kirsch, I. (1985). Self-efficacy and expectancy: Old wine with new labels. *Journal of Personality and Social Psychology, 49,* 824–830.

Klein, D. C., Fencil-Morse, E., & Seligman, M. E. P. (1976). Learned helplessness, depression, and the attribution of failure. *Journal of Personality and Social Psychology, 33*, 508–516.

Kleinke, C. L., Staneski, R. A., & Berger, D. E. (1975). Evaluation of an interviewer as a function of interviewer gaze, reinforcement of subject gaze, and interviewer attractiveness. *Journal of Personality and Social Psychology, 31*, 115–122.

Kobasa, S., Maddi, S., & Kahn, S. (1982). Hardiness and health. *Journal of Personality and Social Psychology, 42*, 168–177.

Koenig, K. P. (1973). False emotional feedback and the modification of anxiety. *Behavior Therapy, 4*, 193–202.

Kolditz, T., & Arkin, R. M. (1982). An impression management interpretation of the self-handicapping strategy. *Journal of Personality and Social Psychology, 43*, 492–502.

Komarovsky, M. (1946). Cultural contradiction and sex roles. *American Journal of Sociology, 52*, 184–189.

Kondas, O. (1967). Reduction of examination anxiety and "stage-fright" by group desensitization and relaxation. *Behavior Research and Therapy, 5*, 275–281.

Kopel, S. A., & Arkowitz, H. (1975). The role of attribution and self-perception in behavior change: Implications for behavior therapy. *Genetic Psychology Monographs, 92*, 175–212.

Korda, M. (1976). *Power: How to get it, how to use it*. New York: Ballantine.

Koriat, A., Lichtenstein, S., & Fischhoff, B. (1980). Reasons for confidence. *Journal of Experimental Psychology: Human Learning and Memory, 6*, 107–118.

Krumboltz, J., Varenhorst, B., & Thoresen, C. E. (1967). Nonverbal factors in the effectiveness of models in counseling. *Journal of Counseling Psychology, 14*, 412–418.

Kuhn, T. S. (1962). *The structure of scientific revolutions*. Chicago: University of Chicago Press.

Kuiper, N. A. (1978). Depression and causal attributions for success and failure. *Journal of Personality and Social Psychology, 36*, 236–246.

Kuiper, N. A., Derry, P. A., & MacDonald, M. R. (1982). Self-reference and person perception in depression: A social cognition perspective. In G. Weary & H. L. Mirels (Eds.), *Integrations of clinical and social psychology* (pp. 79–103). New York: Oxford University Press.

LaCrosse, M. B. (1975). Nonverbal behavior and perceived counselor attractiveness and persuasiveness. *Journal of Counseling Psychology, 22*, 563–566.

Langer, E. J. (1975). The illusion of control. *Journal of Personality and Social Psychology, 32*, 311–328.

Langer, E. J. (1978). Rethinking the role of thought in social interaction. In J. H. Harvey, W. J. Ickes, & R. F. Kidd (Eds.), *New directions in attribution research* (Vol. 2, pp. 35–58). Hillsdale, NJ: Erlbaum.

Langer, E. J. (1982). The value of a social psychological approach to clinical issues. In G. Weary & H. L. Mirels (Eds.), *Integrations of clinical and social psychology* (pp. 3–5). New York: Oxford University Press.

Langer, E. J. (1983). *The psychology of control*. Beverly Hills, CA: Sage.

Langer, E. J., & Abelson, R. P. (1974). A patient by any other name . . . : Clinician group difference in labeling bias. *Journal of Consulting and Clinical Psychology, 42*, 4–9.

Langer, E. J., Janis, I. L., & Wolfer, J. A. (1975). Reduction of psychological stress in surgical patients. *Journal of Experimental Social Psychology, 11*, 155–165.

Langer, E. J., & Rodin, J. (1976). The effects of choice and enhanced personal responsibility for the aged: A field experiment in an institutional setting. *Journal of Personality and Social Psychology, 34*, 191–198.

Langer, E. J., & Weinman, C. (1981). When thinking disrupts intellectual performance: Mindfulness on an overlearned task. *Personality and Social Psychology Bulletin, 7,* 240–243.

Layden, M. A. (1982). Attributional style therapy. In C. Antaki & C. Brewin (Eds.), *Attributions and psychological change: Applications of attributional theories to clinical and educational practice* (pp. 63–82). New York: Academic Press.

Leary, M. R. (1980). *The social psychology of shyness: Testing a self-presentational model.* Unpublished doctoral dissertation, University of Florida.

Leary, M. R. (1981). The distorted nature of hindsight. *Journal of Social Psychology, 115,* 25–29.

Leary, M. R. (1982). Hindsight distortion and the 1980 presidential election. *Personality and Social Psychology Bulletin, 8,* 257–263.

Leary, M. R. (1983a). Strengthening the interface between social and clinical-counseling psychology. *Newsletter of the Society for the Advancement of Social Psychology, 9*(6), 4–7.

Leary, M. R. (1983b). *Understanding social anxiety: Social, personality, and clinical perspectives.* Beverly Hills, CA: Sage.

Leary, M. R. (1983c). Social anxiousness: The construct and its measurement. *Journal of Personality Assessment, 47,* 66–75.

Leary, M. R. (1983d). The conceptual distinctions *are* important: Another look at communication apprehension and related constructs. *Human Communication Research,* 305–312.

Leary, M. R. (1983e). A brief version of the Fear of Negative Evaluation Scale. *Personality and Social Psychology Bulletin,* 371–376.

Leary, M. R. (1985). *Self-presentational functions of socially anxious behavior.* In R. M. Arkin (Chair), Anxiety in interpersonal relations. Symposium presented at the meeting of the American Psychological Association, Los Angeles.

Leary, M. R. (1986a). Affective and behavioral components of shyness: Implications for theory, measurement, and research. In W. H. Jones, J. M. Cheek, & S. R. Briggs (Eds.), *Shyness: Perspectives on research and treatment* (pp. 27–38) New York: Plenum Press.

Leary, M. R. (1986b). The impact of interactional impediments on social anxiety and self-presentation. *Journal of Experimental Social Psychology.*

Leary, M. R. (in press-a). The three faces of social-clinical-counseling psychology. *Journal of Social and Clinical Psychology.*

Leary, M. R. (in press-b). A self-presentational model for the treatment of social anxieties. In J. Maddux, C. Stoltenberg, R. Rosenwein (Eds.), *Social processes in clinical and counseling psychology.* New York: Springer-Verlag.

Leary, M. R., & Atherton, S. (1986). Self-efficacy, anxiety, and inhibition in interpersonal encounters. *Journal of Social and Clinical Psychology.*

Leary, M. R., Atherton, S. C., Hill, S., & Hur, C. (in press). Attributional mediators of social avoidance and inhibition. *Journal of Personality.*

Leary, M. R., Barnes, B. D., & Griebel, C. (in press). Cognitive, affective, and attributional effects of threats to self-esteem. *Journal of Social and Clinical Psychology.*

Leary, M. R., Barnes, B. D., Griebel, C., Mason, E., & McCormack, D. (1985). *The impact of threats to social and self-esteem upon evaluation apprehension and anxiety.* Unpublished manuscript, Wake Forest University, Winston-Salem, NC.

Leary, M. R., & Dobbins, S. E. (1983). Social anxiety, sexual behavior, and contraceptive use. *Journal of Personality and Social Psychology, 45,* 1347–1354.

Leary, M. R., Jenkins, T. B., & Shepperd, J. A. (1984). The growth of interest in clinically-relevant research in social psychology. *Journal of Social and Clinical Psychology, 2* 333–338.

Leary, M. R., Knight, P. D., & Johnson, K. A. (in press). Social anxiety and dyadic conversation: A verbal response analysis. *Journal of Social and Clinical Psychology*.

Leary, M. R., Robertson, R. B., Barnes, B. D., & Miller, R. S. (in press). Self-presentations of small group leaders as a function of role requirements and leadership orientation. *Journal of Personality and Social Psychology*.

Leary, M. R., & Schlenker, B. R. (1981). The social psychology of shyness: A self-presentational model. In J. T. Tedeschi (Ed.), *Impression management theory and social psychological research* (pp. 335–358). New York: Academic Press.

Leary, M. R., & Shepperd, J. A. (in press). Behavioral self-handicaps and self-reported handicaps. *Journal of Personality and Social Psychology*.

Lee, C. (1984a). Accuracy of efficacy and outcome expectations in predicting performance in a simulated assertiveness task. *Cognitive Therapy and Research, 8*, 37–48.

Lee, C. (1984b). Efficacy expectations and outcome expectations as predictors of performance in a snake-handling task. *Cognitive Therapy and Research, 8*, 509–516.

Lee, D. Y., Hallberg, E. T., Kocsis, M., & Haase, R. F. (1980). Decoding skills in nonverbal communication and perceived interviewer effectiveness. *Journal of Counseling Psychology, 27*, 89–92.

Lee, D. Y., Zingle, H. W., Patterson, J. G., Ivey, A. E., & Haase, R. F. (1976). Development and validation of a microcounseling skill discrimination scale. *Journal of Counseling Psychology, 23*, 468–472.

Lefcourt, H. M. (1973). The function of the illusions of control and freedom. *American Psychologist, 28*, 417–425.

Lepper, M. R., Greene, D., & Nisbett, R. E. (1973). Undermining children's intrinsic interest with extrinsic reward: A test of the "overjustification" hypothesis. *Journal of Personality and Social Psychology, 28*, 129–137.

Levenson, R. W., & Gottman, J. M. (1983). Marital interaction: Physiological linkage and affective exchange. *Journal of Personality and Social Psychology, 45*, 587–597.

Leventhal, H. (1970). Findings and theory in the study of fear communications. In L. Berkowitz (Ed.), *Advances in experimental social psychology* (Vol. 5, pp. 119–186). New York: Academic Press.

Levinger, G. (1979). A social exchange view on the dissolution of pair relationships. In R. Burgess and T. Huston (Eds.), *Social exchange in developing relationships* (pp. 169–193). New York: Academic Press.

Levinger, G. (1980). Toward the analysis of close relationships. *Journal of Experimental Social Psychology, 16*, 510–544.

Lewin, K. (1948). *Resolving social conflicts: Selected papers on group dynamics*. New York: Harper & Row.

Lewis, K. N., Davis, C. S., Walker, B. J., & Jennings, R. L. (1981). Attractive versus unattractive clients: Mediating influences on counselors' perceptions. *Journal of Counseling Psychology, 28*, 309–314.

Lewis, K. N., & Walsh, W. B. (1978). Physical attractiveness: Its impact on the perception of a female counselor. *Journal of Counseling Psychology, 25*, 210–216.

Libet, J. M., & Lewinsohn, P. M. (1973). Concept of social skill with special reference to the behavior of depressed persons. *Journal of Consulting and Clinical Psychology, 40*, 304–312.

Lichtenstein, S., & Fischhoff, B. (1977). Do those who know more also know more about how much they know? The calibration of probability judgments. *Organizational Behavior and Human Performance, 20*, 159–183.

Lick, J., & Bootzin, R. (1975). Expectancy factors in the treatment of fear: Methodological and treatment factors. *Psychological Bulletin, 82*, 917–931.

Loftus, E. F., & Loftus, G. R. (1980). On the permanence of stored information in the human brain. *American Psychologist, 35,* 409–420.

Lopez, R. G., & Wambach, C. A. (1982). Effects of paradoxical and self-control directives in counseling. *Journal of Counseling Psychology, 29,* 115–124.

Lord, C. G., Ross, L., & Lepper, M. R. (1979). Biased assimilation and attitude polarization: The effects of prior theories on subsequently considered evidence. *Journal of Personality and Social Psychology, 37,* 2098–2109.

Lorion, R. P. (1974). Patient and therapist variables in the treatment of low-income patients. *Psychological Bulletin, 81,* 344–354.

Lowenthal, M. F., & Haven, C. (1968). Interaction and adaptation: Intimacy as a critical variable. *American Sociological Review, 33,* 20–30.

Lowery, C. R., Denney, D. R., & Storms, M. D. (1979). Insomnia: A comparison of the effects of pill attributions and nonpejorative self-attributions. *Cognitive Research and Therapy, 3,* 161–164.

Ludwig, A. M., & Farrelly, F. (1967). The weapons of insanity. *American Journal of Psychotherapy, 21,* 737–749.

Lueger, R. J., & Petzel, T. P. (1979). Illusory correlation in clinical judgment: Effects of amount of information to be processed. *Journal of Consulting and Clinical Psychology, 47,* 1120–1121.

Lynch, J. J. (1977). *The broken heart: The medical consequences of loneliness.* New York: Basic Books.

Maclachlan, J. (1979). What people really think of fast talkers. *Psychology Today, 13*(6), 113–114, 116–117.

Maddux, J. E., & Barnes, J. (1985). *The orthogonality and relative predictive utility of self-efficacy expectancy, outcome expectancy, and outcome value: A review of empirical studies.* Manuscript submitted for publication, George Mason University, Fairfax, VA.

Maddux, J. E., Norton, L. W., & Leary, M. R. (in press). Cognitive components of social anxiety: An integration of self-presentational theory and self-efficacy theory. *Journal of Social and Clinical Psychology.*

Maddux, J. E., Norton, L. W., & Stoltenberg, C. D. (in press). Self-efficacy expectancy, outcome expectancy, and outcome value: Relative contributions in influencing and predicting behavioral intentions. *Journal of Personality and Social Psychology.*

Maddux, J. E., Sherer, M., & Rogers, R. W. (1982). Self-efficacy expectancy and outcome expectancy: Their relationship and their effects on behavioral intentions. *Cognitive Therapy and Research, 6,* 207–211.

Maddux, J. E., & Stoltenberg, C. D. (1983a). Clinical social psychology and social clinical psychology: A proposal for peaceful coexistence. *Journal of Social and Clinical Psychology, 1,* 289–299.

Maddux, J. E., & Stoltenberg, C. D. (Eds.). (1983b). Interfaces of clinical, counseling and social psychology. *Society for the Advancement of Social Psychology Newsletter, 10,* 1–32.

Maddux, J. E., & Stoltenberg, C. D. (1984a). Where to go from here: Future directions for the interface. *Society for the Advancement of Social Psychology Newsletter, 10,* 34–35.

Maddux, J. E., & Stoltenberg, C. D. (1984b). (Chairs). *Social psychological theory in counseling and psychotherapy process.* Symposium presented at the meeting of the American Psychological Association, Toronto.

Maddux, J. E., Stoltenberg, C. D., & Rosenwein, R. (in press). *Social processes in clinical and counseling psychology.* New York: Springer-Verlag.

Madsen, C. K., & Madsen, C. H. (1972). *Parents/children/discipline.* Boston: Allyn & Bacon.

Mahoney, M. J. (1976). *Scientist as subject: The psychological imperative*. Cambridge, MA: Ballinger.

Mahoney, M. (1977). Publication prejudices: An experimental study of confirmatory bias in the peer review system. *Cognitive Therapy and Research, 1*, 161–175.

Major, B., Mueller, P., & Hildebrandt, K. (1985). Attributions, expectations, and coping with abortion. *Journal of Personality and Social Psychology, 48*, 585–599.

Malkiewich, L. E., & Merluzzi, T. V. (1980). Rational restructuring vs. desensitization with clients of diverse conceptual levels: A test of a client-treatment matching model. *Journal of Counseling Psychology, 27*, 453–461.

Marcia, J. E., Rubin, B. M., & Efran, J. S. (1969). Systematic desensitization: Expectancy change or counter-conditioning? *Journal of Abnormal Psychology, 74*, 382–386.

Margolin, G., & Wampold, B. E. (1981). A sequential analysis of conflict and accord in distressed and nondistressed marital partners. *Journal of Consulting and Clinical Psychology, 49*, 554–567.

Marlatt, G. A., & Rohsenow, D. J. (1980). Cognitive processes in alcohol use: Expectancy and the balanced placebo design. In N. K. Mello (Ed.), *Advances in substance abuse: Behavioral and biological research* (Vol. 1, pp. 159–199). Greenwich, CT: JAI Press.

Marzillier, J., & Eastman, C. (1984). Continuing problems with self-efficacy theory: A reply to Bandura. *Cognitive Therapy and Research, 8*, 257–262.

Maslach, C. (1982). *Burnout: The cost of caring*. Englewood Cliffs, NJ: Prentice-Hall.

Matarazzo, J. D. (1982). Behavioral health's challenge to academic, scientific, and professional psychology. *American Psychologist, 37*, 1–14.

Mathes, E. W., Adams, H. E., & Davies, R. M. (1985). Jealousy: Loss of relationship rewards, loss of self-esteem, depression, anxiety, and anger. *Journal of Personality and Social Psychology, 48*, 1552–1561.

McCroskey, J. C. (1977). Oral communication apprehension: A summary of recent theory and research. *Human Communication Research, 4*, 78–96.

McGuire, W. J. (1969). The nature of attitudes and attitude change. In G. Lindzey & E. Aronson (Eds.), *The handbook of social psychology* (Vol. 3, 2nd ed. pp. 136–314). Reading, MA: Addison-Wesley.

McGuire, W. J. (1973). The Yin and Yang of progress in social psychology: Seven koan. *Journal of Personality and Social Psychology, 26*, 446–456.

McKee, K., & Smouse, A. D. (1983). Clients' perceptions of counselor expertness, attractiveness, and trustworthiness: Initial impact of counselor status and weight. *Journal of Counseling Psychology, 30*, 332–338.

Meecham, W. C., & Smith, H. G. (1977, June). *British Journal of Audiology*. Quoted in N. Napp, Noise to drive you crazy—jets and mental hospitals. *Psychology Today*, p. 33.

Meehl, P. E. (1954). *Clinical versus statistical prediction: A theoretical analysis and a review of the evidence*. Minneapolis: University of Minnesota Press.

Meehl, P. E. (1960). The cognitive activity of the clinician. *American Psychologist, 15*, 19–27.

Meehl, P. E. (1973). *Psychodiagnosis: Selected papers*. Minneapolis: University of Minnesota press.

Meichenbaum, D. H. (1977). *Cognitive behavior modification*. New York: Plenum Press.

Meichenbaum, D. H., Gilmore, J. B., & Fedoravicius, A. (1971). Group insight versus group desensitization in treating speech anxiety. *Journal of Consulting and Clinical Psychology, 36*, 410–421.

Mendonca, P. J., & Brehm, S. S. (1983). Effects of choice on behavioral treatment of overweight children. *Journal of Social and Clinical Psychology, 1*, 343–358.

Metalsky, G. I., & Abramson, L. Y. (1981). Attributional styles: Toward a framework for conceptualization and assessment. In P. C. Kendall & S. D. Hollon (Eds.), *Assessment strategies for cognitive-behavioral interventions* (pp. 13–50). New York: Academic Press.

Metalsky, G. I., Abramson, L. Y., Seligman, M. E. P., Semmel, A., & Peterson, C. (1982). Attributional styles and life events in the classroom: Vulnerability and invulnerability to depressive mood reactions. *Journal of Personality and Social Psychology, 43,* 612–617.

Mewborn, C. R., & Rogers, R. W. (1979). Effects of threatening and reassuring components of fear appeals on physiological and verbal measures of emotion and attitudes. *Journal of Experimental Social Psychology, 15,* 242–253.

Milardo, R. M., Johnson, M. P., & Huston, T. L. (1983). Developing close relationships: Changing patterns of interaction between pair members and social networks. *Journal of Personality and Social Psychology, 44,* 964–976.

Miller, N., Maruyama, G., Beaber, R. J., & Valone, K. (1976). Speed of speech and persuasion. *Journal of Personality and Social Psychology, 34,* 615–624.

Miller, P., Ingham, J., & Davidson, S. (1976). Life events, symptoms, and social support. *Journal of Psychosomatic Research, 20,* 515–522.

Miller, R. L., Brickman, P., & Bolen, I. (1975). Attribution versus persuasion as a means for modifying behavior. *Journal of Personality and Social Psychology, 31,* 430–441.

Miller, R. S. (1986). Embarrassment: Causes and consequences. In W. H. Jones, J. M. Cheek, & S. R. Briggs (Eds.), *Shyness: Perspectives on research and treatment* (pp. 295–311). New York: Plenum Press.

Miller, S. M. (1980). Why having control reduces stress: If I can stop the roller coaster, I don't want to get off. In J. Garber & M. E. P. Seligman (Eds.), *Human helplessness; Theory and applications.* New York: Academic Press.

Millon, T. (1975). Reflections on Rosenhan's "On being sane in insane places." *Journal of Abnormal Psychology, 84,* 456–461.

Mills, J., & Clark, M. S. (1982). Exchange and communal relationships. In L. Wheeler (Ed.), *Review of personality and social psychology* (Vol. 3, pp. 121–144). Beverly Hills, CA: Sage.

Mills, J., & Harvey, J. (1972). Opinion change as a function of when information about the communicator is received and whether he is attractive or expert. *Journal of Personality and Social Psychology, 21,* 52–55.

Mischel, W. (1968). *Personality and assessment.* New York: Wiley.

Mitchell, C., & Stuart, R. B. (1984). Effect of self-efficacy on dropout from obesity treatment. *Journal of Consulting and Clinical Psychology, 52,* 1100–1101.

Montgomery, R. L., & Haemmerlie, F. M. (in press). Self-perception and the reduction of heterosocial anxiety. *Journal of Social and Clinical Psychology.*

Mook, D. G. (1983). In defense of external invalidity. *American Psychologist, 38,* 379–387.

Mowrey, J. D., Doherty, M. E., & Keeley, S. M. (1979). The influence of negation and task complexity on illusory correlation. *Journal of Abnormal Psychology, 88,* 334–337.

Muney, B. F., & Deutsch, M. (1968). The effects of role-reversal during the discussion of opposing viewpoints. *Journal of Conflict Resolution, 12,* 345–356.

Murray, E. J., & Jacobsen, L. I. (1971). The nature of learning in traditional and behavioral psychotherapy. In A. Bergin & S. Garfield (Eds.), *Handbook of psychotherapy and behavioral change: An empirical analysis.* New York: Wiley.

Murstein, B. I., MacDonald, M. G., & Cerreto, M. (1977). A theory and investigation of the effect of exchange-orientation on marriage and friendship. *Journal of Marriage and the Family, 39,* 543–548.

Nadler, A., Altman, A., & Fisher, J. D. (1979). Helping is not enough: Recipients' reactions to aid as a function of positive and negative information about the self. *Journal of Personality, 47,* 615–628.

Napolitan, D. A., & Goethals, G. R. (1979). The attribution of friendliness. *Journal of Experimental Social Psychology, 15,* 105–113.

Nasby, W., Hayden, B., & DePaulo, B. M. (1980). Attributional bias among aggressive boys to interpret unambiguous social stimuli as displays of hostility. *Journal of Abnormal Psychology, 89,* 459–468.

Natale, M., Entin, E., & Jaffe, J. (1979). Vocal interruptions in dyadic communication as a function of speech and social anxiety. *Journal of Personality and Social Psychology, 37,* 865–878.

Nisbett, R. E., & Bellows, N. (1977). Verbal reports about causal influences on social judgments: Private access versus public theories. *Journal of Personality and Social Psychology, 35,* 613–624.

Nisbett, R. E., Krantz, D. H., Jepson, C., & Fong, G. T. (1982). Improving inductive inference. In D. Kahneman, P. Slovic, and A. Tversky (Eds.), *Judgment under uncertainty: Heuristics and biases* (pp. 445–459). Cambridge, England: Cambridge University Press.

Nisbett, R. E., & Ross, L. (1980). *Human inference: Strategies and shortcomings of social judgment.* Englewood Cliffs, NJ: Prentice-Hall.

Nisbett, R. E., & Schachter, S. (1966). Cognitive manipulation of pain. *Journal of Experimental Social Psychology, 2,* 227–236.

Nisbett, R. E., & Wilson, T. D. (1977a). The halo effect: Evidence for unconscious alteration of judgments. *Journal of Personality and Social Psychology, 35,* 250–256.

Nisbett, R. E., & Wilson, T. D. (1977b). Telling more than we can know: Verbal reports on mental processes. *Psychological Review, 84,* 231–259.

Noller, P. (1980). Misunderstandings in marital communication: A study of couples' nonverbal communication. *Journal of Personality and Social Psychology, 39,* 1135–1148.

Noller, P. (1981). Gender and marital adjustment level differences in decoding messages from spouses and strangers. *Journal of Personality and Social Psychology, 41,* 272–278.

Noller, P. (1982). Channel consistency and inconsistency in the communications of married couples. *Journal of Personality and Social Psychology, 43,* 732–741.

Noller, P. (1984). *Nonverbal communication and marital interaction.* Oxford: Pergamon Press.

Noller, P. (1985). Negative communications in marriage. *Journal of Social and Personal Relationships, 2,* 289–301.

Oakes, W. F., & Curtis, N. (1982). Learned helplessness: Not dependent upon cognitions, attributions, or other such phenomenal experiences. *Journal of Personality, 50,* 387–408.

Omer, H. (1981). Paradoxical treatments: A unified concept. *Psychotherapy: Theory, Research and Practice, 18,* 320–324.

Orford, J., & Feldman, P. (1980). Overview and implications: Towards an applied social and community psychology. In P. Feldman & J. Orford (Eds.), *Psychological problems: The social context* (pp. 367–379). New York: Wiley.

Orvis, B. R., Kelley, H. H., & Butler, D. (1976). Attributional conflict in young couples. In J. Harvey, W. Ickes, & R. Kidd (Eds.), *New directions in attribution research* (Vol. 1, pp. 353–386). Hillsdale, NJ: Erlbaum.

Osipow, S. H., Cohen, W., Jenkins, J., & Dostal, J. (1979). Clinical versus counseling psychology: Is there a difference? *Professional Psychology, 10,* 148–153.

Osipow, S. H., & Spokane, A. R. (1984). Measuring occupational stress, strain, and coping. *Applied Social Psychology Annual, 5,* 67–86.

Oskamp, S. (1965). Overconfidence in case-study judgments. *Journal of Consulting Psychology, 29,* 261–265.

Overmeier, J. B., & Seligman, M. E. P. (1967). Effects of inescapable shock on subsequent escape and avoidance learning. *Journal of Comparative and Physiological Psychology, 63,* 23–33.

Palazzoli, M. J., Boscolo, L., Cecchin, G., & Prata, G. (1978). *Paradox and counterparadox.* New York: Jason Aronson.

Parker, D. F., & DeCotiis, T. A. (1983). Organizational determinants of job stress. *Organizational Behavior and Human Performance, 32,* 160–177.

Parloff, M. B., Waskow, I. E., & Wolfe, B. E. (1978). Research on therapist variables in relation to process and outcome. In A. E. Bergin & S. L. Garfield (Eds.), *Handbook of psychotherapy and behavior change* (2nd ed.). New York: Wiley.

Parsons, T. (1951). *The social system.* Glencoe, IL: Free Press.

Passer, M. W., Kelley, H. H., & Michela, J. L. (1978). Multidimensional scaling of the cause for negative interpersonal behavior. *Journal of Personality and Social Psychology, 36,* 951–962.

Patterson, M. L. (1983). *Nonverbal behavior: A functional perspective.* New York: Springer-Verlag.

Patton, M. J. (1969). Attraction, discrepancy, and response to psychological treatment. *Journal of Counseling Psychology, 16,* 317–324.

Paul, G. (1966). *Insight versus desensitization in psychotherapy.* Stanford, CA: Stanford University Press.

Pelton, L. H. (1982). Personalistic attributions and client perspectives in child welfare cases: Implications for service delivery. In T. A. Wills (Ed.), *Basic processes in helping relationships* (pp. 81–101). New York: Academic Press.

Pennebaker, J. W., Burnam, M. A., Schaeffer, M. A., & Harper, D. C. (1977). Lack of control as a determinant of perceived physical symptoms. *Journal of Personality and Social Psychology, 35,* 167–174.

Perlman, D., & Peplau, L. A. (1981). Toward a social psychology of loneliness. In S. Duck & R. Gilmour (Eds.), *Personal relationships 3: Personal relationships in disorder* (pp. 31–56). London: Academic Press.

Peterson, C. (1982). Learned helplessness and attributional interventions in depression. In C. Antaki & C. Brewin (Eds.), *Attributions and psychological change: Applications of attributional theories to clinical and educational practice* (pp. 97–115). New York: Academic Press.

Peterson, C., Bettes, B. A., & Seligman, M. E. P. (1982). *Spontaneous attributions and depressive symptoms.* Unpublished manuscript, Virginia Polytechnic Institute and State University, Blacksburg, VA.

Peterson, C., Schwartz, S. M., & Seligman, M. E. P. (1981). Self-blame and depressive symptoms. *Journal of Personality and Social Psychology, 41,* 253–259.

Peterson, C., & Seligman, M. E. P. (1984). Causal explanations as a risk factor for depression: Theory and evidence. *Psychological Review, 91,* 347–374.

Peterson, C., Semmel, A., von Baeyer, C., Abramson, L. Y., Metalsky, G. I., & Seligman, M. E. P. (1982). The Attributional Style Questionnaire. *Cognitive Therapy and Research, 6,* 287–300.

Peterson, J., Fischetti, M., Curran, J. P., & Arland, S. (1981). Sense of timing: A skill deficit in heterosocially anxious women. *Behavior Therapy, 12,* 195–201.

Petty, R. E., & Cacioppo, J. T. (1981). *Attitudes and persuasion: Classic and contemporary approaches.* Dubuque, IA: Brown.

Petty, R. E., Cacioppo, J. T., & Goldman, R. (1981). Personal involvement as a determinant of argument-based persuasion. *Journal of Personality and Social Psychology, 41,* 847–855.

Pilkonis, P. A. (1977). The behavioral consequences of shyness. *Journal of Personality, 45,* 596–611.

Pines, A., & Aronson, E. (1983). Antecedents, correlates, and consequences of sexual jealousy. *Journal of Personality, 51,* 108–136.

Pope, B. (1977). Research on therapeutic style. In A. S. Gurman & A. M. Razin (Eds.), *Effective psychotherapy: A handbook of research* (pp. 356–394). New York: Pergamon Press.

Powell, F. A. (1965). Source credibility and behavioral compliance as determinants of attitude change. *Journal of Personality and Social Psychology, 2,* 669–676.

Prioleau, L., Murdock, M., & Brody, N. (1983). An analysis of the psychotherapy versus placebo studies. *The Behavioral and Brain Sciences, 6,* 275–310.

Raimy, V. C. (Ed.). (1950). *Training in clinical psychology.* Englewood Cliffs, NJ: Prentice-Hall.

Rands, M., Levinger, G., & Mellinger, G. D. (1981). Patterns of conflict resolution and marital satisfaction. *Journal of Family Issues, 2,* 297–321.

Rappaport, J., & Cleary, C. P. (1980). Labeling theory and the social psychology of experts and helpers. In M. Gibbs, J. Lachenmeyer, & J. Sigal (Eds.), *Community psychology: Theoretical and empirical approaches* (pp. 71–96). New York: Gardner Press.

Raps, C. S., Peterson, C., Reinhard, K. E., Abramson, L. Y., & Seligman, M. E. P. (1982). Attributional style among depressed patients. *Journal of Abnormal Psychology, 91,* 102–108.

Rehm, L. P. (1977). A self-control model of depression. *Behavior Therapy, 8,* 787–804.

Rehm, L. P., & Marston, A. R. (1968). Reduction of social anxiety through modification of self-reinforcement. *Journal of Consulting and Clinical Psychology, 32,* 565–574.

Reich, J. W. (1982). *Experimenting in society.* Glenview, IL: Scott, Foresman.

Reis, H. T. (1986). Gender effects in social participation: Intimacy, loneliness, and the conduct of social interaction. In R. Gilmour and S. Duck (Eds.), *The emerging field of personal relationships* (pp. 91–105). London: Academic Press.

Reis, H. T., Senchak, M., & Solomon, B. (1985). Sex differences in the intimacy of social interaction: Further examination of potential explanations. *Journal of Personality and Social Psychology, 48,* 1204–1217.

Reis, H. T., Wheeler, L., Kernis, M. H., Spiegel, N., & Nezlek, J. (1985). On specificity in the impact of social participation on physical and psychological health. *Journal of Personality and Social Psychology, 48,* 456–471.

Reisman, J. M. (1976). *A history of clinical psychology* (2nd ed.). New York: Irvington.

Renaud, H., & Estess, F. (1961). Life history interviews with one hundred normal American males: "Pathogenicity" of childhood. *American Journal of Orthopsychiatry, 31,* 786–802.

Rhodewalt, F., & Davison, J. (1984). *Self-handicapping and subsequent performance: The role of outcome valence and attributional certainty.* Unpublished manuscript, University of Utah, Salt Lake City.

Rhodewalt, F., Saltzman, A. T., & Wittmer, J. (1984). Self-handicapping among competitive athletes: The role of practice in self-esteem protection. *Basic and Applied Social Psychology, 5,* 197–210.

Rizley, R. (1978). Depression and distortion in the attribution of causality. *Journal of Abnormal Psychology, 87,* 32–48.

Rodin, J., & Langer, E. J. (1977). Long-term effects of a control-relevant intervention with the institutionalized aged. *Journal of Personality and Social Psychology, 35,* 897–902.

Rodin, J., Rennert, K., & Solomon, S. K. (1980). Intrinsic motivation for control: Fact or fiction. In A. Baum & J. E. Singer (Eds.), *Advances in environmental psychology: Applications of personal control.* Hillsdale, NJ: Erlbaum.

Rogers, C. R. (1959). A theory of therapy, personality and interpersonal relationships, as developed in the client-centered framework. In S. Koch (Ed.), *Psychology: A study of a science* (Vol. 3, pp. 184–256). New York: McGraw-Hill.

Rogers, R. W. (1975). A protection motivation theory of fear appeals and attitude change. *Journal of Psychology, 91,* 93–114.

Rogers, R. W. (1983). Preventive health psychology: An interface of social and clinical psychology. *Journal of Social and Clinical Psychology, 1,* 120–127.

Rohrbaugh, M., Tennen, H., Press, S., & White, L. (1981). Compliance, defiance, and therapeutic paradox: Guidelines for strategic use of paradoxical intentions. *American Journal of Orthopsychiatry, 51,* 454–467.

Roll, W. V., Schmidt, L. D., & Kaul, T. C. (1972). Perceived interviewer trustworthiness among black and white convicts. *Journal of Counseling Psychology, 19,* 537–541.

Rook, K. S. (1984). Promoting social bonding: Strategies for helping the lonely and socially isolated. *American Psychologist, 39,* 1389–1407.

Rook, K. S., & Peplau, L. A. (1982). Perspectives on helping the lonely. In L. A. Peplau & D. Perlman (Eds.), *Loneliness: A sourcebook of current theory, research and theory* (pp. 351–378). New York: Wiley.

Rosenbaum, G. (1969). Schizophrenia as a "put-on." *Journal of Clinical and Consulting Psychology, 33,* 642–645.

Rosenberg, M. (1965). *Society and the adolescent self-esteem.* Princeton, NJ: Princeton University Press.

Rosenhan, D. L. (1973). On being sane in insane places. *Science, 179,* 250–258.

Rosenthal, D., & Frank, J. D. (1956). Psychotherapy and the placebo effect. *Psychological Bulletin, 53,* 294–302.

Rosenthal, R., & Jacobson, L. (1968). *Pygmalion in the classroom: Teacher expectations and pupils' intellectual development.* New York: Holt, Rinehart & Winston.

Rosenthal, R., & Rubin, D. B. (1978). Interpersonal expectancy: The first 345 studies. *Behavioral and Brain Sciences, 2,* 377–415.

Ross, L. D. (1977). The intuitive psychologist and his shortcomings: Distortions in the attribution process. In L. Berkowitz (Ed.), *Advances in experimental social psychology* (Vol. 10, pp. 173–220). New York: Academic Press.

Ross, L. D., Amabile, T. M., & Steinmetz, J. L. (1977). Social roles, social control, and biases in social-perception processes. *Journal of Personality and Social Psychology, 35,* 485–494.

Ross, L., Lepper, M. R., & Hubbard, M. (1975). Perseverence in self-perception and social perception: Biased attributional processes in the debriefing paradigm. *Journal of Personality and Social Psychology, 32,* 880–892.

Ross, L., Lepper, M. R., Strack, F., & Steinmetz, J. (1977). Social explanation and social expectation: Effects of real and hypothetical explanations on subjective likelihood. *Journal of Personality and Social Psychology, 35,* 817–829.

Ross, L., Rodin, J., & Zimbardo, P. G. (1969). Toward an attribution therapy: The reduction of fear through induced cognitive-emotional misattribution. *Journal of Personality and Social Psychology, 12,* 279–288.

Ross, M., & Olson, J. M. (1982). Placebo effects in medical research and practice. In J. R. Eiser (Ed.), *Social psychology and behavioral medicine* (pp. 441–458). London: Wiley.

Ross, M., & Shulman, R. F. (1973). Increasing the salience of initial attitudes: Dissonance versus self-perception theory. *Journal of Personality and Social Psychology, 28,* 138–144.

Ross, M., & Sicoly, F. (1979). Egocentric biases in availability and attribution. *Journal of Personality and Social Psychology, 37,* 322–336.

Roth, S., & Kubal, L. (1975). The effects of noncontingent reinforcement on tasks of differing importance: Facilitation and learned helplessness effects. *Journal of Personality and Social Psychology, 32,* 680–691.

Rothbaum, F., Weisz, J. R., & Snyder, S. S. (1982). Changing the world and changing the self: A two-process model of perceived control. *Journal of Personality and Social Psychology, 42,* 5–37.

Rothmeier, R. C., & Dixon, D. N. (1980). Trustworthiness and influence: A reexamination in an extended counseling analogue. *Journal of Counseling Psychology, 27,* 315–319.

Routh, D. K., & King, K. M. (1972). Social class bias in clinical judgment. *Journal of Consulting and Clinical Psychology, 38,* 202–207.

Rubenstein, C. M., & Shaver, P. (1982). *In search of intimacy.* New York: Delacorte Press.

Rubenstein, C. M., Shaver, P., & Peplau, L. A. (1979). Loneliness. *Human Nature, 2,* 58–65.

Rubin, M., & Shontz, F. C. (1960). Diagnostic prototypes and diagnostic processes of clinical psychologists. *Journal of Consulting Psychology, 24,* 234–239.

Rubin, Z. (1970). Measurement of romantic love. *Journal of Personality and Social Psychology, 16,* 265–273.

Sachs, P. R. (1982). Avoidance of diagnostic information in self-evaluation of ability. *Personality and Social Psychology Bulletin, 8,* 242–246.

Sadow, L., & Suslick, A. (1961). Simulation of previous psychotic state. *Archives of General Psychiatry, 4,* 452–458.

Sarason, I. G. (Ed.). (1980). *Test anxiety: Theory, research, and applications.* Hillsdale, NJ: Erlbaum.

Sarason, S. B. (1981). An asocial psychology and a misdirected clinical psychology. *American Psychologist, 36,* 827–836.

Sarbin, T. (1982). The dangerous individual: An outcome of social identity transformations. In V. L. Allen & K. E. Scheibe (Eds.), *The social context of conduct* (pp. 113–118). New York: Praeger.

Sarbin, T. R., & Mancuso, J. C. (1980). *Schizophrenia: Medical diagnosis or moral verdict?* New York: Pergamon Press.

Sawyer, J. (1966). Measurement and prediction, clinical and statistical. *Psychological Bulletin, 66,* 178–200.

Schachter, S. (1959). *The psychology of affiliation.* Stanford, CA: Stanford University Press.

Schafer, R. B., & Keith, P. M. (1980). Equity and depression among married couples. *Social Psychology Quarterly, 43,* 430–435.

Scheff, T. J. (1966). *Being mentally ill.* Chicago: Aldine.

Scheff, T. J. (Ed.). (1975). *Labeling madness.* Englewood Cliffs, NJ: Prentice-Hall.

Scheid, A. B. (1976). Clients' perception of the counselor: The influence of counselor introduction and behavior. *Journal of Counseling Psychology, 23,* 503–508.

Schlenker, B. R. (1973). Social psychology and science. *Journal of Personality and Social Psychology, 29,* 1–15.

Schlenker, B. R. (1975a). Self-presentation: Managing the impression of consistency when reality interferes with self-enhancement. *Journal of Personality and Social Psychology, 32,* 1030–1037.

Schlenker, B. R. (1975b). Liking for a group following initiation: Impression management or dissonance reduction? *Sociometry, 38,* 99–118.

Schlenker, B. R. (1980). *Impression management: The self-concept, social identity, and interpersonal relations.* Monterey, CA: Brooks/Cole.

Schlenker, B. R. (Ed.). (1985). *The self and social life.* New York: McGraw-Hill.

Schlenker, B. R., Forsyth, D. R., Leary, M. R., & Miller, R. S. (1980). A self-presentational analysis of the effects of incentives on attitude change following counterattitudinal behavior. *Journal of Personality and Social Psychology, 39,* 553–577.

Schlenker, B. R., & Leary, M. R. (1982). Social anxiety and self-presentation: A conceptualization and model. *Psychological Bulletin, 92,* 641–669.

Schlenker, B. R., & Leary, M. R. (1985). Social anxiety and communication about the self. *Journal of Language and Social Psychology, 4,* 171–192.

Schmidt, L. D., & Strong, S. R. (1970). "Expert" and "inexpert" counselors. *Journal of Counseling Psychology, 17,* 115–118.

Schmidt, L. D., & Strong, S. R. (1971). Attractiveness and influence in counseling. *Journal of Counseling Psychology, 18,* 348–351.

Schneider, D. J. (1969). Tactical self-presentation after success and failure. *Journal of Personality and Social Psychology, 13,* 262–268.

Schneider, D. J., Hastorf, A. H., & Ellsworth, P. C. (1979). *Person perception* (2nd ed.). Reading, MA: Addison-Wesley.

Schooler, C., & Parkel, D. (1966). The overt behavior of chronic schizophrenics and its relationship to their internal state and personal history. *Psychiatry, 29,* 67–77.

Schuler, R. (1984). *Handbook of organizational stress coping strategies.* Cambridge, MA: Ballinger.

Schulz, R. (1976). The effects of control and predictability on the psychological and physical well-being of the institutionalized aged. *Journal of Personality and Social Psychology, 33,* 563–573.

Schulz, R., & Decker, S. (1982). Social support, adjustment, and the elderly spinal cord injured: A social psychological analysis. In G. Weary & H. Mirels (Eds.), *Integrations of clinical and social psychology* (pp. 272–286). New York: Oxford University Press.

Seligman, M. E. P. (1974). Depression and learned helplessness. In R. J. Friedman & M. M. Katz (Eds.), *The psychology of depression: Contemporary theory and research.* Washington, DC: Winston.

Seligman, M. E. P. (1975). *Helplessness: On depression, development, and death.* San Francisco: Freeman.

Seligman, M. E. P., Abramson, L. Y., Semmel, A., & von Baeyer, C. (1979). Depressive attributional style. *Journal of Abnormal Psychology, 88,* 242–247.

Seligman, M. E. P., & Peterson, C. (in press). A learned helplessness perspective on childhood depression: Theory and research. In M. Rutter, C. Izard, & P. Read (Eds.), *Depression in childhood: Developmental perspectives.* New York: Guilford Press.

Seligman, M. E. P., Peterson, C., Kaslow, N. J., Tanenbaum, R. L., Alloy, L. B., & Abramson, L. Y. (1984). Attributional style and depressive symptoms among children. *Journal of Abnormal Psychology, 93,* 235–238.

Sell, J. M. (1974). Effects of subject self-esteem, test performance feedback, and counselor attractiveness on influence in counseling. *Journal of Counseling Psychology, 21,* 324–344.

Shapiro, A. K., & Morris, L. A. (1978). The placebo effect in medical and psychological therapies. In S. L. Garfield & A. E. Bergin (Eds.), *Handbook of psychotherapy and behavior change: An empirical analysis* (2nd ed., pp. 369–410). New York: Wiley.

Shapiro, A. K., Struening, E., Shapiro, E., & Barten, H. (1976). Prognostic correlates of psychotherapy in psychiatric outpatients. *American Journal of Psychiatry, 133,* 802–808.

Shaver, K. G., Payne, M. R., Bloch, R. M., Burch, M. C., Davis, M. S., & Shean, G. D. (1984). Logic in distortion: Attributions of causality and responsibility among shizophrenics. *Journal of Social and Clinical Psychology, 2,* 193–214.

Shaw, M. E. (1981). *Group dynamics: The psychology of small group behavior.* New York: McGraw-Hill.

Sheras, P. L., & Worchel, S. (1979). *Clinical psychology: A social psychological approach.* New York: Van Nostrand.

Sherman, M., Trief, P., & Sprafkin, R. (1975). Impression management in the psychiatric interview: Quality, style, and individual differences. *Journal of Consulting and Clinical Psychology, 43,* 867–871.

Sherman, S. J. (1980). On the self-erasing nature of errors of prediction. *Journal of Personality and Social Psychology, 39,* 211–221.

Shettel-Neuber, J., Bryson, J. B., & Young, L. E. (1978). Physical attractiveness of the "Other Person" and jealousy. *Personality and Social Psychology Bulletin, 4,* 612–615.

Short, J. F., Jr., & Strodtbeck, F. L. (1963). The response of gang leaders to status threats: An observation on group process and delinquent behavior. *American Journal of Sociology, 68,* 571–579.

Sillars, A. L. (1981). Attributions and interpersonal conflict resolution. In J. Harvey, W. Ickes, & R. Kidd (Eds.), *New directions in attribution research* (Vol. 3, pp. 279–305). Hillsdale, NJ: Erlbaum.

Sillars, A. L. (1985). Interpersonal perception in relationships. In W. Ickes (Ed.), *Compatible and incompatible relationships* (pp. 277–305). New York: Springer-Verlag.

Singerman, K. J., Borkovec, T. D., & Baron, R. S. (1976). Failure of a "Misattribution Therapy" manipulation with a clinically relevant target behavior. *Behavior Therapy, 7,* 306–313.

Skilbeck, W. M. (1974). Attributional change and crisis intervention. *Psychotherapy: Theory, Research and Practice, 11,* 371–375.

Skrypnek, B. J., & Snyder, M. (1982). On the self-fulfilling nature of stereotypes about women and men. *Journal of Experimental Social Psychology, 18,* 277–291.

Slivken, K. E., & Buss, A. H. (1984). Misattribution and speech anxiety. *Journal of Personality and Social Psychology, 47,* 396–402.

Sloan, W. W., Jr., & Solano, C. H. (1984). The conversational style of lonely males with strangers and roommates. *Personality and Social Psychology Bulletin, 10,* 293–301.

Sloane, R. B., Staples, F. R., Cristol, A. H., Yorkston, N. J., & Whipple, K. (1975). *Psychotherapy versus behavior therapy.* Cambridge, MA: Harvard University Press.

Slovic, P., & Fischhoff, B. (1977). On the psychology of experimental surprises. *Journal of Experimental Psychology: Human Perception and Performance, 3,* 544–551.

Smith, T. W., Snyder, C. R., & Handelsman, M. M. (1982). On the self-serving function of an academic wooden leg: Test anxiety as a self-handicapping strategy. *Journal of Personality and Social Psychology, 42,* 314–321.

Smith, T. W., Snyder, C. R., & Perkins, S. C. (1983). The self-serving function of hypochrondriacal complaints: Physical symptoms as self-handicapping strategies. *Journal of Personality and Social Psychology, 44,* 787–797.

Smith-Hanen, S. S. (1977). Effects of nonverbal behaviors on judged levels of counselor warmth and empathy. *Journal of Counseling Psychology, 24,* 87–91.

Snyder, C. R. (1977). "A patient by any other name" revisited: Maladjustment or attributional locus of problem? *Journal of Consulting and Clinical Psychology, 45,* 101–103.

Snyder, C. R., Shenkel, R. J., & Lowery, C. (1977). Acceptance of personality interpretations: The "Barnum effect" and beyond. *Journal of Consulting and Clinical Psychology, 45,* 104–114.

Snyder, C. R., Shenkel, R. J., & Schmidt, A. (1976). Effects of role perspective and client psychiatric history on locus of problem. *Journal of Consulting and Clinical Psychology, 44,* 467–472.

Snyder, C. R., & Smith, T. W. (1982). Symptoms as self-handicapping strategies: The virtues of old wine in a new bottle. In G. Weary & H. Mirels (Eds.), *Integrations of clinical and social psychology* (pp. 104–127). New York: Oxford University Press.

Snyder, C. R., Smith, T. W., Augelli, R. W., & Ingram, R. E. (1985). On the self-serving function of social anxiety: Shyness as a self-handicapping strategy. *Journal of Personality and Social Psychology, 48*, 970–980.

Snyder, M. (1981). Seek, and ye shall find: Testing hypotheses about other people. In E. T. Higgins, C. P. Herman, & M. P. Zanna (Eds.), *Social cognition: The Ontario Symposium* (Vol. 1, pp. 277–303). Hillsdale, NJ: Erlbaum.

Snyder, M., & Cantor, N. (1979). Testing hypotheses about other people: The use of historical knowledge. *Journal of Experimental Social Psychology, 15*, 330–342.

Snyder, M., & Swann, W. B., Jr. (1978a). Hypothesis-testing processes in social interaction. *Journal of Personality and Social Psychology, 36*, 1202–1212.

Snyder, M., & Swann, W. B., Jr. (1978b). Behavioral confirmation in social interaction: From social perception to social reality. *Journal of Experimental Social Psychology, 14*, 148–163.

Snyder, M., Tanke, E. D., & Berscheid, E. (1977). Social perception and interpersonal behavior: On the self-fulfilling nature of social stereotypes. *Journal of Personality and Social Psychology, 35*, 656–666.

Snyder, M., & Uranowitz, S. W. (1978) Reconstructing the past: Some cognitive consequences of person perception. *Journal of Personality and Social Psychology, 36*, 941–950.

Snyder, M., & White, P. (1981). Testing hypotheses about other people: Strategies of verification and falsification. *Personality and Social Psychology Bulletin, 7*, 39–43.

Snyder, M. L., & Frankel, A. (1976). Observer bias: A stringent test of behavior engulfing the field. *Journal of Personality and Social Psychology, 34*, 857–864.

Snyder, M. L., Smoller, B., Strenta, A., & Frankel, A. (1981). A comparison of egotism, negativity, and learned helplessness as explanations for poor performance after unsolvable problems. *Journal of Personality and Social Psychology, 40*, 24–30.

Sober-Ain, L., & Kidd, R. F. (1984). Fostering changes in self-blamers' beliefs about causality. *Cognitive Therapy and Research, 8*, 121–138.

Solano, C. H., Batten, P. G., & Parish, E. A. (1982). Loneliness and patterns of self-disclosure. *Journal of Personality and Social Psychology, 43*, 524–531.

Sonne, J. L., & Janoff, D. (1979). The effect of treatment attributions on the maintenance of weight reduction: A replication and extension. *Cognitive Theory and Research, 3*, 389–397.

Sonne, J. L., & Janoff, D. S. (1982). Attributions and the maintenance of behavior change. In C. Antaki & C. Brewin (Eds.), *Attributions and psychological change: Applications of attributional theories to clinical and educational practice* (pp. 83–96). New York: Academic Press.

Spence, J. T., Helmreich, R., & Holahan, C. K. (1979). Negative and positive components of psychological masculinity and feminity and their relationships to neurotic and acting out behaviors. *Journal of Personality and Social Psychology, 37*, 1673–1682.

Spitzer, R. L. (1975). On pseudoscience in science, logic in remission, and psychiatric diagnosis: A critique of Rosenhan's "On being sane in insane places." *Journal of Abnormal Psychology, 84*, 442–452.

Sprafkin, R. P. (1970). Communicator expertness and changes in word meaning in psychological treatment. *Journal of Counseling Psychology, 17*, 191–196.

Stanley, M. A., & Maddux, J. E. (1985, April). *Self-efficacy and negative mood states: A study of reciprocal influences.* Paper presented at the annual meeting of the Southwestern Psychological Association, Austin, TX.

Stanley, M. A., & Maddux, J. E. (1986). Cognitive processes in health enhancement: Investigation of a combined protection motivation and self-efficacy model. *Basic and Applied Social Psychology, 7,* 101–113.

Starr, B. J., & Katkin, E. S. (1969). The clinician as an aberrant actuary: Illusory correlation and the incomplete sentence blank. *Journal of Abnormal Psychology, 74,* 670–675.

Steenbarger, B. N., & Aderman, D. (1979). Objective self-awareness as a nonaversive state: Effect of anticipating discrepancy reduction. *Journal of Personality, 47,* 330–339.

Steiner, I. D. (1979). Social psychology. In E. Hearst (Ed.), *The first century of experimental psychology* (pp. 513–559). Hillsdale, NJ: Erlbaum.

Stiles, W. B., Putnam, S. M., & Jacob, M. C. (1982). Verbal exchange structure of initial medical interviews. *Health Psychology, 1,* 315–336.

Stokes, J. P. (1985). The relation of social network and individual difference variables to loneliness. *Journal of Personality and Social Psychology, 48,* 981–990.

Stoltenberg, C. D., Cacioppo, J. T., Petty, R. E., & Davis, C. S. (1985). *Career and study skills information: Who says what can alter message processing.* Unpublished manuscript, Texas Tech University, Lubbock.

Stoltenberg, C. D., Maddux, J. E., & Pace, T. (1986). Cognitive style and counselor credibility effects on client endorsement of rational emotive therapy. *Cognitive Therapy and Research, 10,* 237–243.

Stoltenberg, C. D., & McNeill, B. W. (1984). Effects of expertise and issue involvement on perceptions of counseling. *Journal of Social and Clinical Psychology, 2,* 314–325.

Storms, M. D. (1973). Videotape and the attribution process: Reversing actors' and observers' points of view. *Journal of Personality and Social Psychology, 27,* 165–174.

Storms, M. D., Denney, D. R., McCaul, K. D., & Lowery, C. R. (1979). Treating insomnia. In J. H. Frieze, D. Bar-Tal, & J. S. Carroll (Eds.), *New approaches to social problems* (pp. 151–167). San Francisco: Jossey-Bass.

Storms, M. D., & McCaul, K. D. (1976). Attribution processes and emotional exacerbation of dysfunctional behavior. In J. H. Harvey, W. J. Ickes, & R. F. Kidd (Eds.), *New directions in attribution resesarch* (Vol. 1, pp. 143–164). Hillsdale, NJ: Erlbaum.

Storms, M. D., & Nisbett, R. E. (1970). Insomnia and the attribution process. *Journal of Personality and Social Psychology, 16,* 319–328.

Strack, S., & Coyne, J. C. (1983). Social confirmation of dysphoria: Shared and private reactions to depression. *Journal of Personality and Social Psychology, 44,* 798–806.

Straus, M. A. (1980). Wife-beating: How common and why? In M. A. Straus & G. T. Hotaling (Eds.), *The social causes of husband-wife violence* (pp. 23–36). Minneapolis: University of Minnesota Press.

Stroebe, M. S., & Stroebe, W. (1983). Who suffers more? Sex differences in health in risks of the widowed. *Psychological Bulletin, 93,* 279–301.

Strohmer, D. C., & Chiodo, A. L. (1984). Counselor hypothesis testing strategies: The role of initial impressions and self-schema. *Journal of Counseling Psychology, 31,* 510–519.

Strohmer, D. C., & Newman, L. A. (1983). Counselor hypothesis testing strategies. *Journal of Counseling Psychology, 30,* 557–565.

Strong, S. R. (1968). Counseling: An interpersonal influence process. *Journal of Counseling Psychology, 15,* 215–224.

Strong, S. R. (1978). Social psychological approach to psychotherapy research. In S. L. Garfield & A. E. Bergin (Eds.), *Handbook of psychotherapy and behavior change: An empirical analysis* (2nd ed., pp. 101–135). New York: Wiley.

Strong, S. R. (1982). Emerging integrations of clinical and social psychology: A clinician's perspective. In G. Weary & Mirels (Eds.), *Integrations of clinical and social psychology* (pp. 181–213). New York: Oxford University Press.

Strong, S. R., & Claiborn, C. D. (1982). *Change through interaction*. New York: Wiley-Interscience.

Strong, S. R., & Dixon, D. N. (1971). Expertness, attractiveness, and influence in counseling. *Journal of Counseling Psychology, 18,* 562–570.

Strong, S. R., & Schmidt, L. D. (1970a). Expertness and influence in counseling. *Journal of Counseling Psychology, 17,* 81–87.

Strong, S. R., & Schmidt, L. D. (1970b). Trustworthiness and influence in counseling. *Journal of Counseling Psychology, 17,* 197–204.

Strong, S. R., Taylor, R. G., Bratten, J. C., & Loper, R. G. (1971). Nonverbal behavior and perceived counselor characteristics. *Journal of Counseling Psychology, 18,* 554–561.

Strong, S. R., Wambach, L. A., Lopez, F. G., & Cooper, R. K. (1979). Motivational and equipping functions of interpretation in counseling. *Journal of Counseling Psychology, 26,* 98–107.

Strube, M. J., & Barbour, L. S. (1983). The decision to leave an abusive relationship: Economic dependence and psychological commitment. *Journal of Marriage and the Family, 45,* 785–794.

Stuart, R. B. (1980). *Helping couples change: A social learning approach to marital therapy.* New York: Guilford Press.

Stunkard, A. J., & Penick, S. B. (1979). Behavior modification in the treatment of obesity: The problem of maintaining weight loss. *Archives of General Psychiatry, 36,* 801–805.

Sullivan, H. S. (1953). *The interpersonal theory of psychiatry.* New York: Norton.

Super, D. E. (1955). Transition from vocational guidance to counseling psychology. *Journal of Counseling Psychology, 2,* 3–9.

Swann, W. B., Jr. (1985). The self as architect of social reality. In B. R. Schlenker (Ed.), *The self and social life* (pp. 100–125). New York: McGraw-Hill.

Swann, W. B., Jr., & Ely, R. J. (1984). A battle of wills: Self-verification versus behavioral confirmation. *Journal of Personality and Social Psychology, 46,* 1287–1302.

Swann, W. B., Jr., & Hill, C. A. (1982). When our identities are mistaken: Reaffirming self-conceptions through social interaction. *Journal of Personality and Social Psychology, 43,* 59–66.

Szasz, T. S. (1961). *The myth of mental illness.* New York: Delta.

Szucko, J. J., & Kleinmuntz, B. (1981). Statistical versus clinical lie detection. *American Psychologist, 36,* 488–496.

Tavris, C. (1982). *Anger: The misunderstood emotion.* New York: Simon & Schuster.

Taylor, M. S., Locke, E. A., Lee, C., & Gist, M. E. (1984). Type A behavior and faculty research productivity: What are the mechanisms? *Organizational Behavior and Human Performance, 34,* 402–418.

Taylor, S. E. (1975). On inferring one's attitudes from one's behavior: Some limiting conditions. *Journal of Personality and Social Psychology, 31,* 126–131.

Taylor, S. E., & Fiske, S. T. (1978). Salience, attention, and attribution: Top of the head phenomena. In L. Berkowitz (Ed.), *Advances in experimental social psychology* (Vol. 11, pp. 249–288). New York: Academic Press.

Teasdale, J. D. (1978). Self-efficacy: Toward a unifying theory of behavioural change? *Advances in Behaviour Research and Therapy, 1,* 211–215.

Tedeschi, J. T. (Ed.). (1981). *Impression management theory and social psychological research.* New York: Academic Press.

Tedeschi, J. T., & Rosenfeld, P. (1981). Impression management theory and the forced compliance situation. In J. T. Tedeschi (Ed.), *Impression management theory and social psychological research* (pp. 147–179). New York: Academic Press.

Tedeschi, J. T., Schlenker, B. R., & Bonoma, T. V. (1971). Cognitive dissonance: Private ratiocination or public spectacle? *American Psychologist, 26,* 685–695.

Tedeschi, J. T., Smith, R. B., & Brown, R. C. (1974). A reinterpretation of research on aggression. *Psychological Bulletin, 81,* 540–563.

Teglasi, H., & Hoffman, M. A. (1982). Causal attributions of shy subjects. *Journal of Research in Personality, 16,* 376–385.

Temerlin, M. K. (1968). Suggestion effects in psychiatric diagnosis. *Journal of Nervous and Mental Disease, 147,* 349–353.

Tennen, H., Affleck, G., Allen, D. A., McGrade, B. J., & Ratzen, S. (1984). Causal attributions and coping with insulin-dependent diabetes. *Basic and Applied Social Psychology, 5,* 131–142.

Tennen, H., Drum, P. E., Gillen, R., & Stanton, A. (1982). Learned helplessness and the detection of contingency: A direct test. *Journal of Personality, 50,* 426–442.

Tennen, H., Gillen, R., & Drum, P. E. (1982). The debilitating effect of exposure to noncontingent escape: A test of the learned helplessness model. *Journal of Personality, 50,* 409–425.

Tesser, A. (in press). Some effects of self-evaluation maintenance on cognition and action. In R. M. Sorrentino & E. T. Higgins (Eds.), *The handbook of motivation and cognition: Foundations of social behavior.* New York: Guilford Press.

Tetlock, P. E. (1983). Accountability and the perseverance of first impressions. *Social Psychology Quarterly, 46,* 285–292.

Tetlock, P. E. (1985). Accountability: A social check on the fundamental attribution error. *Social Psychology Quarterly, 48,* 227–236.

Thibaut, J. W., & Kelley, H. H. (1959). *The social psychology of groups.* New York: Wiley.

Thomas, A. P., & Bull, P. (1981). The role of pre-speech posture change in dyadic interaction. *British Journal of Social Psychology, 20,* 105–111.

Thompson, S. C., & Kelley, H. H. (1981). Judgments of responsibility for activities in close relationships. *Journal of Personality and Social Psychology, 41,* 469–477.

Timnick, L. (1978, February 26). Birth defects linked to noise from jets? *Indianapolis Star.*

Tinsley, H. E. A., Brown, M. T., de St. Aubin, T. M., & Lucek, J. (1984). Relation between expectancies for a helping relationship and tendency to seek help from a campus help provider. *Journal of Counseling Psychology, 31,* 149–160.

Traupmann, J., Hatfield, E., & Wexler, P. (1983). Equity and sexual satisfaction in dating couples. *British Journal of Social Psychology, 22,* 33–40.

Trope, Y., & Bassok, M. (1982). Confirmatory and diagnosing strategies in social information gathering. *Journal of Personality and Social Psychology, 43,* 22–34.

Truax, C. B., & Carkhauff, R. R. (1967). *Toward effective counseling and psychotherapy: Training and practice.* Chicago: Aldine.

Tucker, J. A., Vuchinich, R. E., & Sobell, M. B. (1981). Alcohol consumption as a self-handicapping strategy. *Journal of Abnormal Psychology, 90,* 220–230.

Turk, D. C., & Salovey, P. (1985). Cognitive structures, cognitive processes, and cognitive-behavior modification: II. Judgments and inferences of the clinician. *Cognitive Therapy and Research, 9,* 19–33.

Turk, D. C., & Salovey, P. (in press). Clinical information processing: Bias inoculation. In R. Ingram (Ed.), *Information processing approaches to psychopathology and clinical psychology.* Orlando, FL: Academic Press.

Turner, R. (1981). Social support as a contingency in psychological well-being. *Journal of Health and Social Behavior, 22,* 357–367.

Tversky, A., & Kahneman, D. (1974). Judgment under uncertainty: Heuristics and biases. *Science, 185,* 1124–1131.

Twaddle, A. C. (1979). *Sickness behavior and the sick role.* Boston: G. K. Hall.

Twentyman, C. T., & McFall, R. M. (1975). Behavioral training of social skills in shy males. *Journal of Consulting and Clinical Psychology, 43,* 384–395.

Tyler, L. E. (1965). *The work of the counselor* (3rd ed.). New York: Appleton-Century-Crofts.

Tyler, L. (1972). Reflecting on counseling psychology. *The Counseling Psychologist, 3*(4), 6–11.

Utne, M. K., Hatfield, E., Traupmann, J., & Greenberger, D. (1984). Equity, marital satisfaction, and stability. *Journal of Social and Personal Relationships, 1,* 323–332.

Valins, S. (1966). Cognitive effects of false heartrate feedback. *Journal of Personality and Social Psychology, 4,* 400–408.

Valins, S., & Nisbett, R. E. (1972). Attribution processes in the development and treatment of emotional disorders. In E. E. Jones, D. E. Kanouse, H. H. Kelley, R. E. Nisbett, S. Valins, & B. Weiner (Eds.), *Attribution: Perceiving the causes of behavior* (pp. 137–150). Morristown, NJ: General Learning Press.

Valins, S., & Ray, A. (1967). Effects of cognitive desensitization on avoidance behavior. *Journal of Personality and Social Psychology, 7,* 345–350.

Vallone, R. P., Ross, L., & Lepper, M. R. (1985). The hostile media phenomenon: Biased perception and perceptions of media bias in coverage of the Beirut massacre. *Journal of Personality and Social Psychology, 49,* 577–585.

Van Egeren, L., Haynes, S. N., Franzen, M., & Hamilton, J. (1983). Presleep cognitions and attributions in sleep-onset insomnia. *Journal of Behavioral Medicine, 6,* 217–232.

Van Riper, C. (1971). *The nature of stuttering.* Englewood Cliffs, NJ: Prentice-Hall.

Wainer, H. (1976). Estimating coefficients in linear models: It don't make no nevermind. *Psychological Bulletin, 83,* 213–217.

Waller, R. W., & Keeley, S. M. (1978). Effects of explanation and information feedback on the illusory correlation phenomenon. *Journal of Consulting and Clinical Psychology, 46,* 342–343.

Waller, W. W., & Hill, R. (1951). *The family, a dynamic interpretation.* New York: Dryden Press.

Wallin, P. (1950). Cultural contradictions and sex roles: A repeat study. *American Sociological Review, 15,* 288–293.

Walster, E., Aronson, E., & Abrahams, D. (1966). On increasing the persuasiveness of a low prestige communicator. *Journal of Experimental Social Psychology, 2,* 325–342.

Walster, E., Traupmann, J., & Walster, G. W. (1978). Equity and extramarital sexuality. *Archives of Sexual Behavior, 7,* 127–142.

Walster, E., Walster, G. W., & Traupmann, J. (1978). Equity and premarital sex. *Journal of Personality and Social Psychology, 36,* 82–92.

Warner, M. H., Parker, J. B., & Calhoun, J. F. (1984). Inducing person-perception change in a spouse-abuse situation. *Family Therapy, 11,* 123–138.

Wason, P. C. (1960). On the failure to eliminate hypotheses in a conceptual task. *Quarterly Journal of Experimental Psychology, 12,* 129–140.

Watkins, C. E., Jr. (1984). Counseling psychology versus clinical psychology: Further explorations on a theme or once more around the "identity" maypole with gusto. *The Counseling Psychologist, 11,* 76–92.

Watson, C. G. (1972). A comparison of the ethical self-presentations of schizophrenics, prisoners, and normals. *Journal of Clinical Psychology, 28,* 479–483.

Watson, C. G. (1975). Impression management ability in psychiatric hospital samples and normals. *Journal of Consulting and Clinical Psychology, 43,* 540–545.

Watson, D., & Friend, R. (1969). Measurement of social-evaluative anxiety. *Journal of Consulting and Clinical Psychology, 33,* 448–457.

Watson, G. M. W., & Dyck, D. G. (1984). Depressive attributional style in psychiatric inpatients: Effects of reinforcement level and assessment procedure. *Journal of Abnormal Psychology, 93,* 312–320.

Watson, J. B., & Rayner, P. (1920). Conditioned emotional reactions. *Journal of Experimental Psychology, 3,* 1–4.

Watzlawick, P., Beavin, J., & Jackson, D. (1967). *Pragmatics of human communication.* New York: Norton.

Waxer, P. H. (1978). *Nonverbal aspects of psychotherapy.* New York: Praeger.

Weary Bradley, G. (1978). Self-serving biases in the attribution process: A reexamination of the fact or fiction question. *Journal of Personality and Social Psychology, 36,* 56–71.

Weary, G., & Mirels, H. L. (Eds.). (1982). *Integrations of clinical and social psychology.* New York: Oxford University Press.

Weeks, D. G., Michela, J. L., Peplau, L. A., & Bragg, M. E. (1980). The relation between loneliness and depression: A structural equation analysis. *Journal of Personality and Social Psychology, 39,* 1238–1244.

Weeks, G. R., & L'Abate, L. (1979). A compilation of paradoxical methods. *American Journal of Family Therapy, 7,* 61–76.

Weeks, G. R., & L'Abate, L. (1982). *Paradoxical psychotherapy: Theory and practice with individuals, couples, and families.* New York: Brunner/Mazel.

Wegner, D., & Vallacher, R. (1980). *The self in social psychology.* New York: Oxford University Press.

Wegner, D. M., Wenzlaff, R., Kerker, R. M., & Beattie, A. E. (1981). Incrimination through innuendo: Can media questions become public answers? *Journal of Personality and Social Psychology, 40,* 822–832.

Weiner, B. (1975). "On being sane in insane places": A process (attributional) analysis and critique. *Journal of Abnormal Psychology, 84,* 433–441.

Weiner, B. (1985). "Spontaneous" causal thinking. *Psychological Bulletin, 97,* 74–84.

Weiner, B., & Kukla, A. (1970). An attributional analysis of achievement motivation. *Journal of Personality and Social Psychology, 15,* 1–20.

Weiner, B., Russell, D., & Lerman, D. (1978). Affective consequences of causal ascriptions. In J. H. Harvey, W. Ickes, & R. F. Kidd (Eds.), *New directions in attribution research* (Vol. 2, pp. 59–89). Hillsdale, NJ: Erlbaum.

Weiss, R. S. (1973). *Loneliness: The experience of emotional and social isolation.* Cambridge, MA: MIT Press.

Weissman, N. M., & Klerman, G. I. (1977). Sex differences and the epidemiology of depression. *Archives of General Psychiatry, 34,* 98–111.

Wells, L. E., & Marwell, G. (1976). *Self-esteem: Its conceptualization and measurement.* Beverly Hills, CA: Sage.

Whalen, C. K., & Henker, B. (1976). Psychostimulants and children: A review and analysis. *Psychological Bulletin, 83,* 1113–1130.

Wheeler, L., Reis, H., & Nezlek, J. (1983). Loneliness, social interaction, and sex roles. *Journal of Personality and Social Psychology, 45,* 943–953.

Whitaker, C. A. (1975). A family therapist looks at marital therapy. In A. S. Gurman & D. Rice (Eds.), *Couples in conflict: New directions in marital therapy* (pp. 165–174). New York: Jason Aronson.

White, G. L. (1980). Inducing jealousy: A power perspective. *Personality and Social Psychology Bulletin, 6,* 222–227.

White, G. L. (1981a). Some correlates of romantic jealousy. *Journal of Personality, 49,* 129–147.

White, G. L. (1981b). A model of romantic jealousy. *Motivation and Emotion, 5,* 295–310.

White, G. L. (1981c). Jealousy and partner's perceived notion for attraction to a rival. *Social Psychology Quarterly, 49,* 24–30.

White, R. W. (1959). Motivation reconsidered: The concept of competence. *Psychological Review, 66,* 297–333.

Wicklund, R. A. (1975). Objective self-awareness. In L. Berkowitz (Ed.), *Advances* / *in experimental social psychology* (Vol. 8). New York: Academic Press.

Wicklund, R. A., & Brehm, J. W. (1976). *Perspectives on cognitive dissonance.* Hillsdale, NJ: Erlbaum.

Wiggins, J. S. (1981). Clinical and statistical prediction: Where are we and where do we go from here? *Clinical Psychology Review, 1,* 3–18.

Wiggins, J. S. (1982). Commentary: Social psychological processes in clinical judgment. In G. Weary & H. L. Mirels (Eds.), *Integrations of clinical and social psychology* (pp. 72–76). New York: Oxford University Press.

Wilcox, R., & Krasnoff, A. (1967). Influence of test-taking attitudes on personality inventory scores. *Journal of Consulting Psychology, 31,* 188–194.

Wilkins, W. (1977). Expectancies in applied settings. In A. S. Gurman & A. M. Razin (Eds.), *Effective psychotherapy: A handbook of research* (pp. 325–355). New York: Pergamon Press.

Williams, J. G., & Solano, C. H. (1983). The social reality of feeling lonely: Friendship and reciprocation. *Personality and Social Psychology Bulletin, 9,* 237–242.

Williams, S. L., Turner, S. M., & Peer, D. F. (1985). Guided mastery and performance desensitization treatments for severe acrophobia. *Journal of Consulting and Clinical Psychology, 53,* 237–247.

Williams, S. L., & Watson, N. (1985). Perceived danger and perceived self-efficacy as cognitive determinants of acrophobic behavior. *Behavior Therapy, 16,* 136–146.

Wills, T. A. (1978). Perceptions of clients by professional helpers. *Psychological Bulletin, 85,* 968–1000.

Wills, T. A. (1982). Decision processes. In T. A. Wills (Ed.), *Basic processes in helping relationships* (pp. 9–11). New York: Academic Press.

Wilson, D. O. (1985). The effects of systematic client preparation, severity, and treatment setting on dropout rate in short-term psychotherapy. *Journal of Social and Clinical Psychology, 3,* 62–70.

Wilson, T. D., & Linville, P. W. (1982). Improving the academic performance of college freshmen: Attribution therapy revisited. *Journal of Personality and Social Psychology, 42,* 367–376.

Wilson, T. D., & Linville, P. W. (1985). Improving the performance of college freshmen with attributional techniques. *Journal of Personality and Social Psychology, 49,* 287–293.

Wine, J. D. (1971). Test anxiety and direction of attention. *Psychological Bulletin, 76,* 92–104.

Wine, J. D. (1980). Cognitive-attentional theory of test anxiety. In I. Sarason (Ed.), *Test anxiety: Theory, research, and application* (pp. 349–385). Hillsdale, NJ: Erlbaum.

Winter, L., Uleman, J. S., & Cunniff, C. (1985). How automatic are social judgments? *Journal of Personality and Social Psychology, 49,* 904–917.

Wolpe, J. (1978). Self-efficacy theory and psychotherapeutic change: A square peg for a round hole. *Advances in Behaviour Research and Therapy, 1,* 231–236.

Wood, G. (1978). The knew-it-all-along effect. *Journal of Experimental Psychology: Human Perception and Performance, 4,* 345–353.

Woodward, H. D. (1972). Self-perception, dissonance, and premanipulation attitudes. *Psychonomic Science, 29,* 193–196.

Woodworth, R. S. (1958). *Dynamics of behavior.* New York: Holt, Rinehart & Winston.

Word, C. O., Zanna, M. P., & Cooper, J. (1974). The nonverbal mediation of self-fulfilling prophecies in interracial interaction. *Journal of Experimental Social Psychology, 10,* 109–120.

Wortman, C. B., & Brehm, J. W. (1975). Responses to uncontrollable outcomes: An integration of reactance theory and the learned helplessness model. In L. Berkowitz (Ed.), *Advances in experimental social psychology* (Vol. 8, pp. 277–336). New York: Academic Press.

Wortman, C. B., & Dintzer, L. (1978). Is an attributional analysis of the learned helplessness phenomenon viable? A critique of the Abramson-Seligman-Teasdale reformulation. *Journal of Abnormal Psychology, 87,* 75–90.

Wright, R. A., & Brehm, S. S. (1982). Reactance as impression management: A critical review. *Journal of Personality and Social Psychology, 42,* 608–618.

Wright, R. M., & Strong, S. R. (1982). Stimulating therapeutic change with directives: An exploratory study. *Journal of Counseling Psychology, 29,* 199–202.

Yuen, K. W. R., & Tinsley, H. E. A. (1981). International and American student expectancies about counseling. *Journal of Counseling Psychology, 28,* 66–69.

Zautra, A. J., Guenther, R. T., & Chartier, G. M. (1985). Attributions for real and hypothetical events: Their relation to self-esteem and depression. *Journal of Abnormal Psychology, 94,* 530–540.

Zeldow, P. B. (1984). Sex roles, psychological assessment, and patient management. In C. Wilson (Ed.), *Sex roles and psychopathology* (pp. 355–374). New York: Plenum Press.

Zimbardo, P. G. (1965). The effect of effort and improvisation on self-persusasion produced by role-playing. *Journal of Expermental Social Psychology, 1,* 103–120.

Zimbardo, P. G. (1977). *Shyness: What it is and what to do about it.* New York: Jove.

Author Index

Subject Index

Springer Series in Social Psychology

Attention and Self-Regulation: A Control-Theory Approach to Human Behavior
Charles S. Carver/Michael F. Scheier

Gender and Nonverbal Behavior
Clara Mayo/Nancy M. Henley (Editors)

Personality, Roles, and Social Behavior
William Ickes/Eric S. Knowles (Editors)

Toward Transformation in Social Knowledge
Kenneth J. Gergen

The Ethics of Social Research: Surveys and Experiments
Joan E. Sieber (Editor)

The Ethics of Social Research: Fieldwork, Regulation, and Publication
Joan E. Sieber (Editor)

Anger and Aggression: An Essay on Emotion
James R. Averill

The Social Psychology of Creativity
Teresa M. Amabile

Sports Violence
Jeffrey H. Goldstein (Editor)

Nonverbal Behavior: A Functional Perspective
Miles L. Patterson

Basic Group Processes
Paul B. Paulus (Editor)

Attitudinal Judgment
J. Richard Eiser (Editor)

Social Psychology of Aggression: From Individual Behavior to Social Interaction
Amélie Mummendey (Editor)

Directions in Soviet Social Psychology
Lloyd H. Strickland (Editor)

Sociophysiology
William M. Waid (Editor)

Compatible and Incompatible Relationships
William Ickes (Editor)

Facet Theory: Approaches to Social Research
David Canter (Editor)

Action Control: From Cognition to Behavior
Julius Kuhl/Jürgen Beckmann (Editors)

Springer Series in Social Psychology

The Social Construction of the Person
Kenneth J. Gergen/Keith E. Davis (Editors)

Entrapment in Escalating Conflicts: A Social Psychological Analysis
Joel Brockner/Jeffrey Z. Rubin

The Attribution of Blame: Causality, Responsibility, and Blameworthiness
Kelly G. Shaver

Language and Social Situations
Joseph P. Forgas (Editor)

Power, Dominance, and Nonverbal Behavior
Steve L. Ellyson/John F. Dovidio (Editors)

Changing Conceptions of Crowd Mind and Behavior
Carl F. Graumann/Serge Moscovici (Editors)

Changing Conceptions of Leadership
Carl F. Graumann/Serge Moscovici (Editors)

Friendship and Social Interaction
Valerian J. Derlega/Barbara A. Winstead (Editors)

An Attributional Theory of Motivation and Emotion
Bernard Weiner

Public Self and Private Self
Roy F. Baumeister (Editor)

Social Psychology and Dysfunctional Behavior: Origins, Diagnosis, and Treatment
Mark R. Leary/Rowland S. Miller

Communication and Persuasion: Central and Peripheral Routes to Attitude Change
Richard E. Petty/John T. Cacioppo

Theories of Group Behavior
Brian Mullen/George R. Goethals (Editors)